We're No
FUN
Anymore

We're No FUN Anymore

*Helping Couples Cultivate Joyful Marriages
Through the Power of Play*

Robert Schwarz and Elaine Braff

Routledge
Taylor & Francis Group
New York   London

Routledge
Taylor & Francis Group
711 Third Avenue
New York, NY 10017

Routledge
Taylor & Francis Group
27 Church Road
Hove, East Sussex BN3 2FA

© 2012 by Robert Schwarz and Elaine Braff
Routledge is an imprint of Taylor & Francis Group, an Informa business

Printed in the United States of America on acid-free paper
Version Date: 20110620

International Standard Book Number: 978-0-415-87187-7 (Hardback) 978-0-415-87188-4 (Paperback)

Library of Congress Cataloging-in-Publication Data

Schwarz, Robert A. (Robert Alan), 1956-
     We're no fun anymore : helping couples cultivate joyful marriages through the power of play / by Robert Schwarz and Elaine Braff.
       p. ; cm.
     Includes bibliographical references and index.
     ISBN 978-0-415-87187-7 (hardback : alk. paper) -- ISBN 978-0-415-87188-4 (pbk. : alk. paper) 1. Marital psychotherapy. 2. Spouses--Psychology. I. Braff, Elaine. II. Title.
     [DNLM: 1. Marital Therapy--methods. 2. Interpersonal Relations. 3. Play and Playthings. 4. Spouses--psychology. WM 430.5.M3]

RC488.5.S39 2011
616.89'1562--dc22   2011005374

Visit the Taylor & Francis Web site at
http://www.taylorandfrancis.com

and the Routledge Web site at
http://www.routledgementalhealth.com

Contents

Foreword

Every therapist has heard these words from couples: "We're no fun anymore." Bob Schwarz and Elaine Braff certainly heard that complaint often enough—and then did something bold about it.

I am so delighted that these two dedicated (and fun!) therapists got together to co-author this important new book. I'm even more pleased to invite you inside, to get lost in the pages, where Bob and Elaine showcase their innovative concepts and strategies for helping couples understand the serious nature of fun and play in happy, healthy relationships. Our field has been in need of such a dynamic book for some time.

As a couples therapist with 30 years experience, I know the importance of fun in life as well as in love. Fun is fuel, and we all know this intuitively. When an invitation arrives, we tear it open, read it, and a typical first response is, *This is going to be fun*! What happens next? Do we put the event on our calendar? Make it a priority? Get energized about it? Look forward to the fun? You bet!

It's this same sense of anticipation and fun-focused attitude the authors want us to use to help couples bring (back to) their relationships. Today, with couples facing longer work hours, a higher cost of living, and outside threats from technological temptations, could there be a greater need for fun? When 80 percent of divorcing couples cite "growing apart" as the reason, and fun is the front line of defense against growing apart, could there be any better time than now for this book?

As Elaine and Bob so expertly point out, fun can't be overlooked when it is one of the primary reasons two people get together in the first place. A couple meets, falls in love—why? Because they are having so much fun together. It's the glue of relationships. Yet therapists know that fun rapidly falls to the bottom of the priority list as a couple's marriage ages. Indeed, most relationships die from neglect, not nuclear threat. The authors show us how to inspire couples to shake up that lopsided priority list and get fun and play back near the top where they belong.

We already know that couples who have fun together are more intimate and more likely to enjoy the sensual, sexual side of love. What couple couldn't use a surefire rocket booster for their sex life? Here, you'll find new ways to spur couples toward more and better sexual fun and play.

Study after study reminds us that to improve a relationship, it's easier to add more positives than eliminate negatives—and that's what Bob and Elaine have outlined here, a concrete plan to motivate couples toward increasing positive interactions. Their work is based on a combination of recent research on brain activity and positive psychology, but broadened by an exciting new approach for the therapy room (and beyond), which addresses overcoming barriers that inhibit couples from play and fun.

Looking for strategies for your couple clients? This book is chock-full of them! As a bonus, therapists get a primer on tools that will help them develop a practice that is itself more pleasurable, productive, and rewarding (Who says therapists can't have fun too?). These two gifted therapists lead the way, showing off their heartfelt hilarity on many pages; but while their subject may seem light-hearted, this book's serious nature cannot be denied.

I find the authors' ideas clever and helpful in so many ways. We owe Bob and Elaine a debt of thanks for putting this long-awaited book in our hands. Now it's our job to read it, heed it, and help couples believe it.

Pat Love, Ed. D.
co-author, *How to Improve
Your Relationship
Without Talking About It*

Acknowledgments

This book only exists because hundreds of couples trusted us with their hearts and souls. We are honored and privileged to have journeyed to those vulnerable places with them. They have been our teachers as well as our clients.

We want to thank Lisa Romeo for her intelligence, gift for words, her amazing editing ability, her coaching, and her patience. We are indebted to her for all that she contributed. Whenever we asked, Victoria Britt lent her watchful eye over our efforts, making sure we said what we meant and meant what we said. Her professional integrity and laser-like clinical knowledge kept this manuscript honest, appropriate, and authentic to the audience. Her contribution was invaluable. Mark Kusnir listened to our ideas, helped us formulate concepts, and smoothed out many edges with his editing skills. His generosity of heart comes through in whatever he touches. We are grateful for his commitment to this book.

Linda Cashdan made valuable contributions to the book and added playful editing touches. We want to thank Don Hartman for offering his keen sense of organization and language skills and Bob Sherman for vetting parts of the manuscript, giving rich feedback and valuable suggestions based on decades of clinical experience. Publisher George Zimmer was the first to show confidence in our book and for that we are humbly indebted. We thank Marta Moldaivi at Routledge for her support and for keeping us on track. Dominick Grundy also offered honest, intelligent feedback, as did Deborah Burrell. Thanks to Judith Simon for her patience and understanding, and lending her editing expertise.

We want to acknowledge Diane Sollee who gave us the opportunity to present our Power of Play Workshops at her "Smart Marriages" annual conference and was dogged in her encouragement that we write this book. Her commitment to the field of marriage education is unflagging. We thank Rich Simon for the opportunity to present our Power of Play Workshops at the Psychotherapy Networker Symposium.

ELAINE'S ACKNOWLEDGMENTS

The irony of writing a book about the value of play is how much it diminished the amount of playtime in my own life! Which means the first person I need to acknowledge is my best friend, playmate, and husband, Hal. Much of this book is a testament to our joyful relationship. I am grateful for his support, literary expertise, and most importantly his patience, love, and devotion.

We are blessed with amazing children and their spouses—Jennifer, Jessica, Adam, Josh, Shoshi, Zach, Peter, Michelle, and Jill who are constant in their love, support, and understanding. And our precious grandchildren who brighten our lives with joy and playfulness.

I deeply appreciate my amazing mother Bea who has given me the gift of unconditional love and the love of play. Special thanks to my sister Sheila for her love and ongoing support, and to my brother-in-law Larry for his enthusiasm for this project.

I thank my professional mentors and teachers, Elaine Rapp, Art Robbins, Milt Shumsky, Werner Ehrhard, Monica McGoldrick, and Lori Gordon for also creating the PAIRS marriage education course and to Morris Gordon for spreading it around the world—bringing joy to so many couples.

I need to thank my wonderful friends for forgiving me when I wasn't available and for making sure I kept some semblance of fun in my life anyway.

BOB'S ACKNOWLEDGMENTS

I want to thank my wife Kim and son Daniel who have been very supportive of the time I have had to re-direct away from them toward the writing of this book. They have always been a source of great joy, love, and fun.

Over the years there have been so many teachers and colleagues who have been a source of inspiration and support and whose wisdom is intermingled on the pages in this book including: Harry Aponte, Jeff Zeig, Steve Lankton, Yvonne Dolan, John Gray, and Maurice Prout. I also want to acknowledge Charlie Johnson who first turned me on to Improv and to my long time Improv instructor Sharon Geller.

About the Authors

Robert Schwarz, PsyD, DCEP, a licensed psychologist and marriage and family therapist, has been in private practice for more than 25 years. The executive director of the Association for Comprehensive Energy Psychology, he is also the author of *Tools for Transforming Trauma* (2002) and coauthor of *PTSD: A Clinician's Guide* (1991) and has published numerous articles and papers. Bob has presented workshops and keynotes internationally to clinicians and businesses. He lives and works in Ardmore, Pennsylvania.

Elaine Braff, M.P.S., A.T.R., is an expressive arts therapist, marriage educator, and relationship coach. She is a Master Leader of the nationally acclaimed marriage education course, PAIRS (Practical Application of Intimate Relationship Skills). A noted expert on relationship skills, Elaine presents workshops on the subject of marriage and the power of play both here and abroad. She has been in practice for 31 years in South Orange, New Jersey.

Introduction

Scene: A young couple in love picks out wedding rings, plans a honeymoon, and signs the long-term marriage contract. The contract reads like this: "After a number of years, the couple will have no fun anymore, no laughs, too little sex, too many household chores and financial responsibilities, time only for their jobs and kids, and oh, yes, harbor anger and resentment."

This sounds like a bad play, but that is what so many couples act out on a daily basis. They arrive in therapy and tell us their anger and resentment are to blame, and that is why they are no fun anymore, why they do not play together anymore. It is our job to tell them the reverse is true: It is not that they do not play or have fun anymore because they are angry and resentful; they are angry and resentful because they do not play together anymore.

ABOUT THIS BOOK

Couples therapists often suggest that their clients go out and have fun together as a break from the "real" work of learning communication skills, using conflict resolution tools, and applying other typical therapy techniques. When the couple takes the suggestion seriously and engages in a playful break together, they often return a week later, glowing, exuberant, and unable to stop talking about what a difference it made. It is as if their relationship morphed from black and white to Technicolor™.

What if this was a more common occurrence in your practice? What if this way of working with couples involved not more work on their part, but more play? What, in fact, if it was all about play? Can couples play their way back together?

This was the central question each of us began to ask ourselves several years ago: What if couples could focus on play and fun, instead of problems, and thus positively transform the context of their relationships? As we each experimented at implementing this somewhat radical but elegantly simple idea in our own separate practices, we were also convinced that play warranted a larger role.

It is not that couples are not playing and having fun *because* they are angry and resentful; they are angry and resentful *because* they are not playing and having fun together.

In case we needed any additional impetus for our inquiry, we had only to compare notes on what was transpiring with the couples we each saw on a daily basis. These couples were like the following: husbands who saw their wives as too preoccupied with the children, wives who felt in second or third place behind the husband's work or golf game, or couples who could not recall having done anything fun or playful together, without the children, in months or even years. Also included were couples who told wonderful stories of how very much in love they were and how often they did fun things together while dating and newly married, but who, by the time they arrived in therapy, could not think of a single enjoyable joint activity in their current lives.

We are *not* suggesting that therapists abandon communication and conflict resolution skills or that family-of-origin issues should be relegated to the unimportant pile. We are suggesting that balancing the hard work of reducing negative experiences with efforts on directly helping couples nurture positive emotions and experiences pays significant dividends. Furthermore, we believe that the ideas presented in this book can be integrated into most forms of couples work. We take a "Yes, and" approach. Yes, you can do what you have always done, *and* you can add some emphasis on helping couples go directly to playing more so they can metaphorically collect $200.

We came to the conclusion that the problem of vanishing play in marriage was epidemic. It was also solvable. Couples could, and have to, reconnect, rebuild, and reimagine their lives based on a foundation of playing together.

As we incorporated playful activities and behaviors in our therapy more frequently, and our couples began to play together, began to lighten up, to smile, laugh, and enjoy themselves, their relationships improved. We are too often part of a culture that does not recognize the value of play in adult life. Due to a work-obsessed ethic and repressive cultural forces, playing is seen as unproductive, frivolous, childish, and unimportant. It became clear that many of our clients were profoundly play deprived.

We formally define *play* in Chapter 1. We use the term broadly, including everything from playing poker to kidding around to engaging in sex. Whatever else it may be, play is a set of activities and interactions that are great sources of joy and connection. What we lose when we do not play are the wonderful faculties and attributes that only play can engender: silliness, laughter, spontaneity, flexibility, risk taking, bonding, joy, and above all, of course, loads of fun.

For play to be deemed *couple's play*, both partners must enjoy the activity and feel that it improves the quality of the relationship (Casado-Kehoe, Vanderbleek, & Thanasiu, 2007). Yet in our work with couples, we see individuals who are in pain because their expectations of what it takes to maintain a healthy marriage are unrealistic. Within our society, there seems to be an epidemic of very high expectations coupled with ignorance. This is seen in the epidemic of obesity and diabetes. Proper nutrition and exercise are to health what creating joy and fun are to relationships. What is clearly lacking is an awareness of each partner's responsibility for bringing these things into the relationship.

Truly mature partners understand what it takes to have a lively, joyful relationship, but they may have let their play skills get rusty. Years of child rearing, career building, and household chores can have this effect. It is for this reason that we decided to write this book; we are both concerned about the detrimental effects that the lack of play can have on relationships. We committed ourselves to helping other therapists understand and develop the tools that will empower them to guide their client couples in rediscovering the profound healing power of play and fun in their lives and in their relationships. If you are a therapist, marriage educator, or coach, you will learn from this book what it takes to help couples transform their relationships from boring and dull to alive and exciting through the incorporation of play in your therapeutic practice.

WHAT TO EXPECT: CHAPTER BY CHAPTER

In Chapter 1, you will discover why play is so vital to couples' relationships as well as to each individual's overall health and well-being. You will see that human beings are built for play, and that we all start out in life playing. In this chapter, we share the research that establishes how essential play is to both individual and marital satisfaction and describe the direct impact these findings have on our work as couples therapists.

Chapter 2 includes the couple's play assessment, which you can use to help couples gain awareness of how increasing the ratio of positive experiences to negative ones, as suggested by researcher John Gottman (1994, 1999), can benefit the relationship. This assessment experience allows couples to see clearly how much (or how little) fun they are having, what they did for fun when they were happier, and when and why it stopped along the way. They will also come to a better understanding of each mate's responsibility to make life happy independent of the partner's contribution to individual happiness. As part of their assessment, a couple is asked to provide an individual and a joint play history and complete a diagram that depicts the amount of play a couple is enjoying together. The assessment is not only an educational component, but also a powerful intervention in itself.

In Chapter 3, we address the barriers to play. We break down each partner's unrealistic marriage and relationship expectations, including beliefs about what marriage should be, and the roles they expect themselves and their partners to play within the construct of their marriage. We also look at individual psychodynamics such as rigidity and control, fear of embarrassment, family-of-origin issues, messages, decisions, beliefs, right and wrong, past negative experiences, insecure attachment, and cultural and economic influences. We provide you with clinical techniques that will enable you to help couples work through their individual blocks as well as those they may have created together.

Chapter 4 explores the cultivation of a playful attitude and how it can profoundly shift a couple's relationship by creating a context of lightheartedness, openness, creativity, spontaneity, risk taking, freedom, flexibility, joy, love, and trust. We describe how everything that happens in the relationship can be experienced within a playful spirit. Playful activities are suggested, some of which may seem small but are framed in such a way to demonstrate the power they can have in enhancing the quality of the relationship.

Chapter 5 encourages shifting our focus from *attitudes* to the specific daily *behaviors* clients can engage in that demonstrate and foster their love, commitment, and enjoyment of the other. Here, you can find the strategies and tools that will help you get your clients to choose to invest time and resources on positive, playful, and joyful activities. Whatever the size, duration, or breadth of a playful activity, engaging in it can profoundly alter the emotional economy of a couple's relationship.

Chapter 6 presents an extensive inventory of the various areas of play. These include outings, athletic pursuits, nature-based activities, cultural events, sex play, board games, social play, caring behaviors, humor play, and more. An added benefit here is that simply presenting the list can have an impact from the first moment a couple begins reading it together. When the inventory is given to both partners, the list begins to jog partners' memories of past pleasurable experiences; they notice the play they have neglected, and it encourages them to start making lists of possible joint activities. This usually stimulates excitement and hopefulness.

Chapter 7 discusses the topic of dating and the misconceptions people have about it, including the distinction between dating in marriage and singles dating. In addition, we explain the mood killers and the mood enhancers of dating so that therapists can learn and communicate them to their clients. It is hoped that once couples understand the mood killers and enhancers, client dating will be an exciting adventure that will reignite the spark that was there in the courtship stage.

Chapter 8 explores sex play, with ideas to assist the couple in integrating their sex lives within the larger field of play, thus making sex less serious within the relationship. Since fun and play are essential components of a healthy sex life, we give you a road map to help couples rekindle their desire for sex, have sex more often, and maintain a satisfying, passionate sex life.

Chapter 9 deals with the role of the therapist in implementing the tools, techniques, and strategies needed to stimulate couples toward more play. We suggest postures and allay fears about how you can be both playful and professional and how you can be a role model for playfulness and authenticity. You will learn how to use humor and playfulness professionally, lighten the intensity that is so often present while doing this work, and make therapy more fun for you and your clients.

We want to be clear from the start. We are not suggesting that the material in this book is the only tool you need to be a good marital therapist or educator. There are many other approaches and therapeutic heritages that you will see inform these pages. But we are suggesting that the power of play and positive emotion, long under-described in the field, can add a package of new tools and approaches to the therapeutic toolbox.

By following the guidelines for play in each chapter, we are confident that you will be able to make an enormous difference in the lives of your clients and move their relationships to more solid footing.

In addition to how it can transform your ability to guide couples, a benefit you may derive from this book is the opportunity to transform your therapy practice by learning how to decrease your stress and have more fun yourself. Rather than becoming frustrated, emotionally drained, and burned out, you will learn about the value of play in your adult life and how to mirror it in your practice.

When couples therapy is going well, it can be a most rewarding experience. However, it also has the potential to be intensely stressful when you cannot get couples beyond their anger, hurt, and resentment, no matter what techniques you employ or theories you use. Every week you wait to see if they did the homework you suggested the week before. Then, they say, "We didn't do it," and blame one another. Or, all the good work you did the week before is squashed because the couple had a big blowout over the weekend. Or, one partner comes to the session with a gripe and then thinks that you and the spouse are ganging up against him or her. They begin to cancel appointments. These scenarios can leave therapists extremely discouraged, of course, so it is our hope that the new approaches we are sharing in this book serve to inspire you and reinvigorate your professional work.

Of course, some of you have probably been integrating play and humor in couples therapy for years, yet you may be looking for more strategies and ideas; you will find them in the pages to come. For others, the use of play in marital therapy may be an entirely new idea and one that asks you to take a risk and leave your comfort zone. Some therapists want to play it safe, not because they fear change, but because they do not want to do anything that may harm clients. However, we ask you to consider that it might be more risky to play it safe by keeping play at bay. You may in fact be depriving the couple of the very thing they need most. Frankly, one of the things that can be most exciting about this approach is the risk aspect—risky in the sense that it allows therapists to use their own creativity and spontaneity in the service of helping clients. After all, therapy is itself a form of play in that we are exploring and playing with possibilities.

Every couple needs to play and have fun; however, we realize that couples therapy is not all fun and games. If couples come into your office with serious problems, such as addiction, infidelity, emotional or physical abuse, mental illness, or trauma, for you to implement humor and play would not be an appropriate treatment strategy—*at least in the beginning.* It would be more important to concentrate on putting out the fire first (which could take some time) and then evaluate when you might want to incorporate play.

As you have most likely experienced in your professional work, when couples finally come to therapy, they may see you as their last hope. They are counting on you to guide them safely out of the mess they have created. We are all aware of the enormity of the responsibility we have undertaken. It is essential for you not only to have the insight to understand the entangled web of issues your clients lay before you but also to develop the skills to provide direction, coaching, and purpose to lead them back to the place where they were joyous and excited to be together, when they dated, laughed, played, and chased one another.

Couples are looking for a therapist who can teach them the tools they need so that they will be able to handle life on their own—tools that will help them to successfully maintain a satisfying, fun, and healthy relationship.

This book is designed to put that tool kit at your disposal. Having these techniques and exercises available to you will provide dynamic, interactive, action-driven ways to guide your clients to what they truly need: a way back to joyful hearts, playful spirits, fun, connection, trust, risk taking, love, and an emotional bank account brimming with love deposits and an abundance of positive experiences. We hope you find the resources that follow are a source of empowerment and joy to you and to your clients.

1

The Power of Play in Relationships and Life
Theory and Research

WHAT IS PLAY?

Defining what we mean when we use the word *play* in this book is a surprisingly difficult task. The word *play* is used in everyday parlance and seems like a simple enough concept. Yet, it has multiple meanings and connotations. In fact, play has more than 90 different meaning variations in the dictionary. It can be a verb, as in to play a game. It can be a noun, such as a Broadway play. Then, there is the adjective *playful* and the adverb *playfully*. If we were to ask you to make a mental picture in your mind of being playful, 10 different people would give us 10 different descriptions.

But, are there a few things on which we can probably all agree? For almost everyone, *play* refers to some type of activity most often associated with positive emotions, such as fun and pleasure. Athletes, musicians, and artists, who more or less "play" for a living, would probably also add that the playing is best when they can get into the zone or a "flow." Csikszentmihalyi (1990, p. 41) explained that "flow helps to integrate the self because in that state of deep concentration consciousness is unusually well ordered. Thoughts, intentions, feelings, and all the senses are focused on the same goal. Experience is in harmony."

One definition of play is that it is an activity that is engaged in for no specific purpose other than generating pleasure and fun (Terr, 1999). While this captures an important aspect of play, it does not tell the entire story. For instance, what about playing music or playing a sport? Certainly, one of the goals of these activities is to generate the positive emotion of fun, but there is a larger purpose involved. There is even effort spent "playing" (called practice) that is often not immediately enjoyable. But, there is also a big emotional payoff with the interpersonal synching that occurs when the musicians are "tight" or the team is playing well together. Perhaps the first example of play in life is the game of peekaboo. On the surface, it looks like a silly activity between parent and child whose only purpose is to create laughter, but there is far more happening. Just because one is not conscious of the deeper purpose does not mean that there is no purpose.

Notice that we said that play has no real purpose other than fun. That assumption may have a huge cultural loading. While we do not talk at length about this in this book, there is a clear subtext that Western culture,* particularly American culture with its roots in Puritanism and Calvinism, is deeply entrenched in a repressed framework that emphasizes a work-only ethic, eschewing the very possibility that play can have any real value. Even those living in the United States who are steeped in other cultures that may have differing attitudes are probably heavily influenced by the rigorous prevailing popular mores concerning work versus play. The one value play has, "fun," is just not that important in that mental outlook. But, do we really need, or want, to stay embedded in that frame?

The more we delve into it, the more we begin to see that this playing concept is not as simple as perhaps we first thought. Is a couple going out on a date engaging in a form of playing? We think so. From our perspective, the concept of play must be broadened. For instance, we include fun, games, pleasure, laughter, and humor as significant aspects of playing.

According to Huizinga (1949), "Play is a voluntary activity or occupation executed within certain fixed limits of time and place, according to rules freely accepted but absolutely binding, having its aim in itself and accompanied by a feeling of tension, joy, and the consciousness that it is 'different' from 'ordinary life'" (p. 28). Most play researchers continue to ascribe to the notion that play is intrinsically motivated and occurs in a "space distinct from reality" (Gordon & Esbjorn-Hargens, 2007). In addition, most play theorists and researchers agree with Bateson's (1972) concept that during interpersonal play there is a meta-message that communicates "this is play."

Play is also "an attitude of throwing off constraint" (Millar, 1968, p. 21). "When we throw off the constraints of a given context, we are free to move, to engage with new contexts as well as to engage the context of our recent experience as an object of play" (Gordon, 2008, p. 6). The attitude of play allows us to shift our awareness so that we can both become aware of our interpretative frames and manipulate them. Many of the qualities of play and playfulness in the following manner were summarized eloquently: "Novelty and risk of a new situation or experience only add to the intensity and pleasure of play. The player is able to be

---

* We want to avoid making sweeping generalizations. Not all Western cultures or subcultures fit this description. And, Western culture is not the only culture that heavily emphasizes work while eschewing play, perhaps as part of its sexually repressive tendencies. The point we are making is that we are embedded in our cultures that inform the family and the individual about what is normal and expected. Often, there is little awareness of this dynamic and even less space to stand back and decide whether to accept such norms.

in control of being out of control and so enjoys a sense of both risk and mastery simultaneously" (Gordon & Esbjorn-Hargens, 2007, p. 217).

Play is a broad-based spectrum of consciousness that includes different degrees of: freedom from constraint, openness, novelty, flexibility, lightheartedness, cooperation, humor, risk taking, trust, creativity, vulnerability, and positive emotion. Play can be a reference to an activity that lasts several hours or a momentary interchange. Play includes both behavioral and attitudinal components, and generally the attitudinal component is the more important one since most behaviors can become playful with the proper attitude. Doing dinner dishes can be a dreadful chore, or it can be a playful shared activity. A normally fun game can lose its "playfulness" when approached with the wrong attitude.

The attitude determines engagement in the playful activity. A certain amount of positive emotion, such as humor, joy, amusement, and interest, must be present. There is a minimum amount of positive emotion needed to activate the transformative chemistry of play. For an activity to remain playful, it must generate even more positive emotion: Play creates positive emotion, and play begets more play.

Play in its many forms is a generator of positive emotion. It is this reciprocal spiral of amplifying positive emotion that makes play so useful in life and in important relationships. The more people play, the more positive emotions are generated, which in turn makes play easier and thus helps to generate even more positive emotion. When partners "are fun" with one another, they expand and broaden their bonds together.

Perhaps the most common association to the word *play* is the idea of "playing a game." It can be helpful to think of a relationship as a game, although not in the cavalier sense of needing to win and another needing to lose, but rather as a mutual activity guided by fair play, engagement, and back and forth. Much marital relationship advice, from Gottman (1999) to Gray (1993, 1995), to this book, is based on the premise that there are "rules" and "guidelines" that lead to successful relationships. Those who follow the rules do well, and those who do not fare poorly; like any other game or sport, attitude is vital. One needs to play the game.

To summarize, play is a broad-based spectrum of consciousness and behavior that includes different degrees of freedom from constraint, openness, novelty, flexibility, lightheartedness, cooperation, humor, risk taking, trust, creativity, vulnerability, and positive emotion that generates increased levels of positive emotion, behavioral flexibility, and interpersonal connection.

POSITIVE PSYCHOLOGY AND POSITIVE EMOTIONS

Since this book is about a strategy that is designed to help couples flourish, it fits well with the mission of positive psychology: to understand and foster the factors that help human beings flourish (Seligman & Csikszentmihalyi, 2000).

Furthermore, it is safe to say that our emphasis on the power of play and humor suggests that we believe in the therapeutic helpfulness of positive emotions. The theory and research in positive psychology support the premise that positive emotions help people, and by extension, couples flourish.

The *broaden and build theory of positive emotions* (Fredrickson, 1998, 2001) has suggested that the function of positive emotions is to help people broaden their thought-action repertoires* and build enduring personal resources. This would be in contrast to negative emotions, which tend to narrow a person's action and thought tendencies. Negative emotions such as fear or anger are highly useful in an *immediate* survival circumstance, leading to a narrowing of choices, to fight or flight. However, the broadened action potentials that come from positive emotions lead to long-standing resource development. Fredrickson (1998) noted:

> Take play, the urge associated with joy, as an example. Animal research has found the specific forms of chasing play evident in juveniles of a species, like running into a flexible sapling or branch and catapulting oneself in an unexpected direction are seen in adults of that species exclusively during predator avoidance (Dolhinow, 1987). Such correspondences suggest that juvenile play builds enduring physical resources (Boulton & Smith, 1992; Caro, 1988, p. 220)

She then cited other research that supported the long-term benefits of play, including building lasting social bonds and attachment (Aron, Norman, Aron, McKenna, & Heyman, 2000); brain development (Panksepp, 1998); and creativity (Sherrod & Singer, 1989). "Two decades of research by Isen and her colleagues suggest that positive affect produces a broad, flexible cognitive organization and ability to integrate diverse material" (Isen, 1990, p. 89) (in Fredrickson, 2001, p. 221).

Broadening response repertoires is a help to couples. There is an old joke: What is the difference between neurosis and health? Health is one damn thing after another, and neurosis is the same damn thing after another. Individuals and couples get caught in highly limited and limiting thought-action patterns. From a theoretical perspective, anything that helps to break a couple out of the repertoire of the same damn thing after another is probably helpful.

Fredrickson and Branigan (2005) found that eliciting positive emotions of joy and contentment increased the thought-action repertoires of subjects compared to controls, and eliciting negative emotional reactions of fear and anger narrowed

---

* A thought-action is a coordinated and connected thought and behavior used to address a life challenge. So, when there is a tree that has fallen and is blocking your way, one thought-action might be the thought: I can climb over this, connected to a memory of previous climbing, connected to various processes in the body that energize the muscles actually to climb the tree, connected to an image and feeling of mastery. One's thought-action repertoire is the entire repertoire of thought-actions available to the person. A person who can only think of solving or approaching a given type of problem one way has a narrow thought-action repertoire.

thought-action repertoires of subjects compared to controls. This finding certainly fits what seems like common sense. The next logical point is: If negative emotions create a narrowing effect and positive emotions create a broadening effect, is it possible then that positive emotions are an antidote to the narrowing effects of negative emotion? Fredrickson and Levenson (1998) referred to this as the "undoing hypothesis." In experimental conditions, positive emotions were found to facilitate more rapid cardiovascular recovery after stress than neutral emotions. Negative emotions had the slowest cardiovascular recovery (Fredrickson & Levenson, 1998; Fredrickson, 2001).

Frederickson and her colleagues also discovered that experiencing positive emotions builds psychological resiliency and activates upward spirals toward emotional well-being. Fredrickson and Joiner (2002) found that individuals who experienced more positive emotion over time developed more "broad-minded" coping skills (a measure of resiliency). Further, the increase in broad-minded coping skills predicted increased positive emotions across time; in other words, it led to the development of a positive upward cycle.

Burns et al. (2008) replicated these findings and found evidence that positive emotions and interpersonal trust also mutually supported each other. The authors found some evidence suggesting that increases in dopamine may be the biological correlate of the beneficial effects of positive emotions on well-being.

Cohn et al. (2009) attempted to unpack happiness and looked at the relationship among positive emotion, life, and resilience. They found that positive emotion was highly correlated with resilience, but life satisfaction was not. They stated the following:

> The finding that positive emotions predict growth better than does life satisfaction is crucial. A wide variety of positive feelings, states, and evaluations predict positive life outcomes (Lyubomirsky et al., 2005), but when momentary positive emotions were disentangled from general life satisfaction, it was the momentary emotions that remained predictive. (p. 366)

They also stated:

> Growth in life satisfaction was predicted specifically by feeling good, not by avoidance of feeling bad. ... However, it appears that positive emotions at moderately high levels (approximately half a standard deviation) can buffer against the effects of negative emotions. (p. 366)

These findings are important both clinically and in the real world of couples therapy because they suggest that it is important to generate positive emotions in the moment on a regular basis. Echoing the work of Gottman (1999), it is not the avoidance of negative emotions (or conflict) that predicts happiness, it is having large enough doses of positive emotion that counteracts the effects of negative emotion.

HOW IMPORTANT IS PLAY IN POSITIVE PSYCHOLOGY?

While we did cite Frederickson's comments on the importance of play as a positive emotion, for the most part play and humor are not seen as that significant in positive psychology texts. Given the emphasis on "happiness" in many positive psychology texts, we find it fascinating, and troubling, that play in all of its forms gets so little airtime. For instance, in the positive affectivity and negative affectivity scale (Seligman, 2002), words such as *playful* or *amused* are not included.

In *Authentic Happiness,* Seligman (2002), the father of positive psychology, focused on the six virtues of wisdom and knowledge: courage, love and humanity, justice, temperance, spirituality, and transcendence. Work, gratitude, and forgiveness get significant page real estate. Yet, the only place that playfulness and humor get any mention is as one of 24 strengths (pp. 157–158). He only discussed play and games in the child-rearing section. In the *How of Happiness,* Lyubomirsky (2007) focused heavily on strategies to increase gratitude and create committed goals. Again, playfulness and humor at best were relegated to ancillary roles.

What are we to make of this? If positive emotions are so important, why not include one of the major sources of positive emotion: play? Frankly, we do not really know the answer, although there may be several explanations. First, most of these scientists are embedded within a work-oriented culture that does not value play outside its importance during childhood. The culture in which science operates seems to dictate that when we grow up we ought to discard childish things, play among them. This bias influences the way the research is conducted and framed. Second, we think we have a much broader definition for what we are terming play. For instance, when it comes to making good marriages better, Seligman (2002) cited Gottman's (1999) work emphasizing the importance of going out on a date at least once a week as well as engaging in affection at least 5 minutes a day. We would characterize these two things as central aspects of play, yet this does not appear to be recognized as such by Seligman. Finally, we suspect that the literature on benefits of play in producing positive emotion and transformative change (e.g., from Huizinga, 1949; to Millar, 1968; to Terr, 1999; to Schaefer, 2003; to Gordon & Esbjorn-Hargens, 2007; to Brown, 2009) simply have yet to penetrate the positive psychology world. It is hoped this book will help to change that situation.

The Ratio of Positive to Negative

In their work with couples, therapists most often focus on attempting to remove or limit conflict and other negative emotions. As a therapeutic strategy, this practice is based on the premise that conflict is fundamentally a negative component within interpersonal relationships. But, is this so? According to researcher Gottman (Gottman, 1994, 1999; Gottman & Gottman, 2010), marital conflict is neither an accurate nor a consistent predictor of marital dissatisfaction. Gottman's research substantiated the knowledge therapists gain from their own clinical experience: Many successful long-term marital relationships have moderate and sometimes even significant degrees of conflict. As therapists, therefore, it is important to acknowledge that conflict reduction does not, in and of itself, engender successful relationships.

A more accurate and useful therapeutic view of the significance of conflict within a marriage is that it is *one* factor among several operating within the relationship dynamic. As for a measure by which marriage success can be more accurately predicted, Gottman (1994) has established that it is the ratio of positive-to-negative experiences that is a more accurate and valid predictor of happiness in a marriage. The common understanding of Gottman's work is that if a relationship is to be healthy and sustainable, it needs to consist of five positive experiences for every one negative (the "five-to-one-rule") (for instance, see Marano, 2004). Couples who are on their way to divorce have a ratio of 0.8 to 1.0 (Gottman, 1994; Gottman & Gottman, 2010). In fact, Gottman's 5 to 1 rule applies to couples when they are *in conflict*. Gottman has stated that in daily living, 20 positive experiences to 1 negative is the target for healthy couples (Gottman, 2011). As clinicians, we have repeatedly used the ratio of 10:1 as the *minimum* target for couples to hit if they want to have very happy relationships.

Frederickson (2009) has suggested that for people to be happy in general they need a ratio of at least three positive emotions to one negative emotion. One could get hung up on which ratio is the correct one, but we do not believe this would be productive. These ratios are not necessarily scored in the same manner. For instance, the Gottman research derives these ratios via the use of relatively objective measures scored by researchers watching videotape. We ask our couples for a felt sense of their experience; they score themselves and come up with the ratio that represents their experience. The critical point for us as therapists is that in a healthy, sustainable relationship, the positives must occur frequently enough to neutralize the effect of the negatives. Furthermore, positive interactions must occur at levels multiple times higher than negatives.

The Opportunity of Play

The importance of positive experiences in a successful marriage makes available to us an enormous therapeutic opportunity. As therapists, we can now reconsider our approaches and reset our sights on helping couples achieve more positive interactions and, by doing so, increase their ratio of positive to negative experiences. If we can do this successfully, we stand a much better chance of helping our clients develop healthy, happy, and sustainable relationships.

Here then lies our challenge: to instill or create positives in the relationships of our clients when these relationships typically and even overwhelmingly consist of negatives. What our client-couples need is not theory or research studies, of course. What they need is hands-on practice, leading to more positive interactions. They need to relearn how to have fun, how to play. This is precisely what we are offering in this book: practical, concrete, teachable therapeutic tools that will help you help your couples increase the number and frequency of positive interactions by helping them to have *fun*, by helping them relearn how to *play*.

Fun and Games and Successful Marriages

Are fun and play so important that they can save a marriage? We believe so, and our position is supported by a great deal of research. Markman and Stanley (1996) initiated a long-term study of 306 Denver area couples. This ongoing study focuses on fun and friendship, and the emerging results support the conclusions of Markman's earlier work that established that the more couples invest in fun and friendship, the happier their relationship becomes. As he puts it, "Fun plays a vital role in the health of a marriage… (but) until recently most relationship research and books for couples widely ignored the role of fun (Markman, Stanley, & Blumbers, 2010, p. 255).

The work of Thomas Bradbury, codirector of the Marriage and Family Development Laboratory and Relationship Institute at UCLA, also points to the fundamental requirement of fun in successful relationships: He has stated, "People in happy relationships generate these [fun] activities, and as they generate these activities, it keeps their relationship strong and healthy and fresh (Joysen, 2008)." In their own survey of the research findings regarding the relationship between successful relationships and play, Lewandowski and Aron (2004) arrived at the conclusion that people who engage in playful interactions in their relationships tend to experience more positive emotions and feel closer to their partners. As a result, such couples are far more likely to arrive at Gottman's (1994) five-to-one ratio of positive to negative interactions and, ultimately, have successful long-term relationships.

For people in both same-sex friendships and opposite-sex romantic relationships, playfulness is associated with interpersonal closeness (Baxter, 1992). Further, Fraley and Aron (2004) found that participating in shared humorous activities increased perceived closeness in initial encounters between people. Aune, Dawson, and Pena (1993) discovered that dyads who engaged in a form of playful behavior, called *persona sharing*, were perceived to be more intimate than dyads not engaged in that behavior. Aune and Wong (2002) found that the consequences of adult play in romantic relationships were heightened positive emotions and increased relationship satisfaction. This work supports the work of Koepecky (1996), who determined that couples who enjoyed playing together counted the playful interaction as a relationship strength, whereas couples who did not engage in playing expressed unhappiness that such experiences were not part of their relationship.

Aron et al. (2000) examined the experiences of two test couple groups; one group was given the task of deliberately engaging in novel, fun-based activities, and the other was given no purposeful, fun-based directives. Over a 10-week period, the study concluded that relationship satisfaction was far greater for those who engaged in the fun and exciting activities compared to … those who did not engage in any special activities.

This research seems to indicate that fun is important for overall marital satisfaction. The romantic narrative is a familiar one, however. People who enjoy spending time with each other are drawn together, date, become engaged, get married, have children. Later, the demands of daily living build up, and fun gets the lowest priority. Soon, it slides out the door entirely. People stop engaging in the very activities that brought them together in the first place. Fun gets short shrift; couples wonder why they are losing the precious spark they enjoyed in the beginning of their relationship. An emerging drought of positive interactions begins to fundamentally alter the emotional economy of the relationship. As the ratio of positive to negative changes, there are fundamental shifts in how each partner views both the relationship and the other partner. "What happened?" they might ask one day. "We're no fun anymore."

Romantic Relationships and Play: A Social Psychology Perspective

According to Arthur and Elaine Aron (1986), at the root of the connection between fun and satisfying and fulfilling relationships is the fact that romantic love fulfills the compelling human need for individual growth and development. The simplest possible explanation of the fulfillment produced by human romantic relationships is that human beings enter into relationships with others in the pursuit of their own individual growth and progression. Their research has focused on romantic relationships as the primary arena for an individual's "self-expansion," and they indicated that romance is a major component of personal development. As the Arons' work suggests, we are drawn to the new, the exciting, and the challenging; we are, therefore, drawn to romance. Human love, then, has its origins in this very desire to grow, to expand, and to magnify. It motivates the formation and continuance of our romantic relationships. It excites us, challenges us, and thereby fulfills us.

The Arons' "self-expansion" model of romance explains why relationships are initially so fulfilling: In the beginning, both partners are deeply engaged in doing new and different things together which engender warmth and good humor. Both, in short, are having fun, playing. As the relationship progresses, however, opportunities to participate in "novel and challenging experiences" diminish. Self-expansion stalls, feelings of boredom and stagnation arise, and relationship satisfaction declines (Aron et al., 2000). The Arons' work concludes that to sustain successful relationships, couples must continue to identify more opportunities to engage in inspiring, exciting, and novel activities together. The couples who discover and engage in such opportunities will be the couples who maintain a flourishing and satisfying relationship (Aron & Aron, 1986).

Conversely, couples who become bored run the risk of experiencing substantially less marital satisfaction as early as nine years into the marriage (Tsapelas, Aron, & Orbuch, 2009). The results established in unequivocal terms the significance of fun and play in marital relationships. As they put it, "It is not enough for couples to be free of problems and conflicts. The take-home message of this research is that to maintain high levels of marital quality over time, couples also need to make their lives together exciting" (Tsapelas et al., 2009, p. 545).

Neuroscience and the Importance of Play, Humor, and Positive Emotions

As we have seen, fun and excitement are fundamental to a successful relationship. Let us call this the good news. The bad news, however, is that the human mind can tend toward the negative. To understand why and to understand the impact of the way we are wired in our romantic relationships, we need to shift our focus somewhat to include the human mind. In the last few years, there have been tremendous strides in the neurosciences that have had a direct impact on our understanding of the importance of positive emotions, including laughter and humor. Neuroscientists have described the bias of the nervous system toward negativity and danger. (Hanson, 2009)

It turns out that Mother Nature is not a fan of relaxation and chilling out on the savanna plains. Evolution has not favored living a high-quality life full of love and peace. Evolution and Mother Nature have favored survival of the genes, and this means alertness and anticipation of danger, of the negative. As a simple example, there are two types of mistakes in life. You can predict that there is no problem or danger when in fact there is. This is the mistake that happy positive optimists make. Or, you can predict there is a problem or danger when in fact there is no such danger. This is the mistake that anxious negative pessimists make. From an evolutionary perspective, anxious negative pessimists live longer. The anxious negative or even aggressive hominid might not be having a lot of fun, but he is far less likely to be taken unaware by the tiger sneaking up in the grass. His genes will survive. The pessimist lives to worry another day. Meanwhile, Harry the hippy dippy mellow caveman ends up as steak tartar, and his genes do not survive.

The evolutionary imperative we just described is structurally rooted in the nervous system. The amygdala, the part of the brain responsible for identifying threats, is primed to label experience negatively: 70% of its cells are tasked with tracking negative events. Furthermore, the amygdala-hippocampal system flags negative experiences for rapid recall. It does not do this for positive experiences. In Seligman's learned helplessness experiments, it only took about six trials of shock training to make dogs become helpless. It took scores of trials to untrain such learned helplessness. The understanding among neuroscientists is that "the brain is Velcro™ for the negative, Teflon™ for the positive." (Hanson, 2009)

Left to its own devices, the nervous system of a human being will tend to respond to the world and the people in the world in negative, fearful, or aggressive ways. The mind is far more likely to recall the negative than it is the positive.

Such fundamental predispositions have profound implications when it comes to long-term relationships.

NEUROPLASTICITY: CHANGING YOUR MIND CHANGES YOUR BRAIN, WHICH THEN CHANGES YOUR MIND

As we have just seen, evolution has selected genes that tend to create brain structures that are biased toward negative thinking and emotions. That is the bad news. The good news, however, is that the mind-brain road is a two-way street. We have the power to influence our brains. The way we habitually think, feel, and believe literally turns our genes on and off (Lipton, 2005) and changes the structures of nerves in our brains (Doidge, 2007; Hanson, 2009; Seigel, 2010). This process is called *neuroplasticity*, and it is a revolutionary break in the traditional understanding of neuroscience.

There is a well-known axiom in neuroscience termed Hebb's rule: *Nerves that fire together wire together.* The more you think negative or anxious thoughts about your partner (or anything else), the more you strengthen that circuit in your brain that makes it easier and more likely that you will think and feel those very thoughts. So, we are not only born with a brain-based negativity bias, but left unchecked, this bias gets amplified and magnified over time.

Of course, the opposite is true as well, and this is our saving grace. The more you look at your partner's face, laugh, and think to yourself, "Wow, I am having a great time with this person," the more you are strengthening the circuit in your brain that makes it easier and more likely that you will think and feel those very thoughts. The latest research on meditation and brain functioning finds that practicing mindfulness and meditation appears to create significant changes in the prefrontal cortex of meditators, solidifying the ability to access and inhabit more positive and sustainably positive states of mind (Davidson et al., 2003).

Another important aspect of Hebb's rule for us here is that nerves that do not fire together unwire. Unused connections between neural axons begin to melt away. This is called *axonal pruning*. If you stop doing the things that make you happy, content, and joyful, the neural connections in your brain that make it more likely for you to engage in those behaviors or even feel the good feeling from doing those behaviors wither and die. If, on the other hand, you stop engaging in negative thinking or negative behaviors, over time the neural circuits that support that negativity will begin to dissolve through axonal pruning. This is the neurological environment we inhabit—as individuals and as couples.

With these principles as a base, Hanson (2009) suggested that creating practices that generate and expand positive feelings are important methods to (a) counterbalance the negativity bias of the brain and (b) maximize the benefits of neuroplasticity. Let us take a moment before we move into a discussion of therapeutic techniques and ask, How does the human animal create positive experiences "in the wild" (i.e., outside a therapist's or coach's office)? How do we do this "normally"? We laugh, we play, and we have fun. We "high five" each other. We hug, we flirt, we have sex, and so on. In simple parlance, we engage in activities that we describe as pleasurable or fun. In other words, we engage in play because it is fun and because it helps balance our brains.

There are other significant neurological benefits from playing and producing positive emotions. One is that these activities produce high and stable levels of dopamine in the brain (Hanson, 2009). Dopamine is involved in helping maintain focus and concentration, positive moods, and learning. Drops or spikes in dopamine make attention shift. What does this have to do with long-term marital satisfaction? When a novel attractive member of the opposite sex walks by, there is a spike of dopamine. The brain says, "What/who is that?" It is not the "devil that makes you do it." It is the spike of dopamine in your brain. If a person's brain has high and stable levels of dopamine, it is less likely to spike. In other words, from a neuroscience perspective, the best way to keep your partner's eyes on you is to make sure your partner has high and stable levels of dopamine. How does one do that? By cultivating novel and playful positive experiences on an ongoing basis with one's partner.

PLAY REWARDS THE BRAIN-BASED
MOTIVATIONAL SYSTEMS IN HUMANS

The brain has three main motivational systems:

1. *The approach system* is pleasure based. This system motivates us to move toward things that feel good. On the positive side, it leads to satisfaction, fulfillment, gratitude, and happiness. On the negative side, it leads to frustration, disappointment, sadness, and discontentment.
2. *The avoid system*: This system motivates us to avoid threats and pain. On the positive side, it leads to safety, security, and self-efficacy and strength. On the negative side, it leads to alarm, anxiety, weakness, helplessness, and pessimism.
3. *The affiliative system*: This system motivates us to attach and maintain relationship bonds and feelings of closeness. On the positive side, it leads to attunement, inclusion, recognition, acknowledgment, friendship, and love. On the negative side, it leads to inadequacy, shame, feeling unloved, disconnected, and aloneness (Hanson, 2009).

Engaging in play and fun with other people, especially a person to whom one is bonded (e.g., a spouse or significant other), is desirable and pleasurable because it rewards the positive side of all three systems simultaneously. From the point of view of the brain and neuroscience, the clinical research that establishes a significant correlation between partners having fun and marital happiness (Markman,

Stanley, & Blumberg, 2010) makes perfect sense. When a couple is having fun together, each person is entraining his or her neural nets to (a) fire off positive emotions and (b) associate his or her partner with happiness and positive experiences. This, then, is the neurology of healthy romantic relationships.

Couples who successfully meet Gottman's 20:1 ratio of positive to negative experiences create a neuroplastic brain entrainment that serves as a protection against the breaching of healthy bonding. First, as Hebb's rule points out, the more couples share positive emotions, the more likely they are to share additional positive emotions. Second, as therapists and educators often witness, individuals who are part of highly distressed couples see their partners as an "other" or even an enemy. Once a partner has been marked or categorized as such, the negative propensity of the brain takes over. Behaviors become coded with greater amounts of danger and distaste. The very same behavior in a partner that several years earlier was seen as something to laugh at or something mildly annoying is now coded and experienced as negative and toxic.

EMOTIONS, NEUROPEPTIDES, PLAY, AND HUMOR

Any feeling that we have is associated with chemicals in our bodies (Pert, 1997). These chemicals are referred to as *neuropeptides* or *informational substances*. Some of them are well known and understood, such as oxytocin, which is associated with the feelings of love and warmth, connection, and relaxation. Others are not even defined. These chemicals, the structures of the brain, and the thoughts and feelings of consciousness all interact, mutually shaping one another. It is not appropriate to say that one causes the other. They coarise and coinfluence each other. Such influence occurs through time in both feedback and feed-forward loops.

Relationships with significant others are uniquely able to generate conflict and negative emotion. Anyone who has ever been in an emotional argument and found themselves unable to calm down has experienced the influence of these neuropeptides. When the emotional engine is racing, often the best you are hoping for is to at least get your mouth out of gear. This is what makes time-outs useful. If you take one and you have been angry and full of the corresponding neuropeptides, you will in time begin to feel the anger wane, feel the effect of the neuropeptide "drugs" wearing off. If neural nets become entrained, it is true that the molecules of emotion associated with those neural nets also become entrained. People who engage in anger frequently either have more anger peptides floating around or have more receptors that react to those molecules; either way, increasingly they find themselves at the mercy of their biological system. Of course, and thankfully, the opposite is also true: People who play, laugh, and create positive emotions will become more prone to those feeling states. So, even if something happens that makes them upset, their biochemistry is such that their reaction will be shorter lived.

Can the neuropeptides of humor, play, and laughter be used as an antidote for the neuropeptides of anger, resentment, and negativity? We believe they can. As we all know, maintaining a sense of humor in the midst of serious relationship conflict allows each partner to think more clearly and to maintain perspective. It also allows each partner to connect and reconnect, to use humor and laughter as a channel of peace, as the means of ending a damaging and ultimately pointless argument or conflict. The more we can laugh at ourselves and not take ourselves too seriously, the more we can let go of our own negativity. In other words, maintaining a sense of humor allows us to repair rifts between our partners and us. These "repair attempts" are one of the most important relationship strategies that successful couples use (Gottman, 1999). Not all repair attempts involve play and humor but consider the following simple case study:

> [Nathaniel and Olivia are in the middle of a fight] The more they talk about it, the higher the decibel level gets. If you were a fly on the wall of their bedroom you would have serious doubts about their future together. Then all of a sudden, Olivia puts her hands on her hips and, in perfect imitation of their four-year-old son, sticks out her tongue. Since Nathaniel knows she is about to do this, he sticks out his tongue first. They both start laughing. As always this silly contest defuses the tension between them. (Gottman, 1999, p. 22)

We postulate that because they influence the three motivational centers of the nervous system, humor and play can be used to rapidly and positively shift human neurobiology, and that this can have a powerfully constructive impact on human relationships. Ordinary human introspection suggests that there are interpersonal cascading effects between people that begin simply with a shift in perspective. Such a shift initiates changes in the brain, body, and energy field of one person, then is communicated to the other through both microcues and energetic field changes that begin to be perceived by the other, initially at the unconscious level. Eventually, a grossly explicit act occurs that is heavily associated with approach, affiliate, and safety connotations, such as Nathaniel's action in the case study. Play then is the elixir and balm that opens or, even better, reopens the heart, lifts the spirit, teaches us cooperation, spontaneity, and creativity; increases the plasticity of our brains; calms our nerves; and expands our humanity. Being playful is being alive and being free, and it is one of the most powerful antidotes to conflict and anger available to us as human beings.*

---

* We do not mean that when one spouse is upset, the other should dismiss or minimize those feelings through humor and playfulness. Relying on that strategy is likely to backfire and become destructive. In the example above, the partners make light of themselves, not each other.

Courtship, Romance, and Play

Fisher (1992) has suggested that the initial experiences of falling in love during the courtship phase of relationships are the emotional sequelae of circulating peptides that facilitate bonding. The problem arises when these chemicals wear off after a couple of years. As the Righteous Brothers put it in a song, the couple loses "that lovin' feeling."

Research examining the courtship phase of relationships suggests that fun and play are essential core components at this stage. In courtship, play is the defining feature of what must be considered among the richest of all possible human experiences. Married couples consistently report that the courtship phase of their relationship was the happiest and most fulfilling of all. In examining the joy and richness couples often experience during the courtship period, Rebecca Abrams, in *The Playful Self* (1997), discovered that courtship is, in fact, indistinguishable from play itself,

> [since it is] characterized by many of the features that also define play: intense absorption, focused attention, joy, the impression that life has value and meaning, an increased capacity for spontaneity and sense of integration and connectedness. Play ... manifests itself through flirting and teasing, and through a particular way of touching and talking. This love-play enables people very quickly to become physically and emotionally intimate. It breaks down inhibitions and builds up bonds. (p. 41)

It is clear, then, that the bliss of the courtship stage of romantic relationships is woven with the threads of fun and playful interactions.

THE POWER OF HAVING FUN USING PLAY, HUMOR, JOY, AND LAUGHTER FOR INDIVIDUALS

Even a modicum of introspection reveals the potent power of play, humor, and laughter to shift consciousness. This is hardly a new idea. Voltaire stated that, "The art of medicine consists of keeping the patient amused while Nature Heals the disease." Nevertheless there is actually relatively little research on the subject. It is often scattered through different domains.

This brings us to Sigmund Freud, the father of psychoanalysis. Terr (1999) explains that Freud understood love and work to be the two singular occupations that allowed human beings to endure what would otherwise be the overwhelming pressures of modern existence. What he failed to consider was the functional power of play in the day-to-day psychological life of the individual. Weiner (1994) concurred, explaining, "most psychoanalytic, neo-Freudian, and even object relations theorists have not viewed play as intrinsically important to adults. Freud saw play and fantasy as motivated by both the projection of wishes and the need to master conflicts and fears through reenactment. Thus, play is a fusion of, or alternation between, primary-process wish-fulfillment and secondary-process ego mastery" (p. 26).

Deeply invested in a theory focused on primary drives and conflicts, Freud greatly underestimated the power of simple and ordinary play, humor, joy, and laughter. As a result, he failed to see that such faculties and experiences create ease of being and positive emotions. Terr (1999) would agree. She pointed out that when it comes to play, Freud missed a key component of human psychodynamics. In her view, play is not only necessary to children's growth but also is a fundamental part of human existence and fulfillment. It is our intention, then, to make a case for prioritizing play and encouraging your clients to make it an integral part of their lives.

The Role of Play in Human Development

From a human being's earliest moments, play is important, far more important than simple acts of playing may appear to the casual observer.

Ackerman (1999) explained the connection between animal and human play. "Play is widespread among animals because it invites problem-solving, allowing a creature to test its limits and develop strategies. In a dangerous world, where dramas change daily, survival belongs to the agile not the idle. We may think of play as optional, a casual activity. But play is fundamental to evolution. Without play, humans and many other animals would perish" (p. 4).

Children learn how to imagine, socialize, cooperate, take risks, follow and establish rules, and engage in make-believe, all within the framework and context of play. They learn how to be themselves by engaging in and observing their own spontaneity. Play in a safe environment allows children to explore the world around them and their internal emotional world. They grow through play by gaining confidence in mastering skills. Children also develop creative skills by experimenting with different roles, develop social and emotional skills by playing with others, gain cognitive and language development (through reading and interpreting directions), and develop physical skills through eye-hand coordination, using small and large muscles.

Terr's (1999) research showed that play has an important function in human childhood development. She stated that "play is necessary to a normal childhood (p. 31)." The simple truth of it is that humans are born with an innate and natural sense of joy and play. An infant's first manifestation of self-expression is, so often, the smile that appears in the third or fourth month of the infant's life. Laughter soon follows. Play is also the defining characteristic in a healthy relationship between mother and child: Mother and baby focus their eyes on each other; mother smiles, baby mimics mother and smiles. They begin to play and are enraptured with each other. They are bonded.

As humans grow from childhood to teenage years and into adulthood, states of play continue to create and reinforce attunement, creativity, and growth.

Developmental psychoanalyst Daniel Stern (2004) described the exquisite intricacies of perhaps the first game that a human baby plays, peekaboo. The game of peekaboo is a complicated dance of interpersonal skills that teaches babies and parents how to attune to each other. Timing is critical. Too slow, and it is no fun. Too fast, it overwhelms. When it is done just right, however, peekaboo brings rounds and rounds of pleasure and interpersonal connections. From early childhood, games and playing form the basic context for learning how to modulate affect, how to explore our own abilities to respond to novel situations, how to practice skills, and how we regulate our attunement with others.

Play is important because it offers human beings an opportunity for growth by allowing us to discover different parts of ourselves that are normally hidden. Through play, we can take risks and test different ways of being in a safe and comfortable way. By so doing, we experience life more deeply, more thoroughly.

At 6 months, babies begin to reach for objects and to explore their physical surroundings. At that time, they also begin to experiment and play with their bodies, focusing on their mouths and vocal chords. By their toddler years, children engage in more rough-and-tumble play (Pankskepp, 1998) and begin to play games. They continue to play throughout grammar school, and studies indicated that they often laugh up to 400 times a day. Then, a change occurs. By the time they have reached junior high school, negative messages about play from parents and teachers have been transmitted and have begun to take effect. They have heard statements like, "It [play] is a waste of time," "Work is the important thing," "Grow up, why don't you?" "Don't be such a child," "That's so childish." Above all, they hear the message that they can play when their work is done.

The golden age of play is over. From that point forward, play is in serious decline. The impulse to play becomes undernourished, impoverished, and censored. Work emerges as the singular life priority. Laughter diminishes—by adulthood, it has dropped to an average of 15 times a day. While this may be normative, it is neither healthy nor optimal. If play is a key component of normal human development, what happens when it declines? What happens when it is fully restricted? Does a child who is deprived of play become dysfunctional?

In the 1960s, Romania's communist dictator, Nicolai Ceauşescu, banned abortion and birth control and offered women financial incentives if they would deliver more children, all to increase the workforce and population of his country. In so doing, he also created a monumental orphan problem, for not only the birth rate increased, but also the number of abandoned children.

In 1989, Ceauşescu fell from power, and the impact of his social experiment was revealed. It has been estimated that the orphan population grew to over 100,000, most living in untenable conditions in orphanages. Although they were fed, the children were not held, played with, or talked to—in fact, some of them were tied to their beds.

Harvard psychologist Charles Nelson, whose research included extensive work among Romanian orphanages, concluded that it is the ordinary child-rearing practices that we take for granted, among them playing with a child, that are the keys to shaping the developing brain (Aslanian, 2006).

THE ROLE OF PLAY AND LAUGHTER: HEALTH

Can playing and laughing help us have healthy, more satisfying lives? In his book *Social Intelligence* (2006), Daniel Goleman explained that human emotions, positive and negative, are shared instantaneously among individuals the moment they arise: "We 'feel' the other ... sensing their sentiments, their movements, their sensations, their emotions as they act inside us." (p. 42) The implications of this biochemical and neurological "sharing" is significant: Without being articulated or otherwise expressed, one human being's inner emotional state affects, influences, and drives another's inner emotional state.

At the center of this neurological interconnectivity are *mirror neurons*. As Goleman explained (2006), these are neurons that make "emotions contagious ... and ensure that the moment someone sees an emotion expressed on your face, they will at once sense that same feeling within themselves." (p. 43) On the basis of Goleman's work, it is clear that each partner in a couple has a strong impact on the physical and emotional health and well-being of the other. Positive interactions prompt the body to secrete oxytocin (the same chemical released during love making), boosting the immune system and decreasing stress hormones. Negative emotions and interaction result in stress, which in turn produces cortisol, which then negatively influences human immune systems. What is remarkable here is that in the sharing of emotions made possible by our mirror neurons, we have the power to affect the longevity not only of our relationships but also of our partner's life.

Norman Cousins, a journalist who wrote for the *Saturday Review*, is another example of the powerful intersection of emotional and physical health. Cousins was diagnosed with a spinal disease and told he had 6 months to live. He took his illness into his own hands and decided to take charge of his treatment by returning himself to a state of play. He found that if he laughed for as little as 10 minutes, he received 2 hours grace from pain. Cousins gathered films and videos of television shows and movies, *Candid Camera*, and the Marx Brothers, whatever he could find that would make him laugh like a child again. Cousins lived another 16 years, and credited his longevity to laughing and heavy doses of vitamin C.

Laugh researcher Robert Provine (2000) rightly pointed out that despite the impact of Cousins's story, it is anecdotal, and in fact there is a paucity of hard research on the health benefits of laughter or humor. He further pointed out that there are huge methodological problems with much of the research. One of them is that there has been little control for the differential effects of humor versus the physiology of laughing itself. Perhaps the findings most often cited come from Berk et al. (1988; Berk, Tan, Berk, & Eby, 1991; Berk, Tan, Napier, & Eby, 1989). Laughter decreased the stress hormone cortisol and improved lymphocyte function (improved the immune system). Humor and laughter have been found to boost antibody (S-immunoglobulin A) levels (Dillon, Minchoff, & Baker, 1985; Martin & Dobbins, 1988; Dillon & Trotten, 1989), which presumably is associated with lower stress.

The importance of play was perhaps best articulated by Dr. Stuart Brown (2009):

> Play allows us to express our joy and connect most deeply with the best in ourselves, and in others. If your life has become barren, play brings it to life again. Yes, as Freud said, life is about love and work. Yet play transcends these, infuses them with liveliness and stills time's arrow. Play is the purest expression of love. (p. 218)

What can we take from the important research into marital studies, neuroscience, and biochemistry we have been surveying? How can we, as therapists, harness the possibilities given to us by the power of play in our day-to-day work when we know only too well that the people who are the partners in the broken down relationships we are trying to heal have developed rigid barriers and defenses, have settled into a moribund and completely *playless* rigidity in their relationships with their partners?

This therapeutic approach, incorporating play in the process of healing and reinvigorating clients' marital relationships, is unique, practical, and appealing. We believe it works and hope you come to believe that states of play can save relationships and marriages and that play can, in fact, utterly transform the state of marriage. In the following chapters, we show you how this can be done.

2

The Couples' Play and Positive Interaction Assessment and Marital Play Deficiency "Disorder"

INTRODUCTION

The assessment tools presented in this chapter are an adjunct to the more traditional general assessment tools couples therapists should already be using early in the process of treating each couple. Conducting an assessment of a couple's play life at the beginning of therapy will give you insight into the couple's probable success at sustaining a happy, lasting relationship and into the success of the therapy experience itself. If all we do is help a couple correct problems, and if they do not move forward to experience any real joy or pleasure together, that couple may stay together, but they will be surviving rather than thriving. We have found that it is extremely helpful to take the time early in therapy to lead the couple through a detailed assessment, to help them look at whether they are currently having fun together at a level that will sustain a healthy, joyful relationship. This discovery helps the therapist assess the presence of fun and play and what resistances or barriers are in the way of the couple's fun. It also provides an opportunity for the couple to become excited about returning to the behaviors and mindset that prevailed during the fun times they had, usually at the beginning of their relationship.

Note that it is not the purpose of this book to describe all of the different aspects and dimensions of therapeutic assessment. In this volume, we concentrate on the role of positive interactions and playfulness in marital health. Therefore, we focus our discussion of assessment on this dimension.

MARITAL PLAY DEFICIENCY "DISORDER"

In the life of a couple, partners may find that somewhere along the way, the spark that was burning brightly when they first met has begun to flicker, wane, and perhaps even die. The fun and joy present earlier in the relationship slowly disappears. Most couples are completely unaware of the process that has gotten them to this point or to pinpoint the turning points and do something about it.

Clients often feel a sense of being understood if the therapists can give their problem a relatable, even a catchy, name. Indeed, in the world of mental health, a problem is not taken seriously unless it is given a name and acronym. So, we have coined one. We say that couples who suffer from a lack of play in their relationship are experiencing marital play deficiency "disorder" (MPDD). There appear to be three stages of this disorder. In real-life practice, the three stages of the disorder appear to be reasonable maps of territory that many of our couples find themselves traversing. These categories should be held lightly without reification.

Stage 1: The couple's relationship is still solid. There is plenty of love and goodwill in the relationship. The couple has fun and sex, but it is becoming stale or routine. The main symptom is one of growing dissatisfaction and boredom. The sizzle is beginning to fizzle. The cause is typically benign neglect.

Stage 2: The spark mostly is gone, except on rare occasions. The lack of play and positive energy has begun to eat away at the fabric of the relationship. There is growing dissatisfaction with the quantity and quality of sex, affection, and fun and an increasing anxiety and resistance to making changes.

Stage 3: This stage is best typified by the sexless marriage. The couple is not even trying to connect anymore as playmates. There is little to no energy put into creating positive and playful moments with each other. Both feel considerable conflict and share a perception that they are just no longer compatible. This couple is well on its way to either divorcing or living in a playless, sexless marriage.

THE COUPLES' PLAY AND POSITIVE INTERACTION ASSESSMENT

To judge the level of MPDD effectively, the following assessment protocol enables the therapist to get a clearer picture of the situation. The (Couples' Play and Positive Interaction Assessment) CPPIA is a process that will assist you in assessing the couple's status. It will help to ascertain the amount of positive interactions in relation to negative ones in the couple's relationship; how much fun they have together; what types and levels of play they experienced earlier in their relationship; what they currently do for play; which play activities the couple shares and which activities each pursues separately; milestones or stressful events that have led to the deterioration of positive interactions; and each partner's individual childhood play history.

This assessment process is *not* simply about the therapist or educator gathering information for treatment. It is much more about helping the couple develop awareness of how the forces and choices they have made in their lives have had an impact on pleasure, fun, and play. Ideally, you will incorporate this assessment tool into your client intake process.

We recognize that there are situations in therapy for which focusing on increasing a couple's playfulness and positive interactions must give way to interventions designed to put out serious burning fires. The most common examples include

- Active physical violence
- Highly volatile cycles of emotional abuse, fighting, rage, name calling
- Untreated trauma and post-traumatic stress disorder (PTSD)
- Uncontrolled addictions
- Significant, uncontrolled, major mental illness such as bipolar disorder, major depression, and psychosis
- Infidelity

These situations call for structure and active therapeutic management, naturally. It is much more important to stabilize these situations by reducing the negative and destructive effects of these problems. The more a couple is in an emotional crisis with high levels of negative affect, the more important it is to immediately work on reducing the negative affect and help the couple to install emotional buffering.

Nevertheless, the approach we are advocating can also be one of the effective tools in the overall arsenal of treatment for couples with these types of issues because one of the reasons such couples are so affectively labile is that they are usually both "starving for positive connection" and reduced to fighting and blaming each other regarding the source of the lack of positive connection. One of the best ways to lower the pressure is to reduce the starvation by increasing positive interaction while lowering the negative atmosphere. However, the more volatile the situation, or the more there is uncontrolled comorbidity of addictions, the more pain and hurt there is over the betrayal of infidelity, or major mental health issues (e.g., bipolar disorder or PTSD), the more that work on building up positive interactions will likely take a back seat to safety and stabilization procedures (which are beyond the scope of this book).

THE COUPLE'S CURRENT EMOTIONAL ECONOMY

During the first session, it is important to take a quick read on the current state of the couple's emotional economy. This is the ratio of positive interactions relative to negative interactions. Is there an abundance of positive interactions compared to the negative interactions? Or, is it the opposite? Is the couple in an emotional drought or famine? Is the economy such that there is barely enough? For each negative interaction the couple experiences, how many positive interactions engage the couple?

In a seminal work, *Why Marriages Succeed or Fail*, Gottman (1994) stated that it is important for couples to have 5 positive interactions to every negative one. From our clinical experience, we have found that truly happy couples have not just 5 but up to 10 positive interactions for every 1 negative interaction. In fact, Gottman said that the ratio actually needs to be 20 positives to 1 negative for couples truly to thrive. The fact is that if a couple is in your office, it is likely the ratio is not even close to 5:1.

It is important to understand that the point of discovering this information has less to do with informing the therapist and more to do with informing the couple and creating a framework to explain their predicament and create a potential road to salvation. In other words, the assessment process and its results become a significant therapeutic intervention in itself.

COUPLES' POSITIVE-TO-NEGATIVE RATIO

When introducing the assessment and discussing the concept of positive-to-negative interactions, you can say the following:

> "Every interaction between the two of you is either positive or negative. The following are a few examples: Helping a partner meet a work deadline is an example of a positive interaction. Criticizing that partner for working too much is negative. Getting into an argument over who is going to pay the bills is negative. Picking up a small unexpected gift and giving it to a spouse is positive.
>
> "We are going to assign a score to each interaction. So, imagine a list of all the positive interactions you have with your partner being on one side of a paper and all the negative interactions you have listed on the other side of the paper; see what that ratio would be. A mild interaction might get a score of 1 in either the positive or negative column. A very strong positive or very strong negative interaction might get a score of 100. Does this make sense? (The couple agrees.)
>
> "Now let us imagine that we can add up all of the positive interactions and put that number in one column, and then we can add up all of the negative interactions and put it on the other side.
>
> "Next, let us boil these numbers down to a simple comparison of the number of positive interactions to the negative ones. This is the ratio on which we focus. A ratio of 3 to 1 would mean that for every 1 negative interaction you experience, there are 3 positive interactions.
>
> "If the ratio was reversed and stood at 1 to 3, you would be saying that for every 1 positive interaction, there are 3 negative interactions. If you thought positive and negative interactions were about the same, you would say the ratio is 1 to 1.

"Now remember, I want you each to think about the interactions that occur between the both of you. Think about what has transpired in the last 3 months. You need to include interactions that originate from your partner toward you and those that come from you toward your partner. Okay?

"I would like each of you to think about this silently for yourself and keep your answer to yourself for the moment. Come up with your felt sense of where you have been as a couple over the past few months and translate that to a ratio of positives to negatives. Take your time and nod your head when you have a ratio in mind."

It is fascinating that couples are usually in the same ballpark with the ratios. Typically, there are three potential types of responses: one positive for every two negative interactions or worse, one positive for every negative, and two or three positives for every negative. The therapist can use these answers to begin to frame for the couple what is happening in a way that increases motivation and hope, leading to a deeper assessment.

UNDERSTANDING THE RATIOS

One to Two or More: One Positive Interaction for Every Two Negative Interactions, or Worse

Couples have at least twice as many negatives as positives occurring (one positive for every two or more negatives). Couples with ratios like this are in desperate shape. They are almost always in Stage 3 of MPDD. They often have little hope that things will improve. They may say you are their last chance. The therapist can respond with the following: "So, two out of three times when you interact, there is a negative charge. I am sure that is not what you signed up for when you got married. This explains why you're so unhappy."

One to One: One Positive Interaction for Every One Negative Interaction

In the situation of one positive to one negative interaction, 50% of the time the interaction is positive, and 50% of the time it is negative. Couples with ratios like this are very unhappy, but they want things to get better, although they are not sure how to make that happen. Couples here are usually in Stage 2 of MPDD. The therapist responds with the following: "So, 50% of the time you interact it has a negative charge to it. I'm sure this is not how it used to be at happier times in your marriage. It's not surprising that your relationship is suffering."

Two or Three to One: Two or Three Positive Interactions for Every One Negative Interaction

Couples with ratios of two or three positive to one negative interaction are unhappy enough to seek an intervention but usually are not in crisis (unless there is some other outside event). This couple has arrived in your office before things have completely deteriorated and are usually in the late phase of Stage 1 of MPDD. They may say they used to be so much happier and want that back. You can respond with the following: "You do have more positives than negatives, but actually the ratio is not high enough to be truly happy. It's easy to see why you are not as happy as you used to be."

THE COUPLE'S EMOTIONAL ECONOMY AND EXPERIENCE

Once a ratio is established, it is important to explain that the higher the ratio is on the positive side, the more likely any single event will be perceived as more positive, even if that event is actually negative, and vice versa. Actions, words, and tone are perceived differently depending on the overall ratio. According to Gottman and Gottman (2010), this is referred to as "positive sentiment override."

In other words, events that do have the potential to "hurt" will actually hurt less because there is a surplus of positive interactions. The couple is more hopeful and loving as well as more inoculated against stress. Likewise, the higher the ratio is on the negative side, the more discouraged, hopeless, and stressed the couple becomes. Everything now looks negative. Individuals lose touch with the love that was present between them in the beginning of the relationship, and they begin to see one another in a more negative light. Gottman and Gottman (2010) referred to this phenomenon as "negative sentiment override." Any slight or slip is experienced as more painful with larger negative meaning, while the very same slight or slip experienced in the context of a lot of positive interaction may not register as negative. But, when the ratio is slanted to the negative, each conflict becomes a major ordeal that can slowly erode the relationship. The longer this situation persists, the more dangerous it becomes. Each partner gradually starts to think of divorce and how he or she might be better off alone or with someone who is kinder, more understanding, and more fun.

Sometimes, the couple does not agree on the ratio of positives to negatives. The question is how much of a difference must exist for it to matter? Our answer is clinical and commonsensical, rather than experimental. If their ratios fall into the same category or are less than 2 points apart, it is not significantly important. For example, he says it is 1:3, and she says it is 1:2. They are still both saying it is a very negative situation. On the other hand, if Alan says it is three positives to one negative, and Jill says it is one positive to one negative, that is clinically significant because they are in fundamentally different categories. He is saying that things are relatively good. She is saying things are relatively bad.

If the couple does not agree, this is actually great information for the purposes of therapy. It usually leads to a highly useful dialogue that unearths salient dynamics. The major question for the therapist to ask is: "What are you aware of in your communications and interactions that your partner is not, which makes you say that the ratio is _____ ?" In this example, Jill replied that she often kept her feelings of hurt to herself, so it was reasonable that Alan was hardly ever aware that what he said and did was often negative to her. Furthermore, she realized that this caused her to hold on to a lot of resentment that made her more sensitive than usual.

THE COUPLE'S BRIEF PLAY PROFILE: ARE WE HAVING FUN?

We ask couples to fill out the following questionnaire designed to determine the degree of fun that currently exists in their relationship. This is an opportunity for the couple to see at a glance what they are doing about fun *now*.

Are We Having Fun?

Score each statement below using the following scale based on how often these activities occur. All interactions are considered to be positive.

1 = Never
2 = Rarely
3 = Occasionally
4 = Often
5 = Always

1. I enjoy my partner's company. _____
2. My partner makes me smile/laugh. _____
3. I make my partner smile/laugh. _____
4. We go out on dates alone together that include fun activities (other than meals). _____
5. We flirt with each other. _____
6. We do novel things together. _____
7. We act silly together when we're alone. _____
8. My partner has a good sense of humor. _____
9. We take trips alone together. _____
10. We enjoy doing the same activities together. _____
11. We plan future fun activities together. _____
12. My partner is open to fun activity ideas I suggest. _____
13. I am open to activities my partner suggests. _____
14. I surprise my partner with something fun to do. _____
15. My partner surprises me with something fun to do. _____
16. We play games together (board/card games, sports, etc.). _____
17. My partner and I joke with or playfully tease each other. _____
18. I am satisfied with the frequency of our sexual encounters. _____
19. I am satisfied with the quality of sex with my partner. _____
20. My partner and I are physically affectionate. _____

Each partner is asked to complete the questionnaire and add his or her scores separately. Next, the therapist asks them to talk about their results together. They are told that this is a time to report, not argue, even if there is a major discrepancy between the scores. If this is the case, it can open up an important discussion. You can encourage them to notice which activities they have scored *never* or *rarely*, where they have scored the same, and where they have scored at opposite ends of the scale.

INDIVIDUAL VERSUS COUPLE'S PLAY

As you are discussing how much fun a couple is currently having, it can be useful also to help them understand the balance between the amount of play that married people engage in as individuals versus what they do together as a couple. We give each person a piece of paper with the following five Venn diagrams shown in Figure 2.1 and ask them to choose which is the closest to their current balance. Sometimes, we ask people to do the same diagram rating for the time when they were first married.

Part A in Figure 2.1 depicts a situation for which essentially all of the fun a person has occurs outside the relationship. This is a diagram of a couple in Stage 3 of MPDD. It leads one to ask, "What is the point of being together as a couple?" This is often the picture of a couple who may be together only for the kids or because of economic reasons or other circumstances that have little to do with mutual desire. It also raises the question of which activities occupy the relatively small overlapping section of joint fun/play? Is there something there to build on? This diagram serves as a stark visual reminder that the couple needs to start redirecting their energies more toward each other than outwardly.

The second diagram, B, is usually associated with either late Stage 2 or early Stage 3 MPDD. All the same questions apply. The person with this diagram still recognizes that there are a few things that bring fun to the couple when together. Very small embers are still burning.

Figure 2.1C depicts the couple having more fun together but not as much fun as each has separately. Since the couple is coming in for help, it suggests that they are in either late Stage 1 or early Stage 2 of MPDD. Again, this suggests that the couple needs to turn toward each other and increase the positive and playful activities together. Generally, if both partners have this chart they have many resources on which they can build.

Figure 2.1D shows a good, healthy balance between self and spouse. This is the figure representing a person in Stage 1 of MPDD. To the extent that this couple is describing their relationship as not fun anymore, it may be indicative that they are no longer enjoying shared activities as much as they each did before. Or, perhaps the nature of their shared time has changed. This could include spending time with children, family, or friends rather than time alone together.

Sometimes you can play and have fun with your partner.
Sometimes you can play and have fun without your partner.
Which picture most accurately reflects the mixture of where you have fun?

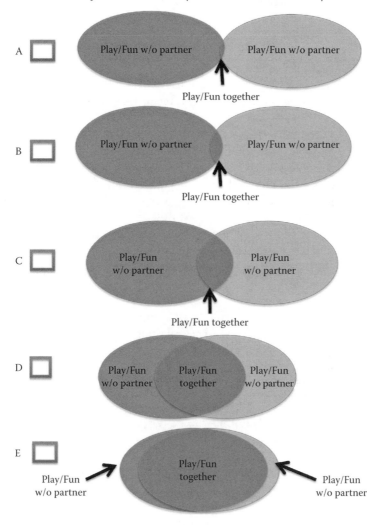

Figure 2.1   Play questionnaire.

Figure 2.1E is a little different. It shows us a situation for which most of the fun a person has comes from inside the relationship, but little fun happens as a separate person. Clinically, this scenario suggests that perhaps the couple is too enmeshed; casually, one might say this couple is "joined at the hip." Often, this is a picture of a couple who is very comfortable together but has become friendly partners with little real passion. Perel (2006) referred to these couples as opting for safety and comfort over eroticism and passion. She suggested that these couples need to add some mystery to their relationship.

THE COURSE OF THE COUPLE'S DETERIORATION OF FUN

Now that you and the couple have discovered what is happening currently, you can ask the couple how long this situation has existed. Whatever the couple says is an opportunity to join (Minuchin & Fishman, 1981) and be empathic. This is usually a good time to educate and reframe the couple's situation. They are told that it is almost impossible to have a happy marriage with such high ratios of negative to positive interactions and with depictions of deriving so much of one's fun activities outside the marriage. However, we point out that by becoming aware of the state of play in their relationship, it can open the possibility of taking positive steps to increase shared fun times together and eventually having a joyous relationship.

The next step is to help the couple reconnect with their past, a time when there was a better ratio and when they spent more fun time together. This can help determine how this deterioration has unfolded over time.

First ask the couple these questions:

- When were you happiest in your relationship?
- What was the ratio of positive to negative interactions then?
- What were you doing then that made the ratio better?

During their first session, Jose and Maria were answering these questions when they recalled that Jose once used to leave love notes on their bathroom mirror for Maria to find. Maria once made delicious gourmet meals at least twice a week for Jose. They recalled one beautiful summer day on Jose's sailboat and how they capsized but laughed about it afterward. They also remembered an overnight at Jose's Aunt Maria's house when they tried a new position while making love in the guest room right next to hers. They had to muffle their voices and had a silent laugh the next morning when Aunt Maria asked, "Did you two sleep well?" However, they could not recall any similarly fun or exciting shared times more recently.

DEVELOPMENTAL MILESTONES AND STRESSFUL EVENTS

At this point, we know what was happening in the couple's life when they were at their best. We know the problem state they are in now, but we need to pinpoint when and how things shifted. We ask, "What happened?" Often, they have no clear sense of how to answer this, so we ask them to track back to developmental milestones or stressful events that may have contributed to the diminishment of fun in their lives. Some couples are surprised to learn that even an otherwise positive event can cause a negative effect on their shared fun. The arrival of children, a promotion at work, a sudden financial windfall—these are thought of as wonderful events, but each can also take a toll on a couple's ratio of positive to negative interactions. So, we set about to make a list of a couple's stressful events. To misquote Captain Renault from the movie *Casablanca:* "The fun has been shot. Round up the usual suspects." The following are examples:

- Birth of children
- Death or illness of family members
- Negative change in career
- Positive change in career
- Moving
- Illness of spouse
- Problems with children
- Children leaving home
- Children getting married
- Accidents or injuries
- Financial loss or hardship
- Spouse returning to college/graduate school

This exercise is about increasing awareness. We want to discuss with the couple how these events and experiences unfolded; what each meant to them both as a couple and individually; and how they coped and managed. Perhaps the most common milestone is when the couple started to have children.

Here is a typical relationship narrative to illustrate:

Andrew explained, "Things started to go downhill with the birth of our first child because after that we focused most of our attention on our child and just stopped going out together. We were always exhausted. But as the kids got older, we just got used to spending all our free time with the children. Somehow, we started to bicker more and more. Now, we are both so angry and frustrated with the whole situation and with each other, and we hardly ever have fun anymore." His wife, Claire, nodded her head in agreement.

Here is another narrative:

Lavinia noted that during the fifth year of their marriage, she developed breast cancer. It was a traumatic experience for her of course, and she naturally became frightened and depressed. But, her trauma was compounded because, she explained, "Don wasn't there for me." She felt abandoned. "He wouldn't take me to the doctor when I needed him. I was shocked. The worst part was that when I was nauseous from the chemo, he would often go to his mother's house to help her fix things instead of staying with me." Lavinia's resentment rose. Many nights, she cried herself to sleep. She and Don became more and more distant. She could not forgive Don for his behavior.

And here is another:

> Mona and Derek married right after college, and she worked to support the couple for the next 8 years while Derek completed medical school and pursued an unusually challenging and competitive, residency, and fellowship program. Even though time and money were in short supply, the couple both recalled that those 8 years were their happiest. They made it a point to use Derek's 1 day off each week to do something fun alone together, even if it was only a picnic in the park. They were living their shared dream, working toward a common goal. Yet, soon after Derek was offered a coveted position at a prestigious research hospital, with a hefty salary in an exciting city, the couple began to fall apart. These otherwise wonderful events—an enviable position, financial security, and a move to a place they both longed to live—put so much stress on the couple, they stopped enjoying one another. They were so consumed with the logistics and adjustments to their new situation, those once-a-week fun days disappeared.

Here is another example:

> When Yves got laid off from his job, he knew he would have severance pay for 8 months, providing security for his family. Soon, he lined up a number of job interviews but got no offers. After 4 months of networking and interviewing, Yves began to worry and often felt depressed. Although she worked part time, Sonya also was concerned about the family's financial situation but still had confidence in her husband. Yves, however, would not discuss things, and they became increasingly distant. To buoy his spirits, Sonya occasionally suggested an inexpensive outing, like bowling, but Yves always insisted they could not afford it. "Don't you understand?" he yelled. "We have to save every penny in case I can't find anything for a while." Yves became more depressed and Sonya more resentful.

The following is a final example:

> Sarita and Ben were married for 26 years and overall agreed they were blessed with great kids, financial security, and good health. Yet, they could not remember the last time they were out on a date together alone. When their last child, Matt, left for college, they came for therapy because both wanted either to bring back the spark in their relationship that had been missing for years or to separate. Both admitted that they felt hopeless about the situation. Sex and intimacy were scarce. They recalled that in the beginning of their marriage they laughed, went out dancing, and had a lot of fun going to concerts and playing poker. Yet, when their first child was born, 4 years into the marriage, they began focusing all their attention on him and the three siblings who arrived later. They put their relationship on the back burner.

Through discussion, we make it clear that stressful milestones can cause a major shift in the fun times a couple experiences together. It is important not to assess blame for who did not handle things well; usually, it is a shared failing for not coping with the milestone as a couple. After opening this discussion, couples are encouraged to see which feelings are still present from the stressful event. Usually, apologies or forgiveness are required, but what a couple needs most is to recognize and acknowledge the stressful event and the role it played in dampening their positive interactions.

RECONNECTING TO PAST PLAYFUL RESOURCES

After getting a picture of the deterioration of play in the relationship, it is important to cycle back and look for resources that have been lost along the way. Here is a set of questions useful for doing so:

- What other activities or interactions have previously been sources of fun, positive emotion, and connection for you as a couple over the years?
- To what extent do you do any of those things now?
- What new activities or interactions have you tried lately to create fun and pleasure?

How a couple responds to these questions is as diagnostic as the information itself. For some couples, simply asking these questions begins to reconnect them to what they used to do, and often they are then more ready to act.

Here are some typical client-couple responses:

Aleta recalled the times that she and Marco sneaked off to the beach at night with a table and chairs, wine glasses, beautiful plates and utensils, and delicious gourmet food. They created a very romantic mood. They lit candles and played music. The sex that followed on those nights was memorable. Marco's eyes lit up, and he looked at Aleta with longing. "Let's do that again," he said. "I can't even figure out why we ever stopped."

Brett explained how he and Luanne had once gone out every Friday for ballroom dancing lessons. They loved learning Latin dancing together and eventually entered small dance contests and often won. When they went to weddings and danced, many people complimented them and asked if they were professional dancers, which always made them laugh. But, they had not danced in more than 10 years. Asked why not, both just shrugged.

For other couples, what rapidly becomes observable is a degree of dysfunction or resistance:

Siobhan talked about being discouraged with her and Liam's recent attempts to put some fun back into their marriage. He had suggested they get season tickets to the local semipro baseball team, which they had done for years but long ago let lapse. But, Siobhan, now in perimenopause, found it too hot to be outside for hours. She instead thought it would be fun to pick up their old hobby of attending antique shows, but Liam did not want to be tempted to spend scarce dollars on antiques, even though he also loved them.

Teresa and Piers were so frustrated with their situation they simply could not think of even one new activity they could try together that might be fun for the two of them. He complained, "She is so rigid; she won't try anything new," while she countered, "But you only suggest things you enjoy and that you already know I don't want to try."

INDIVIDUAL PLAY HISTORIES

Our next goal is to understand the individual play history of each member of the couple. Exploring what people were taught about playing, fun, spontaneity, and so on reveals a wealth of information that is useful for the therapist and the couple.

Never underestimate the power of the question: "What did you do for play as a child?" We use this to powerful effect in all our workshops and couples evaluations. Most of the time, it offers the individual the opportunity to get back in touch with the positive feelings that were present while they played as children. However, sometimes the feelings can be painful.

> During one workshop, Lori raised her hand and began to cry. She said she had stopped playing early in her life because once when playing a game with her father, he got mad at her for winning. She remembered feeling so hurt she vowed that she would never play a game again. She later reported that she did not really understand why she wanted to come to the workshop, but now understood that this childhood experience might have contributed to her compulsive workaholism and incredible resistance to play.

> When Maria and John were asked, "What are your beliefs about play?" they each responded that in their childhood homes, play was something that came after their work was done. It was a reward instead of a necessity. Of course, they rarely played together now as adults because each felt there was always more work to do, and rewards are not necessities.

As mentioned, as part of the assessment, we need to help clients understand that "reasons" or "excuses" may actually reflect some deeper blocks that need to be explored. Like most other aspects of therapy, the area in which to shine the therapeutic light is the client's personal history. If a person was not playful before marriage, he or she will be unlikely to be playful within the marriage.

Depending on your style, you can take a detailed childhood and young adult history as part of this assessment, or you can explore these issues as they arise during treatment. We have designed the questions that follow as a basic approach to the work of uncovering relevant underlying individual factors. This exercise has proven to be extremely illuminating and impactful. It allows clients to get a sense of how their past has shaped their ability to be a playful partner. It is preferable to do this with both people in the room so that each can witness and begin to understand the dynamics of his or her partner. As you are asking these questions, notice the client's body language and inquire about the client's emotional responses.

The following are questions for the client:

- What did you do for play as a child? Can you picture exactly what activities you did? What feelings are you experiencing as you think about this?
- Was the atmosphere in your home a safe, positive, playful environment? If not, was it unsafe, negative, and tense?

- How much laughter and play was there in your house? Who laughed? Was such laughter at the expense of others?
- What was each parent's attitude toward playing and having fun?
- Did you learn that playing was something you did only after your work was completed?
- Were you the first-born child who had the responsibility of taking care of younger siblings?
- Were you laughed at when you did not do well in something such as a sport or a performance?
- What were the messages you heard from parents, teachers, siblings, and so on regarding play?
- What did your parents do for fun?
- What did your family do together for fun?
- Did you have negative experiences playing with friends, siblings, or parents?
- Were you so afraid of looking foolish or making a mistake that you did not try anything new?
- Was play stressful because it was too competitive?

After the couple answers these questions, clinicians can ask follow-up questions to assist the individual who has not learned to play or who has been apprehensive about it, start to see possibilities for future fun and play:

1. How do you think your responses to the questions have affected your ability to play in the past and currently in your relationship?
2. Can you recall a time in your life when you had a fun, joyful, play experience? What worked in that situation?
3. What is stopping you from being able to take slow steps toward playing individually and with your partner?
4. What do you need from your partner with regard to support to help you to begin this process?
5. How might adding more play to your life and relationship benefit your relationship?

In this second chapter of the book, we directed our therapeutic focus to assessment, the first stage of the process of incorporating play into marital therapy. We addressed the following areas in our assessment to determine the couple's shared state of play:

- The couple's current emotional economy
- The ratio of positive to negative interactions
- The couple's original or best emotional economy

- How much fun the couple is currently having
- The course of the deterioration of the couple's playfulness and fun
- The stresses and developmental hurdles that contributed to the demise of playfulness
- The couple's history of play as a possible road map to future interaction
- Responsiveness versus resistance in the couple's ability to reconnect with more playfulness
- Individual play history for each member of the couple

The object of this assessment has been to create (for the therapist and for the client), a necessary map of the couple's past and current state of play. It also is an intervention by

- Stimulating and bringing into awareness the positive feelings of play
- Discovering the importance of play in a healthy relationship
- Motivating the couple to incorporate it into their daily lives
- Giving the couple an opportunity to buy into the idea of starting on a path of cultivating play and, it is hoped, adopting play as a relationship goal

In the next chapter, we focus on the barriers that can inhibit play and playful behaviors. By devoting a therapy session or two to utilizing the assessment tools provided in this chapter, you will be much better equipped to steer your couples through what comes next—reestablishing play to its primary role in the couple's relationship.

3

No Play Zone
Looking at Barriers, Permission, and the Problems of Play

INTRODUCTION

As our playful chapter title suggests, from a certain perspective there is something askew with the objections that clients (and sometimes therapists) make at the outset of counseling with regard to having more playfulness, fun, and joy. It is important to be prepared for this and have an approach to managing these objections so that you can go deeper as your counseling proceeds. Before we delve into the details of the barriers to creating playful and joyful marriages, let us take a brief look at the kinds of objections that clients sometimes make at the outset. We address them briefly now and then spiral down and examine assumptions that underlie them.

Objection 1: *The problems in my relationship are fundamentally too serious and deep to be solved by something as "frivolous" as play.* This objection is actually two objections: The first is that "play" is frivolous, a matter we discuss further in this chapter. The second is that relationship problems are too intense or complex to be resolved by focusing on the positive. In response, we often ask the couple if they have heard the expression, "It is better to light a single candle than curse the darkness." We often ask them what they think this might mean given their anger and resentment. What usually ensues is a reframing of the hidden causality assumption. The assumption we are making here is that the cause of a client's resistance to being more playful is his or her anger and resentment. The alternative hypothesis regarding the cause of the anger and resentment is their resistance to being more playful. Once upon a time, they played more, but as they misunderstood each other and hurt each other, they played less and less. Less play leads to less positive energy, acceptance, love, and so on, which leads to more resentment.

Objection 2: *Play is not productive. It is frivolous and a waste of time.* "Bah, humbug." Remember Scrooge. Remember what happened to him? As we discuss, this is one of the childhood injunctions transmitted via family and culture that lies at the heart of the problem. If a client says this explicitly, therapists looking to get into "deep issues" can jump for joy. The client has just invited you to go directly to the heart of the matter. All you need to say is, "Really, can you please tell me how you have come to know this?" Then, keep asking questions that will lead to all sorts of negative experiences and injunctions.

Objection 3: *We do not have the time. We have work, chores, and obligations with kids.* Of course, they think they do not have time. This is exactly one of the "illusions" that causes so much trouble. It is so easy to get caught up in the grind of life and to forget what makes life worth living. If they are upset enough to come to therapy, it means that their choices are not working for them. If this is the case, they really do need to consider doing something different. The fact is that they are likely spending a ton of energy feeling badly. Once they are playing more, they will actually have more energy and more time to get everything done. They actually can get their work and obligations done and play more at the same time.

Objection 4: *I am too angry and resentful.* This is another great objection that therapists can use to get to major blocks rapidly. It is certainly hard to play when you are angry and resentful. The good news is that if a client says this, he or she has accepted (at least partially) responsibility for personal feelings. The client most likely has good reasons for having resentful and angry feelings, as does the client's partner. They are looking at each other as "the enemy" rather than a teammate. So, the question becomes: Does each one want to keep the resentful angry feelings and have an increasingly bad relationship, or do they want to let go of them? Again, we might focus on the expression regarding lighting a candle in the darkness. There is an axiom: whatever you focus on, you will have more of. Instead of focusing on the increasing darkness, they need to focus on lighting more and more candles.

Objection 5: *We do not enjoy the same type of play, or my partner does not know how to play.* This is another good objection that gives the therapist license to explore the details of the couples play life, their expectations of each other, and each one's individual dynamics.

Almost all people begin life with an innate ability to be joyful and positive. Their desire to expand this experience of happiness and joy culminates, ultimately, in a profoundly powerful decision to join with another individual not only to form a bond, a lifelong partnership, an opportunity to experience greater and newer joys, but also, and importantly, to share personal joy and love with a cherished partner. So often, unfortunately, the joy that was a near-constant feature of the early stages of this bond fades, becomes worn. One day, one or both partners wake with an unsettling realization: "We're no fun anymore. What happened?" they ask. As therapists, it's productive to ask the same question.

This decline in positive and joyful experiences within a marriage arises from multiple factors, some individual, some systemic to the couple, some societal and cultural. In our work as therapists, it is critical that we address the issue of the barriers that arise between an individual and his or her capacity to access and engage in play: those issues that impede and arrest the flow of joy and play so characteristic and necessary in a successful union, those factors that prevent couples from creating new positive experiences in their marriages. It is necessary to remind ourselves, perhaps, that our opportunities to do this work are limited. The truth is that as couples therapists, coaches, and educators, we are granted only a finite amount of time with our clients, 10 to 12 sessions on average (many times, far fewer sessions than that). This makes it imperative that we do everything we can to identify rapidly the barriers to fun and joy that have arisen in our clients' partnerships.

In our approach to the barriers of play, then, we focus our attention on two basic areas: unrealistic expectations about different aspects of marriage and the individual dynamics that create barriers to sustainable, joyful, and playful lives. Based on our own clinical experience, we have come to the conclusion that as clinicians and educators, we best serve our clients by first identifying to what degree a couple is plagued by unrealistic expectations about their marriage and marriage in general. As you will see, many of the things that we are about to address are basic—yet we would argue that they are profoundly important. You may be tempted to simply skip over them to get to the "good stuff," such as the role of deep-seated individual dynamics. Please do not do this. As a therapist, the weight of experience and habitual practice can sometimes be an encumbrance, can allow us to take things, basic things, for granted. To a mechanic, an oil change is basic stuff, hardly worth considering. But to a car owner, it may not be so. This information gap is fine for car owners who just want their car to run smoothly, but it will not do for "marriage owners," who need to know how to make their relationship "run." As therapists, it is important to remind ourselves that many of our "customers" do not have even a basic knowledge about how to care for their "relationship vehicle."

Are you not sometimes amazed at the unrealistic expectations your clients have regarding relationships and marriage? False or unrealistic expectations are so often at the heart of marital strife. The benefits to correcting such expectations are manifold, and as therapists, such an educational opportunity simply should not be ignored. We have found that by first addressing unrealistic marriage expectations we can generate highly useful and positive momentum in our sessions with clients. Another benefit to this approach is that by dealing first with the unrealistic expectations, we can often greatly reduce therapeutic resistance to looking at the individual issues that often underlie them. Resistance is reduced because first we educate and operate under the assumption that both people can engage in new behaviors. This assumption is communicated to the couple either directly or indirectly. We also get intellectual and, it is hoped, emotional buy-in from the couple to shift their behavior based on a set of more realistic expectations. If the couple succeeds, everyone is happy. If one or both people are not successful, this organically brings up the question, "What is preventing me from acting in the way I want to act?"

COMMON AND IMPORTANT BARRIERS TO PLAY: THE SHORT LIST

Within the Partnership: Unrealistic Relationship Expectations

- Unrealistic expectations about what it takes to have a joyous, loving, lasting marriage
- Unrealistic expectations about balancing the roles of parent and spouse
- Unrealistic expectations regarding the responsibility and role of the self and the other partner in creating joy and positive experiences

Outside the Partnership: Individual Dynamics

- Fear of embarrassment, making mistakes, looking silly or stupid
- Viewing the world through the lens of "right" and "wrong"
- Competitiveness
- Fear of loss of control
- Insecure attachment style
- Rigid and inflexible values about how to create positive experiences of fun and joy
- Parental injunctions and life scripts
- Childhood abuse and trauma

UNREALISTIC RELATIONSHIP EXPECTATIONS

Unrealistic Expectations About What It Takes to Have a Joyous, Loving, Lasting Marriage

In the early 1960s, there was a television show called, *Kids Say the Darnedest Things*. Today, we should have a show called *People Have the Strangest Ideas About Marriage*. The more therapists work with couples, the more it becomes apparent to them that this culture creates an appalling set of unrealistic expectations about how to have and maintain a healthy, long-lasting marriage. We simply cannot overstate how significant and problematic this phenomenon is. Here are a few examples:

- Husband and wife agree that their ratio of positive to negative interactions is about 1:1, and they think that is pretty good.
- Husband and wife do not think there is any correlation between them not going out together on a date for over 5 years and their marital discord.
- A husband says that he does not think he has to be romantic with his wife; that is only for dating. They are married now; he should not have to do that.
- A wife says she believes that she does not need to have sex with her husband and thinks that their marriage can still be good.

The good news for us as educators and therapists is that correcting unrealistic expectations is a relatively easy procedure. If these are the only things plaguing the relationship, they are, in fact, fairly simple to repair (especially when, as counselors and therapists, we let go of our brilliant ideas and our need to find "deeper-seated" problems). If, on the other hand, there is more going on under the surface, and there often is, it quickly becomes apparent to all parties.

The biggest problem with unrealistic expectations in a marriage is that when things get difficult, instead of reassessing faulty or illusory expectations, spouses blame either their partners or themselves—and they do so to an increasingly negative degree. As therapists, we must remember that what is driving these problems is, at root, a set of expectations that simply cannot be fulfilled. Our goal in this particular therapeutic area should be to address and correct false or illusory expectations in a psychoeducational fashion so that each partner can develop and invest in new, more accurate relationship expectations. Then, each partner can begin to engage in behaviors that are in alignment with such realistic expectations and, ultimately, create more positive relationships.

The following is a relevant case study:

John and Maria came to therapy complaining that their relationship was boring, dull, and routine. They wanted to be happier and to have more fun together. When they were asked what they did for fun while they were dating, they looked at each other and smiled. Suddenly, it all came back to them.

"We went antiquing, we went to garage sales, we went hiking, we went dancing, we went to the movies," Maria said. John nodded enthusiastically. They became increasingly excited as they spoke. Then, they were asked, "What happened that made you stop doing those things?" John thought for a moment, then responded, "I don't know. Maybe it was because the children were born." Maria added, "Work became more consuming. Responsibilities got in the way."

They were then asked, "Do you think that it was because you got what you wanted? You got married and maybe you put your feet up and started to take the relationship for granted. Perhaps you decided you didn't have to put any effort into it anymore. After all, you had already won the prize. What do you think?" John and Maria looked at each other and then back at the therapist. They agreed. They explained that it was true; they got hitched and then assumed that they "had arrived and could now take it easy." Almost right away, each realized that their relationship was not dead. "You mean it's just that we have become complacent? Wow." Here we can see a relatively healthy couple whose relationship suffered simply from the false idea that once one is married, the work is over, that it should be smooth sailing from that point. This couple spent a total of five sessions in treatment and felt that their relationship was much improved and that they had the tools to make it even better. Most couples therapy is not this easy. However, it does happen, especially when therapists take a resource-based stance.

This point was well illustrated during a therapist training session hosted by Lori Gordon, founder of the PAIRS (Practical Application of Intimate Relationship Skills) Marriage Education Course at the Family Relations Institute in Falls Church, Virginia. Psychiatrist Daniel Casriel compared couples who focus too much on obligations and work to having a pony that is kept in a barn and never ridden. Casriel's advice was to remember to "ride the pony." The pony serves as a metaphor for play and fun in the marriage. The couple diligently cleans the barn but rarely rides the pony. Casriel also suggested that if a couple does not want its pony to grow sick and eventually die from atrophy and disuse, the pony must be taken out of the barn and ridden, as often as possible. Like the need for the pony to be exercised, a relationship needs fun, adventure, and "aliveness" to stay healthy. Those things are clearly present during courtship (it is, in fact, the dominant feature of this period of the relationship), yet over time obligations and work begin to get in the way. The pony sits idle, locked away in a dark stable; as a result, it withers and fades and eventually dies of neglect.

Our experience is that many couples have the misguided expectation and belief that good relationships are self-sustaining, that they go on by themselves without loving attention. To make matters worse, in the last 50 years our expectations have risen sharply about what it is that we should get from our relationships. We expect a great deal more than our parents and grandparents, but do not understand that, in the face of such expectations, our relationships require greater effort to develop and maintain. A belief we often hear from our clients is, "We shouldn't have to work at it. If it's too much work, it's not right for us." Another closely related belief is the following: "Now that I am married, I don't have to do the things I did when I was dating because now I have a commitment from my partner that we will be together." Such unrealistic expectations inevitably create problems for couples. No relationship can last, let alone thrive, without constant attention and maintenance.

We often compare relationships to gardens. What would happen if we planted seeds in a garden and never tended to them? If we do not weed the garden, water it, add some fertilizer or sprinkle a bit of Miracle-Gro once in a while, our plants will eventually die. As it goes with a garden, so it goes with a relationship. With this in mind, we often tell clients, "So, you go to the gym religiously. You lose weight or get into great shape. You achieve your goal. And then, you stop going to the gym, and you expect to stay in shape, right?" And, the client says, "Well, of course not!" This simple analogy creates a useful discussion or teaching point regarding the nutrients and care essential to maintaining and growing a successful relationship.

Let us take this analogy further. It is our contention that it is no coincidence that there is an epidemic of obesity in this country while there is a corresponding epidemic of what we call "relationship fat." The socially inculcated cultural mentality of instant gratification, fast food, get it now, get it on credit, have it all with nothing down has crossed over to infect our relationships. Couples expect to get the great relationship, do virtually nothing to maintain it, and continue to enjoy its fruits. When they fail, they do not reassess their original assumptions; they usually beat up on themselves or each other. Consider Trisha Ashworth and Amy Nobile's latest book, *I'd Trade My Husband for a Housekeeper*.* The book describes the negative effects of unrealistic expectations that women place on themselves. Somehow, they are supposed to have a career, take care of two children, keep the house immaculate, and on and on. Of course, this manner of thinking—this expectation—is doomed to failure; yet, ironically many women today believe they have failed and suffer mentally rather than adjusting their expectations. The truth is that just as women are learning that they cannot have it all, all at once, so must couples realize that they need to choose what is really important in their relationship and then work it, tend to it, nurture it.

These observations regarding the negative impact of unrealistic relationship expectations are fairly obvious to us as therapists. Yet it is also useful to bear in mind that the vast majority of the couples who come for a diagnosis of their marital problems suffer from this set of faulty expectations.

Unrealistic Expectations About Balancing the Roles of Parent and Spouse: Too Many Eggs in the Parent Basket

It has always been true in marriage that after the first child is born, the marriage changes. It is a necessary stage in the life cycle of a relationship for a couple to shift from focusing exclusively on the mate to caring for their child. Yet, this natural shift creates a well-known strain on relationships. In the last few decades, it also appears that many couples fail to adapt to and transcend this shift and instead continue to focus the majority of their energies and attention on the children. Often, as the children grow older, instead of taking up less of the couple's attention and focus, they come to take up even more. The following is a case in point:

> John and Lisa had a healthy, vibrant relationship before the birth of their children. Then, things changed. In therapy, John said, "When Lisa and I do something fun together, it's usually with the kids, going either on bike trips or on a camping trip. We don't ever spend time doing anything that resembles playing when we are alone as a couple." Lisa agreed: "That's really true. It's rare that we make time alone for ourselves to have fun and play."

---

* While catchy, the title alone ought to cause one pause—talk about discounting the importance of a partner.

With very small children, it is normal to have less time and energy to invest in playing with one's partner. One would think that as the children get older and more independent there would be more energy and time to reinvest in the marital relationship. Instead, what we have noticed in our practices is that rather than reconnecting, playing more, flirting more, having more sex after the most difficult phase of child rearing has passed (say, from birth until the age of 5 or 6), couples increasingly make their children the center of the universe: dance lessons, music lessons, soccer, homework, the school play, and so on. To paraphrase Dr Seuss, "They need to be driven here. They need to driven there. They need to be driven everywhere." Modern American parents want to be deeply involved in every aspect of their children's lives at every stage of their children's lives, often to pathological proportions. From kindergarten, rather than energies being somewhat redirected, many couples' energies become directed exclusively toward their children and only secondarily to their work/career. What is left for the marital relationship is, frankly, the leftovers.

This problem is becoming so ingrained in our culture that many couples even continue this laser-like focus on children into their offspring's young adulthood. These days, colleges complain that mommy or daddy keeps calling up professors to ask why their little darling only got a B on the midterm. Is it any wonder relationships lose their spark and partners lose each other in the arid desert their once mutually focused partnership has become?

Whatever the sociological causes for this phenomenon, the conditions that arise from it do not produce happy, long-term marriages or well-adjusted children. Parents need to provide their children with a strong, healthy, loving marital model. Children need to see their parents having fun together, being affectionate and playful. So often, parents sacrifice their marital relationship "for the good" of their children. While they might think that giving up dates and intimate time with each other is a necessary, even a noble, thing, they should understand that by doing so they often sacrifice and even damage their children's own relationship future. So much about parenting is modeling, after all. They need love from their parents, yes, but they also need love between their parents. Such love is critical to children's development, their sense of who they are, their sense of well-being, their sense of what love and respect actually are. To put a marriage on hold to raise children is not only detrimental to the marriage but also extremely damaging to the children in the household and often results in their children replicating such joyless marriages as adults.

Another thing we commonly hear from couples is "We're buddies. When we hear this, it should be a red flag. The question to ask is, "When did you *stop* being *lovers*?" If the excitement and passion are gone, it is vital that the couple be told that they are now vulnerable to affairs or divorce. Childproofing a marriage during the parenting years is a necessity, or the couple will eventually see their marriage slip away and die.

Unrealistic Expectations Regarding the Responsibility and Role of the Self and the Other Partner in Creating Joy and Positive Experiences

There are three major misunderstandings and unrealistic expectations in this area:

1. "My partner is supposed to fill in all the blanks I have in myself and fulfill me."
2. "Even if I am no fun anymore as an individual, we should be having fun as a couple."
3. "My partner needs to make up for everything others did to me in the past."

"My Partner Is Supposed to Fill in All the Blanks I Have in Myself and Fulfill Me"

That a partner is to fill in the blanks and fulfill a spouse is a culturally created fantasy/expectation that is at the core of virtually every love song ever written: Think about the lyrics to so many of the most popular songs of our culture about love, romance, and breaking up. Invariably, the lovesick partner croons about how he or she would be lost, incomplete, unable to function, or even unable to survive without the other.

This appalling and illusory message is pumped out by the gallon by our romantic films, television, movies, romance novels, Hallmark cards, and especially our advertising geniuses. The idea may be a cultural product, but people ingest it and often have it reinforced for them in their first experiences of romance in adolescence and young adulthood, when they have partners who seemed somehow to bring something out of them that was better and worthwhile. People get a little older, get hitched, are happy for a while. Then, the bloom wears off, and they find themselves looking back to that rosy and soft-focus memory. Soon, they begin to fantasize that since their current spouse is no longer making them completely happy, things would be better if only they could just find the absolute right person who could bring out the best in them 24/7/365. We end up having to break the news to our clients that this perfect mate fantasy is part of the "cherries" problem. Here is how it goes:

> "If you have ever played casino slot machines, you know that fairly often you pull the lever and two cherries appear on the win line. A few coins drop into the winnings tray. The point of the cherries is to keep you at the machine and keep putting money into it so that you will eventually lose all of your coins. Learning theorists call this *intermittent variable reinforcement* (IVR). You get the reward at random times. Since you never know when you will get it next, you keep repeating the behavior. If you are training a rat (or human), once the rat learns this behavior through IVR, it

is hard to get rid of it. This is what happens with this fantasy. Every once in a while, we do find someone who seems to meet this you-complete-me expectation, or our partner does something that makes us feel great or fulfills us in some way. Every time that happens, this fantasy is reinforced. So, it is really hard to get rid of it even though it is a losing bet."

If only the problem stopped there. It is one thing to note or even expect that *sometimes, once in a while,* one's partner will do something that makes the other partner really happy or fulfills the partner. It is quite another thing to come to expect that this kind of experience is part of one partner's *duty* to the other.

What is even worse is that individuals confuse the trigger of a response with the source of the response. One partner does something and the other partner feels great, so that person thinks that his or her partner is the source of feeling good. This is an error. The fact is that a person is the sole and singular source of his or her feeling good, feeling bad, feeling anything. One partner's actions or presence may stimulate something inside the other, but the partner is not the source. To the extent that one person attributes the good feelings to his or her partner, the more likely it is that this person will become demanding of the partner. Furthermore, this person will be much less likely to look at him- or herself and his or her thoughts, feelings, attitudes, and behavior as the real reason why they feel good.

As we discuss in this chapter, it is important to help each partner in the couple to realize that he or she is responsible for creating his or her own good feelings. If both partners hold themselves responsible for creating positive feelings, then each is more likely to be happy more of the time.

It is at this point in the educational process that a client often asks, "But aren't I at least partly responsible for making my partner happy?" Here is how we respond:

"Look at it this way. Your partner jogged in new shoes and now has a sore foot. You are not responsible for the sore foot. You are responsible for not stepping on the foot. As a marital partner it might also be kind and helpful if you offer your partner a footstool and maybe an ice pack for the foot. Maybe, you can offer to make dinner so your partner can rest the foot. Partners who have entered into a marital relationship do need to understand that part of this contract is that they can and even should offer kindnesses to each other. Otherwise, what is the point of being in a relationship? But, offering kindnesses is not the same as being responsible for making the other person happy."

The main point of this discussion is to help the two people in the couple return to what they knew when they were dating or newly married: to see that much of what keeps a relationship vibrant is giving energy freely (measured in terms of behavior, feelings, and attitudes) to the other as a "gift" of love rather than as a response to a demand that must be fulfilled. As soon as a partner expects that it is his or her partner's "duty" to make him or her happy or to fill a gap, then what once might have been a freely given gift quickly turns into an obligation for the other person.

When people marry, they bring expectations with them that often conflict. This is absolutely typical. A case in point is the following:

> In one particular therapy session, Barbara complained that she was missing novelty and excitement in her life. She said she spent her days with her young children and often felt bored and needful of interaction with other adults. She held out an expectation that her husband Phil would want to go out and do fun things with her after work and on the weekends. Phil, however, worked on Wall Street as a trader for a hedge fund and was constantly involved in intense work. He also frequently had to entertain clients at fine restaurants. His daily life was already full of novelty and excitement. By the time he came home, he wanted quiet, stability, and relaxation. This had become a barrier to the couple's play. They were seeking very different things. The roles could be reversed, of course, with a wife whose work involved travel and lots of social contact and who, consequently, wanted only to relax when she got home on nights and weekends, while her husband was looking to take outings together.

"Even If I Am No Fun Anymore as an Individual, We Should Be Having Fun as a Couple"

This barrier is rather straightforward. Your client is an unhappy, unfulfilled, lonely person who does not know how to have fun on his or her own. How will he or she be in a relationship? The answer is exactly the same, of course. In dealing with such an individual, therapists must seek to find out how playful, joyful, or positive this person was before the marriage or relationship started. It is often the case that one person in the partnership believed that somehow his or her love would transform the other from an Eeyore into a Tigger.* Such rescue fantasies are almost always doomed to failure. A more common issue is that individuals get sucked into the day-to-day grind of living and stop doing the very activities that were a source of life energy, pleasure, and excitement for them. They cut themselves off from whatever passions and joys they were able to engage in and then wonder why they are so stressed out and why things are not as fulfilling as they used to be.

It is not unusual to discover that people did engage in at least a few activities that once energized them and gave them joy and pleasure, but that they then stopped engaging in them. The result is that they are unhappier than they used to be. They bring this lower level of satisfaction with their own lives into the life of the partnership. And, since they do not realize what is happening, they tend to misattribute (Schachter & Singer, 1962) decreased levels of joy and happiness to their relationship. Ironically, there is often a grain of truth to their misattribution. Likely it was the couple's relationship or their children that provided the context for the individual to stop doing what gave him or her joy or pleasure. Most often, however, it was the individual who took the step on his or her own

---

* For those who have never read about Winnie the Pooh, Eyore has a temperament that is congenitally slow, negative, and pessimistic, whereas Tigger is always fast, excited, and positive.

instead of having been pushed or urged by the spouse into abandoning pleasures. It is only in a limited number of cases that the spouse put pressure on a partner to stop engaging in individual creativity or fun.

Identifying these basic facts needs to be the first focus of treatment. The second step in the intervention is to encourage individuals to shift their energies so that they begin to allocate time for "feeding" themselves. The ubiquitous protestation that there "is not enough time" is almost always a false objection. This claim means either "I do not believe the investment of time in this activity will benefit me enough to warrant the time I will spend doing it" or "I do not deserve to spend this time on myself." Both beliefs are worth exploring. On closer examination, they typically either dissolve under the weight of scrutiny or lead to a beneficial review of individual dynamics.

"My Partner Needs to Make Up for Everything Others Did to Me in the Past"

Left unexamined, one's history can easily destroy joy and pleasure between partners, which act as a barrier to play. How is it that a couple can be having a wonderful time together laughing and feeling close, then suddenly, everything turns sour? One partner has had an intense reaction to something said or done by the other probably because of a disappointing past experience that the partner was now hoping the spouse could make up for. The partner who has had the strong reaction feels perfectly justified. The good time is over. Playing halts, and what is left for both partners is pain and disappointment rather than joy and optimism.

Gordon (1993) referred to Boszormenyi-Nagy's coined term, the *revolving ledger* (1984), to describe how an individual's expectations in a relationship are often determined by that individual's own past relationships with parents, siblings, lovers, former spouses, and friends. He posited that as we go through the revolving door of life, we accrue emotional debits and credits. Building on this work, Gordon (1993) explained: "In effect we hand our partner a Revolving Ledger from our past and punish them for what others did or did not do." (p. 239) When the bill goes unpaid, there is potential for misunderstanding, upset, anger, resentment, and disappointment. This dynamic can show up in any aspect of a relationship, but we are confining ourselves to how it can often show up during couples' positive play together like a penalty red card in soccer, and one of the partners is thrown out of the game.

Here is an example:

New parents Cathy and Brad had little time for dating but did hire a sitter so they could attend a neighborhood New Year's Eve bash. They enjoyed getting dressed up, talking and laughing together, and the company of adult friends. When Brad went to refresh his drink, Cathy soon noticed him in the next room talking with an attractive woman she did not know. Cathy tried to concentrate on her own conversations, but she was distracted watching Brad, who appeared to move physically closer to the unknown woman. Eventually, Cathy asked the host to tell Brad she was not feeling well and had gone home. When Brad arrived home shortly after, Cathy yelled that their party-going days were over and, possibly, so was their marriage. Brad was stunned and wanted to explain that the woman was a mother of three, and he was simply telling her funny stories about their newborn. In therapy the following week, Cathy traced the source of her extreme reaction to her first marriage. Her ex-husband was an incurable flirt and eventually left Cathy for a younger woman he met at a party. After exploring her family history, she realized that her father had left her mother, creating a pattern of abandonment that was handed down from another generation. Brad had become her enemy. She was making Brad pay for what her father did to her mother.

In this example, Cathy was unaware she was making Brad pay for the debts inflicted by others in the past. Gordon (1993) noted, "The Revolving Ledger is a metaphor for transference and projection—for feelings from the past that affect behavior in the present by attaching to whomever is there." (p. 239)

The key to resolving this type of barrier is awareness about the hidden expectations and debts from past close relationships. The tried-and-true tools of education counseling and therapy are used to gain this awareness.

The ledger metaphor can be a useful tool when used in conjunction with a three-generation genogram (McGoldrick, 1985) after constructing the basic structure of the players. The goal is to see what each person on the genogram has contributed to the ledger (at least from the perspective of the client). If a couple like Brad and Cathy comes in with this type of big upset, the clinician can use what happened as a first approximation of what might be "owed." The basic questions to be filled out for each person on the genogram are as follows:

1. What were the relationships like of your parents and grandparents on both sides? Conflictual, close, or enmeshed? Were there any stressful events within those relationships?
2. What patterns, if any, do you see through the generations?
3. How do you think these patterns have affected you regarding joy and fun in your present relationship? What debt was not paid?
4. What needs to happen for you to build trust and heal the past so that you can have a playful, fun relationship with your spouse?

This exercise can bring awareness to the unrealistic expectations and debts that are perceived to be owed. The goal is to forgive the debts or at least stop expecting the partner to pay all the interest owed that becomes a roadblock on the path to positive play in perpetuity.

INDIVIDUAL DYNAMICS

In our examination of the role of unrealistic expectations about marriage so far, we have yet to comprehensively address the underlying question, What is the root cause of such expectations? The answer is that most often the core beliefs that underlie these expectations arise from the client's family of origin and from his or her social or cultural matrix, the individual's dynamics. So often, marriage is idealized as a construct capable of providing individuals with everything they need, everything that is missing. Such an idealized view goes back to a Disney view of the world. Snow White looks into the well and wishes her prince will come. And guess what? He does!! And, of course, they live happily ever after. This is not a realistic narrative for any long-term human relationship, is it? Add to this the fact that in the last 20 years or so relationship expectations have skyrocketed, and you have a genuine recipe for disaster.

Unfortunately, most people have never witnessed or had modeled for them a healthy, loving, and genuinely playful relationship. The marriage people most "study" is that of their parents. Family histories play a central role in our view of the role of play and positive experiences in life. Because people are not aware of the degree to which their early history is influencing their present lives, they come up with other, circumstantial, and often illusory reasons for not investing in fun and play or their partnerships.

Individual Barriers to Fun and Play

In the following discussion, you will find some of the most common individual barriers to being playful and joyful. You will probably find that the categories we have used often overlap and reinforce each other. Depending on your theoretical orientation, you might be inclined to see several barriers as examples of a higher-order pattern. You may also notice that as we move down the list we are moving from relatively more "surface structure" or "normative" descriptions or constructs to "deeper structure" or "more pathological" descriptions or constructs.

Fear of Embarrassment, Making Mistakes, Looking Silly or Stupid

Fears of embarrassment, making mistakes, or looking silly are some of the great killers of creativity of all kinds (von Oech, 1983). Making mistakes is a fundamental part of any creative and learning process, yet the need to avoid making them drains the joy out of any activity. An individual's worry that others will see him or her as silly or stupid is, of course, a projection of that individual's own feelings and evaluations. These reactions are a reflection of this individual's lack of self-acceptance. The fantasy that one's partner will love us unconditionally can never be fulfilled when we are so conditional in our own acceptance of ourselves.

The following is a concrete example:

> When Marty and Carol were discussing the idea of going ballroom dancing because Carol loved to dance, Marty made a face. "She doesn't like the way I dance. The last time we went dancing, Carol said I have no rhythm." Carol responded coldly with, "I don't care. I want to dance." Marty replied, "I don't feel comfortable doing it." Marty's fear of embarrassment here was palpable and

a considerable barrier to undertaking this new activity. In cases such as these, partners need to be encouraged to come to the rescue with encouragement and support. Carol, for example, might have said, "I'm sorry that I said that. It was insensitive. I just want to be with you. Why don't we try again, Marty? We can do this, and we can have fun."

As we can see from this example, individuals sometimes avoid revealing aspects of themselves to their partners for fear of ridicule. This has the effect of inhibiting growth and intimacy. If I am a bad dancer, I tend to avoid dancing because I believe myself to be awkward. If I can become willing to accept my awkwardness (real or imagined) and to look like a klutz with my partner, I can then allow him or her to see and appreciate me as willing to take risks. We will have an opportunity to laugh together, learn to dance together. When I do participate and my partner does not ridicule me, I get an opportunity to feel safe with my partner, and I get to feel more competent at dancing. Finally, I get the opportunity to discover that it is worth being willing to make mistakes to have a more fulfilling and joyful life.

Although these tendencies to avoid certain types of activities often have childhood antecedents, most people are unaware of this fact. These fears, rooted in childhood, can be deadly to the creation of joy and happiness. They can also block creative solutions to life challenges. There is enormous therapeutic power in educating individuals and couples about the origins of their avoidance behaviors, thus giving them permission to embrace mistake-making as part of living and enjoying a more joyful life.

Imagine a couple, Kim and Alex, we will call them. Against considerable avoidance instincts, Kim and Alex go to karaoke together. The truth of it is that they are absolutely dreadful singers. Yet, despite their shared lack of ability, they laugh and have fun with each other as they sing. Are they not engaging in and living out the wish for unconditional love and having fun at the same time? They may be creating irritation and even dread in their audience, but much more important, they are embracing the opportunity to experience the joy and wonder of mutual acceptance and love. This is the kind of opportunity available to your clients when you can help them move beyond their avoidance behaviors created by their personal history.

Viewing the World Through the Lens of "Right" and "Wrong"

Some people have a strong tendency to view the world in terms of whether a situation, person, or thing is "right" or "wrong" rather than seeing it as either working or not working or simply consisting of differing preferences and choices. This tendency can be viewed as an aspect of a personality style, or it can be understood as a learned system from childhood, usually springing from a repressive and dogmatic orientation. Many religious teachings are framed using such a right/wrong paradigm. Underlying such a perception of the world is, most often, the belief that human beings have impulses that need to be controlled from the outside, and that people cannot regulate themselves with their internal values. Again, a childhood lived in such an environment can profoundly inhibit the capacity to play.

It has been our experience that many individuals have little awareness about the negative impact their right/wrong perceptual orientations have on their lives. This lack of awareness, unfortunately, often acts to limit their ability to have fun in life and relationships. It can also be the source of relationship power struggles. Therapy in this area needs to include enough questioning to bring about needed awareness, along with education about alternative ways to perceive and describe value preferences.

Here is another narrative that illustrates the kinds of problems that can arise when at least one partner in a relationship is "play inhibited":

> Juan and Teresa, two clients, were enjoying an evening at a small dinner theater where they had just watched and laughed at a comedy. On the way out of the theater, Teresa, who was completely taken by the main character's wacky behavior, pratfalls, and silly jokes, began to mimic some of the funnier scenes from the play. She was laughing out loud, walking a zigzag line through the parking lot, and inviting her husband to play along. Juan, however, believed that conducting oneself this way in public was wrong; he chided Teresa for acting like a child and for embarrassing them in public. Juan's rigid perspective of what constitutes right and wrong behavior quashed their golden opportunity to expand and amplify what had, until then, been a wonderfully fun and playful evening together.

Competitiveness

Some people feel compelled to win. For them, a game is only "fun" in terms of winning or being the best. In point of fact, they rarely have fun. And, their spouses rarely have fun with them. We have encountered the next scenario many times. The names change, the games (tennis, bridge, bowling, etc.) change, but the story is always the same.

> Sally and Roger are playing doubles tennis. If either Sally or Roger begins to play badly, Roger becomes increasingly tense and upset. If Sally makes mistakes, he glares at her during the game. They get into horrific fights after the game. Sally complains that Roger does not know how just to have fun. Roger says that she is not supporting him because she does not take it seriously enough. Sooner or later, they stop playing tennis together, which leads to further distancing.

The other variation on this motif is that both people are competitive, and they get so busy trying to beat each other they forget to laugh and enjoy each other's company. While such determination might be useful for a professional athlete (and there are arguments against this idea as well), it is rarely useful in marital and long-term personal relationships.

Even when—or maybe especially when—both partners are fiercely competitive individuals, the couple needs to guard against negative behaviors that often crop up around issues of play. These include extravagant displays of one-upmanship, sarcasm, mocking the other's physical or mental sporting abilities, and rubbing in one's success for hours or days afterward.

If the couple is in your office complaining of anxiety, depression, significant marital discord, or simply that "they are no fun anymore," and there is such a high level of competition, this is an appropriate barrier to address.

Fear of Loss of Control

The fear of losing control has many different sources and can be experienced at different levels of intensity for an individual or as a couple. It usually is a defensive adjustment that sits on top of one of the other blocks we have been discussing. As a block to play and playfulness, this fear leads to an added layer of rigidity. The person who consciously or unconsciously fears the loss of control has the following rules: Control keeps you safe; you must stay on guard and tense to stay in control. Allowing yourself to go with the flow of being in the moment, experiencing pleasure, spontaneity, or intimacy takes you off guard duty, leaving you out of control, and therefore is unsafe. The intensity of the need for control will determine how much flexibility an individual has before this dynamic enters the picture.

The fear of losing control can certainly inhibit many areas of pleasure, including sexuality in all of its forms, from flirting, to intercourse, to orgasm. It can make trying new things difficult and inhibit responding to a partner's novel behaviors. It restricts spontaneity and the ability to be in the moment. The need to remain in control often leads to negative judgments and attempts to manipulate others lest they do something that appears to be "out of control."

The following example illustrates this point:

Kirk and Nadia are lying on the couch in front of a fire, enjoying a glass of wine after both putting in a full day at their jobs and getting the children settled into bed. They reach for one another, cuddle, and begin kissing. Kirk reaches under Nadia's sweatshirt, and his hand finds her sports bra. Impulsively, he suggests that they both change into "something a little bit more enticing." Kirk jumps up and is halfway to the bedroom, thinking he will surprise his wife by wearing the silk pajamas they bought on their honeymoon, but Nadia is still on the couch. She is upset because she interprets Kirk's suggestion not as a playful invitation, but as a way to control her clothing choice during foreplay. Further, she is irritated by what she thinks is Kirk's need to see her in alluring clothing in order to have sex. In reality, Kirk was already excited just sitting next to his wife and hugging and had only made the suggestion to change so that they could both feel more sexy and turn an ordinary evening into something special. She thinks that a husband and wife should not need anything to stimulate their desire, and her rigid ideas about what is right and wrong in initiating sex shut down any possibility of intimacy that night.

Insecure Attachment Style

Research has shown that problems with secure attachment can be a significant impediment to smooth affect regulation and relationship functioning. A quick glance at some of the most relevant findings will point out significant ties between attachment and how successfully couples play together.

Attachment theory (Bowlby, 1969) has become increasingly relevant in understanding couple interactions (Johnson, 2004; Siegel, 2006, 2010). For the purpose of this book, we are interested in how attachment problems influence the way that couples will interact when engaging in playful activities.

Compared to more securely attached people, individuals with high attachment anxiety showed lower recall for positive events (Gentzler & Kerns, 2006), showed less performance improvement after positive emotion induction (Mikulincer & Sheffi, 2002), and interpreted their partners' negative actions in more threatening ways and their positive behaviors in less-positive manners (Collins, 1996; Collins, Ford, Guichard, & Allard, 2006).

People with avoidant attachment styles reported lower positive affect during daily social interactions (Pietromonaco & Feldman Barrett, 1997); they showed no performance improvement after positive emotion induction (Mikulincer & Sheffi, 2002) and had lower recall for recent positive events in their own lives (Gentzler & Kerns, 2006).

The original study to measure attachment was conducted with children (Ainsworth, Blehar, & Wall, 1978) and ironically was built around play. The study, "Strange Situation," began with children between 12 and 18 months old playing in a room with their mother. The mother leaves, and a stranger enters. When the mother returns, researchers concluded that if the child went toward the mother for comfort and felt soothed, the child was considered as having a secure attachment. According to Siegel (1999), this means that the child trusts and feels safe with the mother, and the attachment system is a "safe haven." Hazen and Shaver (1987) suggested that "romantic love is an attachment process" and is a "biosocial process by which affectional bonds are formed between adult lovers, just as affectional bonds are formed earlier in life between human infants and their parents." (p. 511) For our purposes, we discuss the three attachment styles that were explored: secure attachment, anxious/ambivalent attachment, and avoidant attachment and their affect on romantic relationships.

Since attachment styles developed at a young age continue into adulthood, it is not a surprise that lack of secure attachment can negatively affect a partner in a couple feeling at ease engaging in playful activities with one's spouse. A securely attached individual can play with his or her partner, be comfortable spending time alone or with friends, and then reunite with his or her partner with ease for more play another time. An individual with insecure attachment may find it difficult to part with his or her mate; might fret, worry, or become suspicious while they are apart; and could behave in a hostile manner when they are reunited.

Other characteristics typically associated with securely attached adults are also vital to a couple's ability to play together. Play that is invigorating for couples involves positive emotion, novelty, and risk taking with one's partner. Securely attached adults do not have particular problems with these characteristics. They trust their partner to be supportive and feel comfortable with closeness and independence and can balance both because they trust and feel safe. Securely attached people feel good about themselves, their partners, and their relationship and can explore their world easily with curiosity. They are willing to take risks and experience novelty because they have the ability to regulate their emotions and trust that their partners will protect them. These characteristics enable them to be cooperative and open to participating in playful, joyful, and exciting experiences. On the other hand, an insecurely attached person will interpret a partner's need for alone time as threatening because it feels like a form of abandonment. These individuals also typically mistrust their partners, do not feel safe with them or feel comfortable with closeness, all of which will inhibit the trusting spirit necessary for exploring new situations during play.

Anxious/ambivalent attached adults will be uncomfortable taking risks or trying something new and have difficulty regulating anxiety when things do not go as planned. They usually have stronger negative reactions to new situations, do not trust their partner to protect or soothe them if they are upset, and compensate by seeking increased levels of intimacy. An ambivalently attached adult will tend to seek approval from his or her partner, is overly dependent, and displays a lot of worry and intense emotional expression in his or her relationship.

> Miranda and Jeff had a big complaint: Each time Jeff suggested a new, playful activity the couple had never tried, Miranda either balked, agreed with a high level of reluctance, or participated with a degree of duress. If he did manage to convince her to try something new, any little problem would set off her anxiety, such as when they went hiking and Miranda's new boots caused a blister. "She gave up on the hike immediately, saying she never should have agreed to it. We had a first aid kit with us, and I wanted her to sit down and take off her boot to see if I could devise something to help ease her pain and make it possible for her to at least walk comfortably back to the car at a slow pace. But, she just stalked off ahead of me, limping and crying and complaining." The therapist suggested that Miranda was likely exhibiting the long-term effects of an ambivalent attachment from her childhood, and her behavior had little to do with Jeff or the hiking situation. Once the couple understood this, in future outings they were able to handle any unexpected problems more carefully; Miranda agreed not to storm off or call it quits, and Jeff agreed to slow down the pace of new activities because Miranda needed to feel safe in new situations.

Those with an avoidant attachment style will also have blocks in their attempts at being playful. They have a strong need to be independent and often suppress their feelings. These individuals distance themselves and are unaware of their feelings of anxiety, so at times when they are afraid, they pull away. Often numb to their feelings, these people tend to be inauthentic and create distance from their partner when they feel rejected. They might back off rather than take a risk. Usually, this type of person not only has a block to playing, but also has barriers to forming intimate relationships. They are not in touch with themselves, their partners, and fun.

> Felicia and Armando admitted that they rarely did anything playful together because Armando seemed to prefer time alone. Getting him to agree to an evening out or a weekend afternoon doing something fun was always a chore for Felicia. "It's not that he has to work so many hours. He just says he's not interested in doing whatever I suggest, and then he spends that time alone watching TV or reading the paper—things he could do later. When I ask why he won't go do something with me, he just shrugs and gets quiet." Armando noted that it wasn't that he craved all that time on his own, but that he just never thought about it much. By talking about these scenarios, the couple's therapist realized that Armando was likely exhibiting an avoidant attachment style developed during his youth. This couple's homework assignment was for Felicia to suggest three different outings over the next week and for Armando to say yes to at least one. In this way, he had some control over the choice but didn't have the option of constantly pushing his wife away.

How do we deal with the diverse histories of clients so deeply affected by the level of attachment they developed so long ago? As therapists, first we need to educate the couple and explain attachment styles so that they become aware of what may be causing their current behavior. Identifying and understanding the different attachment styles that both partners have brought to the marriage can be a great benefit for the therapist and clients. Armed with an insight into each partner's attachment style, a therapist will be more able to help clients understand one another and make specific, on-target suggestions. When both partners in a couple understand their own individual attachment style and what problems it may be causing, they can move forward by communicating their feelings, building trust, and selecting appropriate playful activities to do together.

Play is an ideal way to help heal partners' attachment wounds from the past. Playing together and taking graduated risks acts as a "corrective emotional experience" (Alexander, 1961) that is an embodied, enacted way of becoming securely attached, especially if processed as an example of being safe and secure as partners. The more comfortable the couple bond, the more they will choose to participate in fun experiences with one another. If play becomes an integral part of a couple's life together, positive experiences will accumulate.

Rigid and Inflexible Values About How to Create Positive Experiences of Fun and Joy

He likes action movies; she likes romantic comedies.

He wants just to lie on the beach and relax; she wants to do things and visit places.

He wants fresh air; she wants Times Square.

It may be true that opposites attract. But, when rigid and inflexible people who do not share the same values and criteria about how to create positive experiences of joy and fun become a couple, life gets more complicated. Two factors must be in place for this barrier to become a significant problem. First, the couple needs to have disparate likes and dislikes with relatively little overlap. If both partners like the same things, it does not matter if they are rigid and inflexible.

Second, one or both of them needs to be relatively rigid and inflexible in terms of trying new things or stretching. The couple will end up bickering and arguing over what to do to have fun. For couples with this problem, there is little flow. Everything is a negotiation, if it even gets to a level of negotiating. Vacations become more of a source of stress than fun. Or, it becomes a kind of parallel vacation. Togetherness is limited. Often, one or both of the people are relatively immature and self-absorbed. They focus on what is the most fun at the moment, and that gets the full priority. They fail to account for the benefit of togetherness. Often, they cannot even enjoy a choice for togetherness. For instance:

> Alex agrees to go snowshoeing with Martha, but he just can't stop thinking about the downhill skiing he is missing. He keeps making negative comments about the experience and how he could be having so much *more* fun skiing. Martha is sorry that he came along. Alex will not be having sex later that night.

One way to work with this type of problem is to help the person become less self-absorbed and more "selfish."

Therapist:	Alex, on a scale of 1–10, how much do you like skiing?
Alex:	"Ten."
Therapist:	On the same scale, how much fun is snowshoeing?
Alex:	A 6.
Therapist:	So, snowshoeing can be fun, but skiing is the best for you.
Alex:	Right.
Therapist:	Alex, on the same scale, how much fun is it to be with Martha laughing and having a great time together?
Alex:	Anywhere from an 8 to a 10.
Therapist:	Was it an 8 to 10 when you went snowshoeing?
Alex:	No, not even close.
Therapist:	What got in the way of you two having a blast together?
Alex:	Well, because I was in a bad mood, because I wanted to go skiing.
Therapist:	So, you gave up a probable 10 in skiing. And, you could have had an 8–10 with Martha having fun, but because you were pouting that did not happen. Is that right?
Alex:	(exasperated) Yes, I guess so.
Therapist:	I forgot to ask: How do you rate good sex on the same scale?
Alex:	A 10 of course! (smiling)
Therapist:	(turns to Martha) Men, we are such simple creatures. (Everyone laughs.) So, Alex, when you came back from the snowshoeing, how was the sex that night?

Alex:	We did not have sex that night because we had been fighting. I get it. I get it. You are saying that if I had not been so focused on the skiing, I could have a lot of fun with Martha, including having sex.
Therapist:	Bingo.
Alex:	I guess I need to be less selfish.
Therapist:	Actually, you need to be *more* selfish.
Alex:	You're kidding, right?
Therapist:	No, I am very serious. When you focused on just going skiing, you were more like a self-absorbed teenager. But now you are realizing that you can be a more mature man who takes care of the self in a much larger and deeper way. You can have fun, cultivate a context for you and your wife to be closer, and of course you and she could have great level 10 sex. In other words, you and Martha need to be more selfish, but you need to widen your definition of what is good for the self.

Another variation of the problem of disparity of likes and rigidity requires that one or both people cannot tolerate and accept those differences. No room exists for doing separate things. For instance:

Jaycee just likes to relax on the beach. Kevin wants to go sailing. He knows that Jaycee is scared to be on a boat. He is more than willing to go sailing by himself and let her read her book on the beach. Jaycee, on the other hand, feels that Kevin should stay with her. If he goes sailing for the morning, when he meets her for lunch he gets nothing but hostile looks and complaining.

When a couple comes into your office with this type of issue, one option is to help them explore and accept personal differences and the possibility of having fun alone and sharing afterward; if that is not tolerable, as in this case, work with his or her attachment issues (see Johnson, 2004).

Parental Injunctions, Decisions, and Life Scripts: "Don't Play, Don't Be a Child, Don't Feel, Don't Be Spontaneous, Grow Up!"

Children are naturally open, curious, and spontaneous, yet unfortunately, the circumstances of early childhood provide rich opportunities for children to shut down their natural ability to feel free and to play. Messages from parents, teachers, or other adults often become ingrained in children. Painful personal experiences with family members, teachers, friends, and classmates provide opportunities for people to conclude that it is best to suppress their natural playful instincts.

During one session, Maria and John were asked to close their eyes and recall the messages they got from their parents regarding fun and play. After a little while, Maria said her parents told her that work was most important, and play was a waste of time. She was asked if she believed that. She replied, "I'm not sure." When John was asked the same question, he responded by saying that the messages from his parents were that "Grown ups need to be responsible and productive. Play is for children." Since both had their playful instincts suppressed during childhood, it is no wonder this couple had not spent an evening out together on a date for as long as either could remember.

Herb Goldberg, author of *The New Male-Female Relationship* (1983), addressed the issue of harmful parental injunctions:

> Generation after generation has glorified the work obsession as a virtue and ultimate validation. Parents transferred their play repressions to their children. They rewarded the offspring who worked hardest and took on the greatest responsibilities earliest. These children were looked on with favor as the best and most mature. Parents could be truly proud of them. These parents were extinguishing in their children the play capacity that, if maintained and expressed, would threaten to expose their own frustration and unhappiness over not being able to let go and be playful. (p. 193)

This, then, is the prevailing and culturally imbued emotional landscape inhabited by many of our clients during childhood. Let us look at some examples of parenting that devalue play:

> Billy, a client, shared in therapy that his parents operated a grocery store and worked nearly 7 days every week. From the time Billy was 8 years old, he would help his father in the store after school and on weekends. Naturally, this did not permit Billy to have any free time for having fun and playing with friends. In addition, he never saw his parents laughing or going out together. The message he took with him into adulthood was that "working is the most important area of life, and there is simply no time for play and fun."

> Another client, Jennifer, complained that her husband, Robert, would criticize her for being too silly and for being "way out." Asked to explore what messages he had in his head that got in the way of him being more "silly" or "way out," Robert described how he colored fanciful scenes with way-out colors until he was about 8 years old. Then, one day, his father picked up his artwork and with a look of what Robert perceived as utter disgust and with a derisive tone in his voice said, "Why are you using these absurd colors? That is not the way things look!" Robert reported that even as an adult, he could still feel his father's "look and tone."

> Jill, another client, described that her mother was very ill when she was between the ages of 9 and 11. She was given many chores to do to help, but she often did them singing or playing, until one day she was told to be quiet and stop playing around because it would bother her mother. Now, when Jill and her husband do chores together, she views them as drudgery and resists his attempts to lighten the mood.

> Another couple, Tom and Julia, often got into fights around the topic of pleasure and waste. Julia usually took the position that it was good to do something for fun, while Tom felt it was wasteful, and that there were more important things on which to spend their money. Tom explained that he had grown up in a very religious, repressed, and stoic family for whom the very idea of doing things for fun was seen as wasteful at best and sinful at worst.

> When a discussion regarding having fun and playing in her relationship came up in therapy, Lisa mentioned that it had always been difficult for her to play because of her childhood and all the time she spent caring for her siblings. She was a "good girl" and would do anything to please her parents, but she definitely felt that this role had deprived her of having anything like a "normal" childhood. While her friends were out playing together, Lisa was always at home babysitting. Eventually, she found herself becoming increasingly resentful. As an adult, this childhood

experience turned out to be a significant causal factor in her inability to give herself the pleasure of experiencing spontaneous fun with her partner.

These examples illustrate that early childhood experiences can have a profound impact on the ability to play as an adult. If we are to help our clients have a more playful future, we must often address these scripts, decisions, and injunctions.

Childhood Abuse and Trauma

The effects of childhood abuse and trauma have been written about extensively (Briere, 1996; Courtois, 1988; Dolan, 1991; Maltz, 1992; Schwarz, 2002; van der Kolk, 1987). Any thorough clinical understanding of an individual should include a trauma history. While most therapists think of trauma as problematic because it creates damage, the bigger problem with trauma is that it cuts us off from our resources (Schwarz, 2002). For our purposes here, the resources in question may be feelings of safety, enjoying the positive sensations of the body, sexuality, trust in oneself, trust in members of the opposite sex, positive beliefs about one's worth, and positive expectations about life, to name a few.

The nature of trauma can range from a single incident lasting a few minutes to multiple events lasting years. Traumatic events can be of devastating intensity and violence, or they can be insidiously subtle. For our purposes, we are concerned with how the experiences act "virally" on the client. To what extent do they "take over the DNA" and run the show? A classic example might be the effects of the Great Depression. Many now elderly people feel compelled to work and are compulsively avoidant of spending time and money on pleasure because the experiences of that time are still active in their mind. Another example is the effects of sexual abuse. Many people cannot enjoy sex or even sensual touch because it either reminds them of the pain of being sexually abused or on a deeper level stimulates self-disgust or guilt about feeling sexual pleasure because they felt sexual pleasure during abuse.

These examples of trauma are what Schwarz (2002) called Big T traumas. There are of course many examples of little t traumas. Little t traumas do not include being raped or physically abused, but are experiences that are too negative for a child or person to process at that moment. Or, to put it another way, the person becomes overwhelmed because he or she does not have enough resources to cope effectively with a difficult situation; this might include shaming experiences at school.

While a full discussion of trauma treatment is beyond the scope and purpose of this book, it is useful to remember the saying: "Trauma cannot be destroyed, but it can be dissolved in a sea of resources" (Schwarz, 2007, p. 67). Effective trauma treatment involves eliciting and stabilizing sufficient resources to allow the processing of traumatic events in a positive context (Briere, 1992;

Herman, 1992; Schwarz, 2002). Furthermore, effective trauma treatment seeks to reconnect that person with a positive and meaningful life (Herman,1992; Schwarz, 2002).

To the extent that traumatic incidents need to be addressed to remove barriers to treatment, it is helpful to frame the therapeutic approach here as "restoring and reconnecting with one's ability to feel pleasure and joy, to be playful and sponta-neous." Such an approach tends to increase therapeutic motivation and minimize regression. More than once we have said to people, "The best revenge is living well." A good example of this type of work is Wendy Maltz's *The Sexual Healing Journey* (1992). Maltz describes how couples can work together as a team to help the survivor of sexual abuse reconnect in a positive manner with sexual feelings.

TREATING BARRIERS TO PLAY

Now that we have described some of the more common barriers to play, the ques-tion is how to treat them. The answer is you treat these issues the same as you would any other problem or resistance. In fact, you should simply use the approaches you already use. We have found that we tend to work on these issues in four lay-ers, usually in order: (a) education and increased awareness, (b) permission and choice, (c) behavioral work, and (d) emotional work, psychotherapy, energy work, EMDR (eye movement desensitization and reprocessing), and so on.

> **Education and increased awareness.** The fact is that most people have little knowledge or awareness about the patterns in their lives. Awareness and mindfulness are powerful tools for change. Simply becoming aware of the fact that they are being driven by events in the past often frees people to behave differently. Becoming deeply mindful of the costs of certain attitudes and actions or inactions often motivates people toward change.
>
> **Permission and choice.** If it has not become clear by now, we do not advo-cate a stance of neutrality when it comes to play and joy. As therapists and experts, we often act as role models. In terms of Jungian archetypes, we are king and queen and give blessings. We give our clients permis-sion and provide hope and encouragement to take a few risks, to make new choices, and to remove the hidden shackles of a repressive society. The good news is that many people just need a little permission.
>
> **Behavioral work.** Our clients need to do something differently. Without changing the action, nothing much will change. We give homework. We prescribe new actions. Those actions may be small, or they may be large. The new behaviors need to become frequent and consistent. Couples are debriefed about what happened. Special emphasis is placed on what worked. We catch people doing something right and reward them by acknowledging their progress.

Emotional work, psychotherapy, energy work, EMDR, and so on. Sometimes, the first three approaches simply are not enough to overcome blocks. It is hoped that you have any number of tools in your clinical tool kit. Sometimes, people need to work more deeply, more emotionally, or in a more focused manner on specific memories or schemas. The kinds of interventions that we recommend here include family sculpting (Satir, 1983); Gestalt two-chair techniques (Perls, 1973); redecision work (Goulding & Goulding, 1979); EMDR (Shapiro, 1995); energy psychology (Diepold, Britt, & Bender, 2004; Feinstein, 2004; Gallo, 1999); mindsight (Siegel, 2010); and emotional focused therapy (Johnson, 2004), to name a few.

Cultivating virtuous circles of positive energy. Both couples therapy and education are a spiraling process. More awareness leads to different choices that generate new behaviors and experiences that can be reinforced with new awareness. As a couple starts to make shifts, we continuously act to link positive actions and awareness with beliefs, identity statements and future expectations. If a couple takes a risk and goes to karaoke, the following type of interview occurs:

Therapist:	So how did the karaoke go?
Kim:	Oh my gosh, it was so scary at first. But then it was so much fun.
Therapist:	That's great. Alex do you agree with Kim that it started off scary and ended up fun.
Alex:	Well Kim was more nervous than I was. I just reassured her like we discussed that no matter how bad we were, I would still love her.
Therapist:	Did that help Kim?
Kim:	It certainly did. It made me feel really close to Alex.
Therapist:	Like you could count on him.
Kim:	Yeah!
Therapist:	(To Alex) Sir Knight, it would seem that the lady now knows that chivalry is not dead.
Alex:	(Laughs and smiles at Kim.)
Kim:	It really did feel like he was up there protecting me.
Therapist:	So, the next time you want to take a risk at something, do you think that you would be less or more likely to imagine that Alex would be there to protect you no matter the outcome?
Kim:	I definitely see him more as someone who would be there for me rather than laugh at me like my brother did.
Therapist:	Alex, how do you react to knowing that Kim sees you more like a knight than a sadistic clown?
Alex:	It feels great. It is much better than her not trusting me.
Therapist:	That is great. So, can you guys see yourselves taking a few more risks together as a team, laughing and having fun? (Kim and Alex laugh, nod their heads.) I think this calls for a celebratory hug. (They hug.)

In this chapter, we explained the many barriers to play. We organized them into three main categories: (a) unrealistic expectations about what it takes to have a joyous, loving, lasting marriage (b) unrealistic expectations about balancing the roles of parent and spouse; and (c) unrealistic expectations regarding the responsibility and role of the self and the other partner. The individual barriers include (1) fear of embarrassment, making mistakes, or looking foolish; (2) viewing the world through the lens of right and wrong; (3) competitiveness; (4) fear of loss of control; (5) insecure attachment; (6) parental injunctions and life scripts; and (7) childhood abuse and trauma.

We have presented a number of treatment strategies that you can integrate with your own methodologies for problem resolution that will allow you to better identify and treat the forces that prevent your clients from having more fun and joy in their relationships.

4

Cultivating a Play-It-Forward Attitude

INTRODUCTION

We turn now to the first stage in the use of play within the context of marital therapy. At this stage of the therapeutic process, the therapist has already devoted time and resources to conducting an assessment of the client-couple's capacity for play. The goal here is to build on and expand the existing playful resources that exist within and between the clients.

THE CHARACTERISTICS OF A PLAYFUL ATTITUDE

If a therapist is to foster and encourage play successfully in the couples' relationship, a question that might naturally arise is: What is play, anyway? Play is, above all, a way of being, a way of navigating one's life. Play is a state of mind that includes different degrees of: freedom from constraint, openness, novelty, flexibility, lightheartedness, cooperation, humor, risk taking, trust, creativity, vulnerability, and positive emotion that generates increased levels of positive emotion, behavioral flexibility, and interpersonal connection. When one or more—preferably more (ideally all)—of these characteristics of being are present in both partners, caring occurs, intimacy arises, love transpires. Play is best understood as a broad-based phenomenon, so broad that it is best seen as constituted by a whole family of attitudes.

An underlying playful attitude and spirit make it much easier to incorporate play and joy into one's daily life. As therapists, we know how much attitude and spirit drive behavior through internal motivation. Undoing and overcoming the habits and states of mind that inhibit a human being's inborn playful spirit require conscious and conscientious effort and practice. Over time, this work becomes self-reinforcing, sustaining, and transforming. It is imperative that we learn how to teach couples how to develop and return to their playful spirits so that they can reap the benefits of incorporating the positive elements of play and joy into their daily lives. Remember the motivational saying: "It is not what happens to you; it is what you do with what happens to you"? If you are to incorporate play successfully into your therapeutic work with couples, your need to help each individual in the relationship accept the truth of this statement.

It is not sufficient simply to tell couples that they need to "lighten up" or have a more playful attitude. Nor is it sufficient to give them a list of behaviors or activities in which they need to engage. What we really want to do is to help couples cultivate an internally driven motivation that nurtures a playful way of being. Without this internal motivation, the couple is not likely to create sustained change. Since this is a tall order, we follow the Ericksonian dictum, "When the going gets tough, break it into smaller parts" (Zeig, 1985, p. 34). We believe that there are seven interlocking characteristics that make up or support a playful attitude. There are five main characteristics that make up a playful attitude and two additional ones that support and nurture the positive energy that feeds the ability to be playful. To help instill a playful attitude toward life in their clients, therapists must help them as individuals, as couples, and as families to begin to practice and adopt these seven interlocking characteristics:

1. Embrace whatever comes their way and whatever they are doing; find ways of acting that incorporate as much fun and joy as possible (rather than resisting, rejecting, being negative). Actively look for and privilege opportunities and points of view that lead to humor, laughter, and connection (rather than righteousness, anger, and disconnection).
2. Embrace the "yes, and" principle of improvisational comedy.
3. Choose to invest time and resources on positive, playful, and joyful activities small, medium, and large.
4. Nurture adventures in "letting go" and in appropriate risk taking.
5. Develop/nurture a sense of humor about their foibles and the foibles of their family members. Do not let them take themselves so seriously.
6. Nurture an "attitude of gratitude."
7. Be in the present/forgive.

EMBRACE WHATEVER COMES THEIR WAY AND WHATEVER THEY ARE DOING

Find Ways of Acting That Incorporate as Much Fun and Joy as Possible

Couples and individuals describe a variety of contexts and situations in which they bicker or resist each other. When it comes time to do the dishes, to pay the bills, or to go visit their in-laws, they can do so without being annoyed, with a sense of fun and play and optimism. Therapists need to help clients identify those situations that so often lead to negativity. Once identified, the therapist can help clients explore new intentional approaches that can turn a previously negative context into a positive one. The question we teach our couples to ask themselves is: "How can I/we do this with a playful or positive attitude?" Whenever confronted with a "negative" context (e.g., paying bills, doing housework, etc.), the question must be asked. Even if an answer is not immediately found, asking the question begins to help people become more mindful of their negativity. Doing so will help them begin to shift the energy for that moment. When an answer is found, it can provide a specific reference point and metaphor for living life more playfully.

Let us use the example of doing dishes. A wife might complain that her husband does not do his share. He might complain that when he does, she is stressed and becomes annoyed with him because he is not doing it right. As a result, he avoids doing his part.

Let us model the therapeutic approach we are advocating:

Therapist:	So, Debbie, you don't like doing dishes, and you want John to help. And John, you don't want to help Debbie with dishes because she is so negative when you do help?
John:	Exactly.
Debbie:	I guess so.
Therapist:	So, this is a perfect example of the principle of embracing everything as an opportunity to approach life with fun and joy. Debbie, assuming that John was working with you, how could you make doing dishes more fun?
Debbie:	Doing dishes is never fun. It always reminds me of my mother nagging me.
Therapist:	Can you hear your mother in your head?
Debbie:	Yes.
Therapist:	Change her voice to that of Donald Duck.
Debbie:	She laughs.
Therapist:	How could you bring that laughter into the kitchen?
John:	I could do my impersonations while we are doing dishes.
Debbie:	(Laughs) That would be funny. You would do dishes in character?
John:	I guess. Sure. If we were having fun, I would not mind doing the dishes with you. We could take turns washing and drying.

Actively Look for and Focus on Opportunities and Points of View That Lead to Humor, Laughter, and Connection

If all the world's a stage, maybe we can make the drama that is our life into a comedy or, at the very least, blend in some comic relief. It is true that some people are "humor impaired," but this is not a genetic disability. It grows out of a series of blocks that develop through living. Humor impairment can be corrected over time through conscious and diligent practice. An individual can create contexts for laughter, for example, by watching a comedy he or she enjoys or a funny movie. Many people never put themselves in premade humorous contexts such as this. Other people do so but do not do it often enough. Our technologies make available to us a wide variety of comic materials. Is it not time we started putting them to good use?

Telling and listening to jokes is another great way of generating humor and laughter. People can look together at anthologies of cartoons. The Internet now makes it possible to share these materials easily with friends and family. Can we not also use this as a medium for fighting humor impairment and for creating contexts for humor and laughter? Developing and maintaining a sustainable playful attitude requires that our clients invest time and energy in its pursuit. Otherwise, they are at risk for falling back into the "nose-to-the-grindstone" approach to life.

How a couple or family plays a game of Scrabble, Monopoly, or dominoes is a good measure of taking opportunities for humor. Is it all business, or is there a lot of joking around? Can someone put down a silly made-up word just for laughs without losing a turn? Are the rules more important, or is the fun and connection more important?

Can we not, as therapists, assume (when necessary) the role of Mary Poppins and remind people that a "spoon full of humor makes the medicine go down"? Our clients actually appreciate this reminder to have fun in their lives. As one person in a couple said, "I know it is silly, but it really changes the mood in the family when we sit with the kids and watch *Seinfeld* episodes. We all laugh, and then the next day at breakfast people keep making references to the program, and we crack up again."

Therapists need to encourage clients to search for humor in everyday life and to share it with their partners. Not the kind of humor that is cutting or that occurs at the other's expense. We are speaking here of positive and playful humor. When our clients begin to align themselves with the comedy of everyday life, they will find that comical events occur all day long. Mistakes happen; people say and do the "darndest" things. Children are a perennial source of humor. If approached with the right attitude, gender differences alone are good for several laughs a day.

Many couples get deeply lost in the day-to-day business of raising children. Yet, children can provide a plethora of particularly pleasing punch lines. Does the family have a culture that emphasizes telling humorous events of the day, or even finding ways to make things more amusing? A simple game for families is using alliteration just as we did two sentences ago ("plethora of particularly pleasing punch lines").

Even the dreaded poor judgment of teenage boys (and girls) can provide opportunities to have moments of connection and learning. When a teenager describes an example of using poor judgment, instead of immediately getting upset, yelling, or lecturing, the parent can say: "Oh, you had an NFL moment." The first time a teenager hears this, he or she will stop and say, "What are you talking about?" or "What does football have to do with it?" This novel statement piques the teenager's attention, and his or her brain is prepared for learning. The parent says, "NFL means no frontal lobe." Everyone laughs. The parent can then go on to explain how the frontal lobe is the part of the brain that is responsible for foresight and planning, and that it is not fully developed yet in teenage boys (or girls). The parent can continue and talk about how the teenager needs to work on engaging his or her frontal lobes.

This type of stance opens the door for coming back to this issue repeatedly in a manner that is amusing and, more important, supportive of the positive connection between the parent and the teenager. Frontal lobes do not fully come on line until after 20 years old, and there is not much we can do about it. We can use those NFL moments as opportunities to be accepting and connected and not take ourselves so seriously (see Characteristic 4).

The research on "positive or optimistic attitude" discussed throughout the literature of positive psychology has significant relevance for this principle. Although 50% of a person's happiness is predetermined by personal make-up (genes, temperament, etc.) and is not amenable to change and only 10% of that person's happiness is determined by outside circumstances (money, beauty, job, etc.), a full 40% of a person's happiness is determined by intentional activities (Lyubomirsky, 2007). The intentional activities that we prescribe to our couples mirror Lyubomirsky's work. We agree with Lyubomirsky (2007) that this 40% is more than enough for couples to improve their relationships fundamentally. The point, though, is that individuals and couples must actively engage in "accepting whatever comes their way" in a manner that incorporates as much fun and joy as possible. They must do this in an ongoing manner.

EMBRACE THE "YES, AND" PRINCIPLE OF IMPROVISATIONAL COMEDY

The two words that are the greatest enemies of creativity, joy, cooperation, and connection are *no* and *but*. Yet, the words *Yes, and* have the opposite effect. One of the reasons that we are such fans of improvisational comedy is that it is a great metaphor for life and uses the *Yes, and* principle. In improv, actors are confronted with an obstacle or a challenge. They have no script, and they must cooperate with each other to address and deal with the situation.

When one actor says something to another, it is called "an offer." This *yes, and* principle can also work in therapy. In improv, if an actor says, "Oh no, there is a herd of pink elephants with wings heading our way," the other actor must say "Yes" to this premise and then build on it. For instance, the actor might say, "Yes, and it is a good thing I have my special flying pink elephant saddles. Now we won't be late for the wizards' convention."

In improv, the more specific the offer is, the better it is for their fellow actors. Whatever anyone says in an improv scene is right. They are simply not allowed to say, "No, that is not correct." The *yes, and* principle demands that they accept the offer (saying "Yes") and then build on it (the "and ... "). The greatest improvisational therapist was the psychiatrist Milton H. Erickson. When a psychotic patient in the hospital came to him and said, "I am Jesus Christ!" Erickson replied, "I hear you know something about carpentry." He then gave the man some carpentry work.

Here, we can see that Erickson accepted the offer of the client. Erickson said, "Yes." Then, he built on that offer by saying "And ... we have need of a carpenter." Imagine the result had Erickson said, "No, you are not Jesus; you are psychotic." He would not have established a relationship with the client. The therapeutic opportunity would have dissolved. If the second actor in the previous scenario says, "There is no such thing as pink winged elephants," the scene dies.

How many potentially positive and playful experiences are shut down by couples and families refusing the "Yes"? Here is a script that models how couples commonly negate offers and lose the opportunity to say "Yes" and therefore to play:

Husband: Let's go out this weekend.
Wife: I don't know. I am not in the mood.

Or,

Wife: Will you help me clean the house this weekend?
Husband: Do I have to do that? You know how I hate that kind of work.

Or perhaps,

Husband: I was thinking of planning a trip for next summer.
Wife: Next summer? That is so far away. I can't even begin to think about that now. I am too overwhelmed with the kids.

Another example might be the following:

Wife: I was thinking of getting theater tickets.
Husband: What? You know we can't afford that!

As we have seen so often in our work with couples, dialogues and interactions such as these lead to nothing but friction, resentment, and eventually, fighting.

When therapists teach clients the *yes, and* training exercise, they give couples the opportunity of creating, not negating. This approach, used therapeutically, can lead to completely new forms of fun and entertainment. Here are some typical instructions:

"At this point, I would like the two of you to do an exercise. The name of this exercise is 'yes, and.' It will help you do several things. First, it will help you play together in a cooperative manner. Second, it will teach you how to accept and build on whatever your partner says. Third, it will help you both be more creative. Finally, you are going to have fun.

So, here is how we do it. In a minute, I am going to ask you two to create a 'food dish from another planet.' Tom, you are going to start. You are going to say one characteristic of this food. It can be anything. Whatever you say is right. Beth, whatever Tom says, you say 'Yes, and' and then you add one thing. Then Tom, you respond to what Beth says by saying, 'Yes, and' and then add another characteristic. You keep going until I tell you to stop. Remember you get to say whatever you want. Your job is to accept and build on what your partner says. Have fun; be creative!"

The principle at work here is modeling for couples how they can learn to accept each other's offers and, even better, to build on them. Such interactions build and sustain cooperation and a sense of teamwork. They also engender the spirit of playful creativity within the relationship dynamic. When we use such a therapeutic approach, we encourage couples simply to play and to let go of pre-conceived notions and behaviors. When such work is done during a session, there is lots of laughter. If either partner has trouble letting go, this also becomes grist for the therapeutic mill.

Here is a script that demonstrates "the food dish from another planet" exercise:

Husband: This dish starts off with sliced tree limbs.
Wife: Yes, and they are soaked in oil for 1 day.
Husband: Yes, and then they are seasoned with a ton of habanera-like peppers.
Wife: Mmm. Yes, and then they are roasted with eyes of newt and pickled Martian rats for 3 hours.
Husband: Yes, and then the whole thing is served over a bed of wilted rhubarb leaves.
Wife: Wonderful! Finally, it is topped off with a sauce of melted moon cheese mixed with salted Saturn ring dust.

A silly exercise? Perhaps. Instructive, imaginative, playful, creative, open ended, infinitely variable, and expandable fun? Absolutely.

Yes, and is a technique that can be adopted for use in many different situations and contexts. Couples can, for example, be encouraged to play at home or even to incorporate their children in their play. For it to be integrated into daily life, couples should be advised that they need to cue each other about the principle. This can be done on the initiation of a conversation. The wife might say, "Let's do a 'Yes, and ...' about what we want to do this weekend. When one partner is sliding into a negation, a 'No,' the other partner can remind him or her of their agreement to employ the *yes, and* principle in their marriage. For example, if the wife says: "I was thinking of planning a trip for next summer," and the husband's response is along the lines of "What? You know we can't afford that," the wife can in turn respond "Honey, remember we agreed to do 'Yes, and.' So let's do '*Yes, and*' about how to take a trip on very little money."

The amazing thing is that comedic improv scenes thrive on conflict. In real life, the *yes, and* principal defuses conflict. An example is as follows: A husband comes home late for dinner. The wife is annoyed.

Wife:	Darn it Tony, you are late, and you didn't call.
Husband:	Yes, that was very rude of me. And, now I am going to have to make it up to you (winks).
Wife:	Yes, you are buddy boy, but it is not going to be the way you expect, dear one (winks back).
Husband:	Really?
Wife:	Yes, really. You are going to have to clean the oven to make this up to me.
Husband:	Okay. And I suppose you want me to do it naked.
Wife:	(Laughing now). The thought had occurred to me. We will save the naked part until after you clean the oven.
Husband:	Yes, Ma'am.

As you can see, the *yes, and* principal of accepting an offer and building on it has ramifications for all facets of life for which a therapist is attempting to nurture nascent creativity and encourage teamwork, whether that be at home with a partner or with children or in the world of business.

CHOOSE TO INVEST TIME AND RESOURCES ON POSITIVE, PLAYFUL, AND JOYFUL ACTIVITIES SMALL, MEDIUM, AND LARGE

The principle of investing time and resources in positive, playful, and joyful small, medium, and large activities is at the very heart of this book. Intention is a good beginning, but it is not enough. Individuals must commit to action. Sometimes, the action is large, but many times the action is small (such as simply saying, "Thank you"). The point is that most people lose sight of the many possibilities that lie just at their fingertips. To the extent that they do commit to action, they will often focus only on higher magnitudes of playful or joyful activity. They will plan the 1- or 2-week vacation, for example, but forget about the importance of weekly outings. They will focus on creating date night on a weekly basis, but neglect to play board games or to take a moment before going off to work to connect with their spouses. Individuals, couples, and families need a healthy mix of small, medium, and large joyful activities. By the end of the book, you will have learned about a wide range of activities (both large and small) that all work to help couples cultivate joy and playfulness.

There is a highly porous boundary between activities and behavior that are positive and caring compared to playful and humorous. For our purposes, there is little point in attempting to separate them. Smiling, laughing, and touching are examples of "small things" that could easily fit into the play or positive or caring framework. They are so important that we are going to discuss them in the next chapter. Other small things include short, friendly phone calls, small notes or cards, telling a joke or making a funny comment or story, using a pet name, giving a compliment, or saying "I love you" or another declaration of affection. All of these relatively short and brief actions contribute to the positive side of the five-to-one ratio.

Four most important times of the day: For years, we have suggested to our couples that they maximize the return on their investment (of energy) by making sure they engage in these small positive activities at four important times of the day: waking up, leaving home, coming home, and going to bed. These transition times often set the stage for the feeling and tone for hours to come.

Medium-size activities can include activities such as going out on dates of all shapes, sizes, and times. This could range from the dinner at a restaurant to a movie, to going for a long walk together; playing sports together; sitting in front of a fire; having meaningful conversations about life, dreams, and plans; having sex; and so on. These types of activities require more sustained attention, effort, and often some planning. They can also lead to more meaningful intimacy and awareness of the inner world of the other.

Large-size activities usually require a lot of planning and take up considerable time. Romantic weekends and major vacations are classic staples of this category. Not only is it the time itself to do the activity, but also it is the time and attention in planning the activity that makes these things "large." It is the intention to create a positive experience for the other that makes these things special. If a husband plans a weekend trip to the Daytona 500 race but the wife hates NASCAR (National Association for Stock Car Auto Racing), the effort does not count. He is simply being self-absorbed.

NURTURE ADVENTURES IN "LETTING GO" AND IN APPROPRIATE RISK TAKING

We all have playful impulses and thoughts running through our heads. Nurturing appropriate risk taking includes experimenting with, accepting, and expressing these thoughts and impulses in appropriate contexts. People who are not playful have a tendency to overcontrol these impulses and thoughts for fear that they are wrong, "bad," and unacceptable.

People who have a healthy, playful attitude develop a comfort with going out of their comfort zone. They know that nothing ventured is nothing gained. People who do not have a healthy playful attitude are often restricted by fears of making mistakes or of looking foolish or being wrong. The tendency to be overcontrolled can certainly be explored therapeutically. But, here we want to focus on nurturing adventures in letting go. These adventures can be as simple as encouraging clients to try a new type of food, a different restaurant, or painting a wall in a room with a bold color. Trying any new activity can be an adventure in letting go, such as going to the opera or learning a sport together, when such activities are uncharacteristic and uncommon. Other classic examples include the following:

> Doing karaoke and hamming it up as much as possible (if you already do this and you are a ham, it does not really count).
> Taking a class in comedic improv (they are available in many cities; to find them, google "improv classes").
> Taking a dance class together.

Adventures in letting go can include trying a different sexual position or a different sexual act. Simpler still, an adventure in letting go can be an honest attempt at becoming more willing to look silly. Here are a few examples of exercises that an individual or a couple can do to explore adventures in silliness.

- **Doofus bowling:** Go bowling with the intention of looking silly. The classic move is to take the ball and walk up to the foul line. Turn your back toward the pins. Bend down and look through your legs toward the pins and then bowl the ball through your legs. Note: In this or any other position, make sure to take care of your back and any other body parts. Try not to drool on the bowling lane from laughing so much.
- **Foreign accent:** Go out to dinner or participate in any other activity, but for the entire night (or at least a prearranged amount of time), speak in a foreign accent.
- **Pretending to meet for the first time:** This is a classic game that couples play and is a great game for when couples go out on a date alone together. The couple arranges to meet somewhere and pretends that they do not know each other. They flirt and get to know each other from a different frame of reference.
- **Ministry of Silly Walks:** This game is taken from the British television show *Monty Python's Flying Circus*. Each partner develops his and her own silly way of walking. They then walk down the street doing the walk. It generally only lasts about 30 seconds. Couples usually are laughing hysterically.

If a therapist assigns these types of exercises, it is important to stress four things: (a) The client is likely to feel anxious. That is normal, and the client should do the assignment anyway. (b) The assignment is not about doing something well. It is about taking risks and being more comfortable feeling silly. It simply does not matter how well a person does the assignment. In fact, if they do it well, they may be defeating the purpose of the assignment. (c) Partners should laugh *with* each other, not at each other. (d) The clients probably will feel silly and even embarrassed. That is the point, and that means that they are headed in the right direction.

There are two potential problems with this type of exercise. The first is that the client or couple simply cannot do it and will feel like a failure. This should be reframed as feedback about the amount of blocks that exist and becomes grist for the mill. The second problem is that the person does do the exercise, and for some reason his or her level of shame skyrockets; instead of the exercise neutralizing the fear of silliness, it has the opposite effect. How could this happen? One example is if a couple tried to do doofus bowling in a lane next to league bowlers who did not have a sense of humor and became belligerent.

Since the goal is to "nurture adventures in letting go," both therapist and clients must respect where the "adventure" is. For some people, walking down the street doing silly walks or "doofus bowling" is just never going to happen. It would not be an adventure to do it; it would be a trauma. To try to make it happen would actually be counterproductive. Following guidelines from solution-focused therapy (de Shazer, 1985, 1988), the therapist needs to help the couple nurture small changes in letting go. The therapist can ask the scaling question, "On a scale of 0–10 (where 0 is you are never silly and 10 is you are silly all the time), where are you in being silly?" Perhaps the husband says he is a 3. The adventure might be to help the husband and wife work on moving from a 3 to a 4 on the scale. The point is to encourage internal motivation for taking "appropriate risks." The couple gets to decide what is "appropriate."

DEVELOP/NURTURE A SENSE OF HUMOR AND ACCEPTANCE ABOUT THEIR FOIBLES AND THE FOIBLES OF THEIR FAMILY MEMBERS

Do Not Take Yourself So Seriously

One could make a good case for the idea that most psychological problems stem from a lack of acceptance of some aspect of ourselves. Ergo, the more we accept ourselves, the healthier we will be. Since two thirds of all couples' complaints are not solvable (Gottman, 1994), the principle of learning acceptance becomes the only real solution. The fact is that we are imperfect beings with all sorts of foibles. From our point of view, acceptance often includes letting go of our seriousness about ourselves, which leads to letting go of critical judgments of self and other. Colloquially, we can say that we need to develop a sense of humor about ourselves. When we can chuckle and play with our own personality quirks as well as the personality quirks of our spouse, we can have a lot more fun in life.

Here is an example:

Anthony was a good guy. However, his insecurity often caused him to act a bit like a know-it-all. Whenever anyone would explain something, Anthony would respond, "I knew that!" His wife had talked to him about this. She particularly did not like when he would do this to her. Anthony realized she was correct. As they talked about this issue, it became clear that half the time he did not even realize he was saying, "I knew that!" To break this unconscious habit, Anthony and his wife used the following intervention technique: He made a conscious choice to find the most obvious and ludicrous contexts in which to look in her eyes and purposefully say, "I knew that!" In turn, she responded, "Yes, you did." Then, they would both laugh. After a few months running this intervention procedure, Anthony's "know-it-all" responses vanished entirely.

Another example is the following:

Janet often snapped at Steve for no apparent reason. As a result, Steve felt shocked and hurt. Janet understood that her behavior was destructive, yet she also knew that it would be difficult for her simply to stop her behavior. Because she wanted to break this bad habit, she came up with a solution. She decided that every time she snapped at Steve, she would immediately follow it up with a hug. The solution worked beautifully. It brought Janet and Steve closer together, helped her more clearly see what she was doing, and helped and healed Steve's hurt. Eventually, by applying this technique, Janet stopped snapping entirely, and Steve became relieved and happy.

One significant benefit of looking at relationship problems through the lens of gender differences (Gray, 1993; Tannen, 1990) is that it helps us stop taking ourselves so seriously. When John Gray (1993) described men as "Mr. Fix It" and women as "the home improvement committee," it gets people to laugh at themselves rather than become defensive or attacking. It also helps them be less judgmental of the other. Whether it is understanding gender, cultural, or individual differences (e.g., Myers-Briggs typology), it is crucial for Spouse A to realize that the very "weird," "strange," "different" behavior of Spouse B makes sense for Spouse B and is not designed specifically to upset, annoy, or hurt Spouse A. In fact, once understood from a certain perspective, these things are usually quite funny.

The Sitcom Intervention

Another way to help couples with this principle is to target little behavior patterns that serve as flash points for much bickering using the sitcom intervention. The goals for such an intervention are threefold: (a) Reduce the negative side of the positive/negative ratio by neutralizing flash points that create a disproportionate amount of negativity; (b) model and teach a method for stepping back and getting perspective; and (c) create or strengthen the ability to have a sense of humor about oneself and one's partner. For instance,

Husband:	(With a raised voice and sharp tone) I can't stand it when she moves my stuff. I can't find it!
Wife:	(Also with a raised voice) Well, if you did not leave it everywhere, I would not need to move it. And, I don't like you talking to me like that.
Husband:	Well, if you would stop being so defensive and actually tried to cooperate, I would not get so annoyed.
Therapist:	So, let me get this straight. You guys have lots of fights about the moving of things?
Wife:	All the time. He is really nasty about it.

Husband:	I have become nasty because you do not listen. I had to search for an hour for my Day-Timer because you moved it and you put stuff on top of it.
Therapist:	That sounds like it was a big inconvenience.
Husband:	You ain't kidding.
Therapist:	Julia, I can see that when Manny raises his voice, it hurts your feelings, and you don't feel respected.
Wife:	You got it.
Therapist:	And this kind of fight happens several times a week. And, each time you are upset at the other for at least an hour if not more?
Husband:	Oh, yes.
Wife:	Definitely.
Therapist:	It seems to me that there are a number of aspects to this problem. But, let me make sure I understand something. If you step back a bit, would each of you say that the fights you have about this are toxic to your relationship, and compared to major life issues, this problem of moving things or not is relatively small? And, you would like not to fight so much about it?
Husband:	Yes.
Wife:	Yes.
Therapist:	Okay, so let me ask you to imagine something. It might sound kind of weird. Can you bear with me? (Couple nods.) Imagine the scene about the Day-Timer but imagine it as if you were watching a sitcom on TV.
Husband and Wife:	(Start to laugh.)
Husband:	Oh no, that is actually funny.
Therapist:	But, you were really mad a second ago. What happened?
Husband:	It is hard to take it so seriously when you think of it as a sitcom.
Wife:	Yeah, the entire thing does not seem worth the fight. It is just one of these things that we each do.
Therapist:	Exactly, instead of "men are from Mars," we could say women are movers and men are leavers.
Husband:	Yeah, compared to Julia, I am more messy, and I do leave things around.
Wife:	I definitely pick things up and put them in their place. I guess that makes me a mover. (Chuckles)
Therapist:	So, you have a choice. You can turn this thing into a control battle or a battle about who is being less respected. You can have these nasty fights several times a week. Or, you can have a sense of humor about yourselves. Manny, you can lighten up on the tone and the hostility when Julia moves something; you acknowledge that you are a bit messy and that it stresses Julia. Julia, you can lighten up on the defensiveness about being a mover and acknowledge that sometimes when you move things it stresses Manny because he does not know where they are. This may just be your own personal sitcom from now until you are old people rocking on the porch together.
Wife:	Yeah, I am going to move your hearing aids when you leave them out. (Laughs)
Husband:	What did you say? (Laughs)

Do you develop acceptance as a result of not taking yourself so seriously, or do you not take yourself so seriously as a result of developing acceptance? In fact, this is a complicated and interesting question. However, we are going to choose sides and suggest that it is best if therapists help each member of the couple to be more accepting of the other and take the self less seriously. It is crucially important that the therapist should set a good personal example by not taking him- or herself too seriously. We often advise therapists that they should have several good self-effacing personal teaching stories about the importance of not taking oneself too seriously. What are yours?

NURTURE AN "ATTITUDE OF GRATITUDE"

When people experience gratitude on a daily basis, they will find it much easier to be playful. As we all know, after a few years of marriage, spouses commonly begin to take each other for granted. This is to be expected, but it can also prove detrimental, allowing the partnership to lapse into robotic routines. The very comfort that arises within long-term marriages—the sense that "this is someone I do not have to impress, someone with whom I can totally be myself"—can itself rob a marriage of its vitality by causing spouses to be less interested in doing things for their partners, less appreciative when things are done for them. Instead of thinking of little surprises that might brighten a partner's day, they become far more likely to concentrate on doing things for people they want to impress in the outside world.

Habitual behavior in the marriage can erode gratitude. One partner does this, the other is responsible for that, neither is grateful, neither is thankful to the other. Worse, nagging can occur when a responsibility or chore goes uncompleted. Acrimony is the result. The first step toward decreasing acrimony and enlivening a marriage is profoundly simple; it is what mothers tell their young children: "Say 'Thank you.'"

Expressing gratitude for the little things spouses do to give each other pleasure and to fulfill their obligations within the marriage partnership—whether that be making dinner, bringing over a morning cup of coffee, or calling from work to find out how the day is going—can revitalize both the day and the marriage.

Many people erect walls to protect themselves from being hurt. The underlying belief is that "if I take a risk and open my heart to you and share my deep gratitude to you, you might hurt me." This overly protective attitude can harden the heart and distance a spouse from his or her partner. Such a person may stay safe, but will also become disconnected from deep feelings and from the deep feelings of the partner. This is critically important work for us as therapists. We must encourage couples to take risks and begin the practice of opening or reopening their hearts to each other. By cultivating an attitude of gratitude, it is possible to help clients not only change their mood but also change their lives by becoming more optimistic, healthier, and ultimately happier.

In the beginning of our sessions, we often ask each person in the couple to appreciate the other. Such a practice helps create a more loving and joyful context in which even negative feelings can be expressed. Repeat this exercise at the end of the session to make sure there is a loving connection between the two when they leave. Couples are willing to comply, and it is crucially important that they leave the session bonded.

Outside the sessions and in the midst of the family/work tensions of everyday life, partners can become so self-focused that they neglect to open up to each other. Under such circumstances, a simple expression of gratitude can make a vast difference. Here is a client-based example:

> Charles was not in a good mood. It was the holiday season and the busiest time of the year for his wife, Cheryl, who ran a gift shop. He had arrived home after 6, and not only was Cheryl absent again, he discovered after he released the babysitter that there was little in the house to feed their three sons for dinner.
>
> He grabbed two old boxes of macaroni and cheese from the back of the cupboard and began preparing—both the macaroni and an angry scenario. Cheryl would tell him this was not a healthy meal, and he would tell her that she had left him little choice. What else was there to make? What is more, he would inform her, she was not the only one with a heavy workload these days.
>
> Charles had worked himself into a state of fury by the time Cheryl finally walked in. Carrying a bag of groceries, she looked exhausted. Her jaw dropped when she saw the boys munching their macaroni and cheese, however. "You fed them!" she gasped, her eyes lighting up.
>
> "Well," he began, "you know, just mac ... "
>
> "You are a godsend," she whispered, throwing her arms around Charles's neck. "I had no idea it was getting so late! Thank you, thank you!"
>
> Charles's body relaxed, welcoming the internal shift that had taken place and changed him from angry husband to godsend. "Anything in that bag for us to eat?" he asked playfully.
>
> "Yes," she whispered, backing up and smiling up at him, "later."

As we can see from this common enough scenario, the power of gratitude lies in the fact that it is a double positive. For the people expressing it, gratitude amplifies their awareness that something special has been done on their behalf—something thoughtful, beneficial, pleasurable, unexpected, or useful, it does not matter. For the receiver, to benefit from an expression of sincere gratitude is to experience recognition, an accolade. The gift of gratitude brings euphoria for both the giver and the receiver. However, as we know, receiving thanks is difficult for some people. Self-esteem influences the degree to which a person can "let in" an expression of appreciation. Low self-esteem, a belief that I am not worthy of praise, can cause a person to block gratitude. This is another area of work for therapists; within a marriage and without, it is just as important to receive thanks graciously as it is to give thanks. It is a gift to the giver as well as the receiver.

Gratitude not only shifts a person's mood but also causes a shift in their partner's mood. Often, a simple "Thank you" can help others feel valued and worthwhile. It reinforces behaviors we want and need to increase, as well as creating an atmosphere of goodwill and sincerity.

Gender differences may also have an impact on one partner's ability to show emotion and offer thanks to the other, as pointed out in the study "Gender Differences in Gratitude" (Kashdan et al., 2009). The researchers said evidence shows women find expressing gratitude less difficult and less costly compared to men (pp. 11–12).

Imagine what a difference it would make if you could help couples encourage and empower each other through the expression of thankfulness. It is helpful to encourage clients to cultivate an attitude of gratitude so they form the habit of thanking their partner for positive behaviors on a daily basis. The key is to do so with sincerity and openheartedness, not simply as a perfunctory gesture. To cultivate and begin to embody this skill takes time and practice. Remember, for some people this will come more naturally and more easily because they may have a more generous spirit or because they benefitted from a gratitude-oriented family culture as children.

Also, bear in mind that for it to have a strong impact, both depth and sincerity are required. The truth of it is that communicating gratitude successfully is an art. Ask couples to write down some things from the past or present that they want to thank their partner for now. After they finish, ask them to follow these instructions:

- Sit facing each other.
- Clear your mind.
- Be present.
- Have an intention to have your partner get this communication.
- Speak slowly.
- Focus on the other person.
- Look into your partner's eyes lovingly.
- Speak with sincerity, staying connected to your heart and your partner's heart.
- Emphasize your feelings of joy and love.
- Take turns sharing your gratitude with the other.
- When both partners are finished, they should share a hug.

BE IN THE PRESENT/FORGIVE

We include forgiveness or letting go of resentment in our list of characteristics for developing a playful attitude because resentment is like a superweed that can choke even the most skillfully cultivated garden of love and joy. Forgiveness as a choice informed by the belief that relationship happiness is the ultimate goal. Why should a person forgive? Because holding on to resentment blocks positive emotions, thoughts, and behavior. Not forgiving prohibits a couple from connecting and finding harmony within each other. Resentment makes fun difficult, if not impossible. Psychologist Fred Luskin, director of the Stanford Forgiveness Project, links forgiveness with improved physical health, lower stress levels, more successful relationships, and fewer feelings of hostility (2009, pp. 32–33).

A partner who has the capacity for forgiveness is a significant asset in any relationship. Goodwill is the essential ingredient in this work. Goodwill is one partner's manifestation of positive regard for the other. It is the mechanism by which a partner finds it possible to forgive.

Let us look at how this can play out:

> Cindy and Joe had plans to go out to dinner to a new restaurant. They had planned to leave at 6:00 p.m. for a 6:15 reservation. Cindy was home by 5:30. At 6:05, Joe was still not home, so Cindy called him on his cell phone but could not reach him. She began to get very tense and annoyed. By 6:30, Joe was still not home, and Cindy was fuming. At 6:45 when Joe walked in the door, Cindy yelled furiously, "Where have you been? You knew we were supposed to leave at 6:00. You are so inconsiderate!" Joe apologized, of course, but Cindy would not accept it. She said, "It's too late now. I don't want to go." Then, she went to work on her computer. Over time, Joe made numerous attempts to connect with Cindy, but she would not budge. This went on for several days until finally Cindy started to talk to Joe again and to let her anger go.

If Cindy had shared her anger and disappointment and had found it in herself to forgive Joe immediately by using goodwill, they might have had a wonderful evening and, possibly, wonderful and healing sex afterward.

Luskin notes that refusing to forgive can lead to distance and criticism that "can erode love and goodwill in both partners and over time spells death for the relationship" (p. 52). He also outlines four stages of forgiveness which are useful to consider – In stage 1, a person is "filled with self-justified anger and hurt" and blames the partner, by stage 2, one realizes the pain associated with this stance is not worth it and begins to move past it; at stage 3, a person realizes it will feel good to forgive and chooses to do so; finally, in stage 4, forgiveness occurs, concurrent with understanding of a partner's human tendency to make mistakes (pp. 60–65).

We build on Luskin's work by reminding couples that forgiveness is not something we do *for* others, and it doesn't erase the past or signal that the pain was not real. Rather, forgiveness is a state of mind, achieved as a gift to oneself, because it allows a person to move forward with an open heart.

In the work of helping your clients cultivate more playful attitudes, what you are doing is to help them learn to focus both on what is good in their partners and good in themselves, to learn to understand the power of play and goodwill within their partnership. By doing so, you can help them dissolve the destructive patterns that can erode the relationship, to replace the darker attractions of anger and resentment with a more positive aspiration toward goodwill and good feeling. Invoking the higher goal of the relationship bond and shared happiness can help.

Helping the client-couple cultivate a playful attitude is an enormously positive process because such shifts in underlying perspectives and perceptions bring along with them a shift toward a more constructive and loving orientation. It is only the first stage of an important two-stage process: first playful attitudes, then playful behaviors. In the next chapter we build on the work here by focusing on practical actions and behaviors that are manifestations of playful attitudes.

5

Playful Practices That Pack a Punch

INTRODUCTION

We repeatedly get the same question from clients: "We love the idea of having more play in our marriage, but how do we fit play into our busy day?" The elegant part about incorporating play is that it begins with small acts—words, behaviors, and gestures that take little time but make a significant difference. In Chapter 4, we described the internal attitudes and values that tend to drive behaviors. Without the internal motivation, attempts at behavior change tend to run out of gas quickly or are perceived as shallow and without meaning.

In this chapter, we now shift our focus from attitudes to specific daily behaviors. Here, we zoom in on the third characteristic from Chapter 4: Choose to invest time and resources on positive, playful, and joyful activities small, medium, and large. We are going to focus on the small daily activities. (In Chapter 6, we deal with the medium and large activities.) It certainly is important to cultivate a playful attitude. But for it to truly count, this internal shift must become manifest in the actual behavior of couples. Couples must demonstrate in terms of behavior, words, and actions their love, commitment, and enjoyment of each other.

People often think of the "small stuff" in life as irritating annoyances that we have been advised not to "sweat" (Carlson, 1997). But, there is also much small stuff in life that has the opposite effect—small acts that please and delight. We keep coming back to the importance of creating positive emotions that have the power to move a couple toward, and then beyond, the 5:1 positive-to-negative interactions ratio. It is simply hard to get there without small daily positive transactions. Focusing on these specific actions can be both diagnostic as well as therapeutic. By zeroing in on these behaviors, clinicians and clients discover areas for improvement and build experiences and initiate practices that perpetuate positive pairing. Building on existing small behaviors helps a couple move from a fair or good relationship to a great relationship. When couples come to you at a time when their relationship feels negative, it is even more important to encourage them to start with positive small acts. There is usually less resistance to begin incremental changes that so often lead to substantial payoffs.

What follows are concrete and daily practices that expand and grow from the playful attitudes we outlined. The four key areas are as follows:

- Smiles, greetings, laughter, and silliness
- Caring behaviors, loving words, and affectionate touch
- Flirting, mystery, surprise, and romantic acts
- Acknowledgment, enthusiasm, and delight

SMILES, GREETINGS, LAUGHTER, AND SILLINESS

Small changes precipitate structural shifts. As chaos theory postulates, the simple action of the wings of a butterfly in Beijing brings rain to New York. The power of small changes of behavior in relationships is no different. As an example, let us examine the power of the simplest of all human expressions, the smile.

We have all seen partners who rarely smile at one another. This is no small thing. A smile can tell someone so many positive things: "I feel happy," "I'm happy to see you," or "I like you." It allows the partner to feel warm and safe. It is an invitation to play. A smile is other directed. It changes a partner's focal point from "inside my own head" to "you."

In our work with couples, we emphasize the importance of smiling for these reasons and more. We believe a smile as part of greeting one's partner at crucial times during the day is enormously helpful. An early morning smile sets the tone for the whole day, a reassuring send-off when each heads out into the world. A smile is a positive way for two tired people to greet each other at the end of the day and says, "I am happy to be here with you. I look forward to our evening together. I am present now in your life and intend to leave my preoccupations behind me. Come join me." Right before bedtime, a smile can say, "I enjoyed my time with you tonight. I wish you a peaceful sleep." At any time of day, for the person smiled on, the smile radiates pleasure, affection, love, warmth, and sunshine.

For couples who want to be more connected, a key benefit to a smile is that it so often triggers a reciprocal smile. Such a small thing might strike some of us as insignificant, but the impact of the smile can be enormous. "Smiles have an edge over all other emotional expressions: the human brain prefers happy faces, recognizing them more readily and quickly than those with negative expressions—an effect known as 'the happy face advantage'" (Leppanen & Hietanen, 2003, in Goleman, 2006, p. 44).

Jillian dismisses the smile as a marketing tool. "Ticket-takers, waitresses, salespeople, they all smile because they have to be polite," she says. "The good thing about being married as long as Danny and I, is that home is where we let it all hang out. We don't have to be polite." Consider however, which bodes better for Jillian and Danny's night? Danny greeting Jillian with a frown, eyes rolling, saying, "And you think you've had a bad day?" or Danny greeting Jillian with a smile that tells her she is an oasis in his life, and that he intends to be one in hers?

Here is an important question: Do life's problems—the grumbling points—overshadow happiness because there are more problems than good or because we grant them higher status? In the couple's world, is home a place for the expression and sharing of joy, or is it a place designated primarily for the unloading and articulation of problems—the complaint box in both partner's day? Smiling and its associated behaviors, such as softening of the eyes, can melt tension and act as an effective repair attempt that can short-circuit potential negative escalations. For instance:

Susan and Stephen were traveling in a foreign city and thoroughly enjoying themselves—looking at maps, making plans for an afternoon walk—when Stephen said something that annoyed Susan, and she let him know it. Instead of taking a walk together, he stormed out of the hotel. Susan paced for a while, but then grabbed her coat and ran after him. Knowing the route they had planned, she took a shortcut. When she saw him in the distance, she called out the nickname she used for him. Stephen turned around, startled. She waved and smiled, and he waved and smiled back, suddenly happy to see her. Her smile said, "I want to be close to you. Let's stop this nonsense." His smile said, "I agree. Let's make this fun!"

To help a couple gauge the role smiling can play in their happiness quotient, we suggest you ask couples to answer a few key questions:

- In what daily situations would you like your mate to smile at you more frequently?
- Can you envision yourself shifting from a neutral greeting to one that is accompanied by a smile? How do you feel when you smile?
- What holds you back from greeting your mate with a smile?
- How does it feel when your spouse smiles at you? Would you like to have that feeling more often and, in turn, allow your spouse also to have that feeling more often?

Laughter is a stress reducer and connecting force between people under duress. When a person laughs for 20 seconds, it causes the heart rate to double and remain elevated for 3 to 5 minutes. When it returns to normal, that person's heart rate, blood pressure, and breathing are reduced to lower levels than they were before the laughter, in turn causing a reduction in overall body tension. Laughing also lowers the levels of stress hormones circulating in the blood. The power of laughter in a marriage is that it can help protect a relationship from the ravages of negative emotions and destructive conflicts. Laughter in this context flows from the playful attitude of not taking oneself so seriously. Following interpersonal neurobiology (Seigel, 2010), if one person starts to laugh, it tends to create an interpersonal cascade of brain-based relaxation.

Lynn and Dave had been married, and happy together, for 42 years. At one difficult point, however, work-related anxieties were making each irritable. They had started quibbling about everything, including the route they took to their jobs each morning. For about a week, Lynn kept insisting they would get there faster via Norton Street. Dave, the driver, always ignored her, turning down Logan instead, which he said was quicker.

One morning, Dave was feeling sorry for his wife, who had not been sleeping well and looked stressed out; so to please her, he turned left onto Norton Street, then hit the brakes. A huge tree—a victim of the storm the night before—had fallen across the street, blocking all traffic. He heard a giggle. It grew in intensity. He turned to his right just as his wife erupted into raucous laughter. He also laughed—delighted at the joy suddenly reflected in her eyes. As they laughed together, Lynn leaned over and kissed Dave's cheek because she knew why he chose Norton Street and because the ridiculous obstacle in front of them underscored the fact that they had both been taking their ride to work far too seriously.

When a partner laughs, his or her spouse will not only laugh but will also connect. When people laugh at the same thing, their brains become synchronized, and they communicate the deeper emotion of joy without words. They become emotionally attuned to one another and are more likely to get a particular point across when they substitute humor for a lecture.

Harry and Martha had the usual male/female issues about the bathroom. Harry felt a bathroom was where you drop wet towels on the floor; leave the toothpaste open on the sink, oozing from the tube; and leave the toilet seat up after relieving yourself. After all, it was just a bathroom. Martha, on the other hand, felt a bathroom should be neat and attractive, and that even a man who grew up with four brothers could learn to put the toilet seat down when he was finished. The "bathroom issue" was not a big issue; nevertheless, it caused a good bit of grumbling.

Then, one day Harry went into the bathroom, raised the toilet seat, and found himself staring at a picture of his wife glued to the underside of the seat, with the word *Please*? He burst out laughing. What a nut that Martha was! Still smiling, he put the toilet seat down when he was finished and picked his towel up off the floor. Here was an ongoing conflict handled and healed with humor and laughter. Yes, it takes creativity to come up with such humorous solutions, but the benefits are remarkable.

A therapist can urge a couple toward more laughter in a number of ways, and asking a few pointed questions can get things rolling:

- How often do the two of you laugh? Are those times limited to watching a funny TV show or comedy movie, or do you laugh at things each other says or does?
- When one of you finds something funny, do you find a way to tell the other as soon as possible so you can share the laughter?

- Think of some instances when you recently shared a good belly laugh. What were the circumstances? How do you think you can create more of those opportunities?
- Do you purposely try to elicit a laugh from your partner at least once a day, even with something as small as pointing out a funny typo or laughing over something that went awry, like a burned burger?

Silliness is a behavior that is spontaneous, absurd, or foolish, but in a good-hearted way, never mean spirited. Being silly often involves plain old clowning around; it is something that children do easily without inhibition. Adults, on the other hand, might judge silly antics as immature and dismiss them as childish. We suggest otherwise. We are big proponents of the benefits of being silly. If done for fun and at appropriate times, it can be freeing and bonding for couples. And, laughter, which we have already shown to be a great contributor to happiness, often results immediately and directly from silliness.

> One day a year or so ago, Stuart said to Charlotte, "I am so lucky to have you," and Charlotte added, "I am lucky, too." Immediately following this, they both put their right arms out to the side as singers do and spontaneously began to sing the rest of the song. This became a ritual and now is always followed by belly laughs.

The key here is that both partners enjoy it. Remember that it is not couple play if one of the spouses is not enjoying it.

> Barbara complained that Frank would often talk to her in a baby voice. This was a big turn off for her. The more Frank continued with this behavior, the angrier Barbara got. Instead of creating laughter and fun, which was Frank's original intention, it caused anger for Barbara and conflict between them.

Every human being has a unique idea of what makes for acceptable and appropriate silly fun. Clinicians must be sensitive to personal and social norms of clients. Inhibitions and self-consciousness can set upper limits on the amount of silliness in which a person can engage. On the other hand, people will sometimes spontaneously create a silly scenario out of something totally unexpected. Still, some exploration may be in order. One can ask a couple the following:

- Can you remember the last time the two of you enjoyed acting silly together?
- What kinds of situations seem to bring out the silly nature in your spouse?
- When are some possible times or situations that naturally occur in your lives that may offer the chance to be really silly together?
- Have you ever joined in with your children or with other couples when they seem to be having some silly fun?

CARING BEHAVIORS, LOVING WORDS, AND AFFECTIONATE TOUCH

Caring Behaviors

The importance of performing small acts of caring has been discussed by many (Chapman, 1992; Gordon, 1993; Gray, 1993; Hendrix, 2007; Markman et al., 2010). Gray (1993) defined acts of caring as specific behaviors that demonstrate caring for the other person, such as giving cards, writing small notes, pouring a cup of coffee, doing the other's chores, giving flowers, and so on. He also suggested that there are gender differences in how caring acts are defined. Gray described how women prefer an ongoing stream of small acts of caring. As Gray put it, if a man gives a woman a dozen roses at one time, he gets 1 point. If he gives her one flower at a time each week over 12 weeks, one per week, he gets 12 points. Following ancient principles of the feminine (yin) and the masculine (yang), Gray suggested that maintaining the energy of a relationship is furthered when the man actively does acts of caring for the woman and the woman actively receives that energy and gives back appreciation to the man. While some may see this as too stereotypical, our clinical and personal experiences suggest the utility of this approach.

Chapman (1992) said that emotional love languages are defined by the receiver and are particular to each person. What makes one person feel loved may not be what makes the other feel loved. He stated that a person's behavior is affected by the amount of love the person experiences from his or her mate. Chapman asserted that there are five different love languages: physical affection, acts of service, quality time, words of affirmation, and gifts.

To illustrate this in the PAIRS (Practical Application of Intimate Relationship Skills) Marriage Education Course (Gordon, 1993), each participant fills out a form listing these five love languages. Within each of these categories, each person lists his or her preferences and from that list creates a list of 12 behaviors the person would like to experience. They are directed to list only behaviors, and not attitudes, because attitudes cannot be measured. For example, they cannot ask a mate to be more reliable. This is an attitude. Instead, they must translate this into a behavior, such as "Be on time or call me if you are going to be late." After the lists are completed, the couple is requested to exchange lists. Each mate then puts his or her partner's list in a place where it can be visibly seen every day. Each partner is asked to perform three of the behaviors their partner requested every day for their mate. When contemplating the lists, partners are reminded that instead of giving their partner what they themselves like, they are asked to give their partner what the partner has indicated on his or her list that makes that partner feel special and loved. This is another excellent way to make love deposits in the emotional bank account, keeping the ideal ratio of five to one.

Carissa and Sean grew up in different countries in families that valued different kinds of interactions. For Sean, feeling loved can take the form of Carissa stocking up on unusual fruits and vegetables during the summer, her giving him the occasional back rub, and accompanying him to rugby matches. Carissa could not care less about most of these things, but over the years she has come to recognize that they are important to Sean, and doing them makes him feel loved and cared for as an individual. Along the way, Carissa challenged herself to learn a few delicious recipes using the ingredients Sean loves. While she still does not love rugby, she has found other wives she enjoys talking with on the sidelines. Sean learned that showing his love and care for Carissa should include grilling her favorite sausages in the summer, calling her during the day from work just to ask how she is and telling her he loves her, and bringing her coffee in the morning. He discovered that while grilling the sausages, which he does not care for, he could also toss on a steak for himself; now, they joke about having "steak-and-sausage" nights. He set his cell phone alarm to remind him to phone Carissa each day after lunch and now finds himself looking forward to those exchanges. After he makes his morning coffee, Sean now remembers also to bring Carissa a cup.

To help couples get insight into what each other regards as a behavior that shows caring, we might ask each partner to consider the following:

- What small acts do you wish your mate would do that might make you feel cared for?
- Do you know what small acts of caring your mate might wish from you?
- Can you think of at least one way each day to perform small caring acts for your spouse?

Loving Words

Ah, loving words—what happens to the whispered endearments, sweet nothings, and romantic language couples employ so often during premarital and post-honeymoon days? Verbal exchanges of loving words and phrases are one way couples play with one another: If I say this, what will she do—laugh, smile, kiss me, say something equally loving in return? The long haul of a marriage, and possibly children, often pushes a couple's use of loving words to the periphery of their conversations—or off the edge altogether.

Partners who speak to one another as if they are roommates or business partners, or even just casual friends, rob their relationship of some of the most intimate and private moments possible. When a couple communicates in a loving manner—including the choice of words, tone of voice, and coded meanings—they are indicating that they still see the other as a playmate, someone who they intend to have fun with and with whom a special bond is shared. Often, it is only one's spouse who is permitted to call someone a certain nickname. When a mate addresses his or her spouse as "honey" or "sweetheart" or greets the spouse on the phone with "Hello, lover," the mate signals that there is still a playfully loving attitude at work.

Affectionate Touch

In a marriage, reaching out to touch makes the couple's world a better place. Nonsexual touch, often referred to as bonding, between partners acts as a tonic, greasing gears that will help bring the couple closer. The need to touch and be touched, to hold and nurture, and to be embraced and comforted, is overwhelming, as evidenced by the famous studies of ignored orphan babies in Romania and Russia, as well as Harlow's (1958) pivotal primate work. In his "mother" monkey study, the need for affection and physical touch outweighed even the yearning for food.

As we consider the role of play in helping couples heal, we need to ask how much a couple's degree of touching can contribute to their playing successfully. The absence of loving physical contact is frequently at the heart of client complaints and a reason they do not play: "I'm too angry to touch him. If I touch him, he always assumes I want sex when I just need to be held." Willard Harley, marriage expert, agreed with women. He said, "Because men tend to translate affection into sex so readily, I put the emphasis on sexless affection." He said that men do not realize that women need that kind of affection to want to have sex. Often, a man's response is, "I'm just not an affectionate guy, and I don't touch her because I'm afraid I'm going to get rejected." Harley's point is that if men do not give women that type of touch, they will not get the amount of sex they want.

Early in working with the couple, the therapist should suggest an increased touching agenda. The couple may resist, but we believe increased touch is essential to creating playful experiences. Hugging is a good example; it is an important touch that women need. Harley (1986/2001) pointed out that women are much more comfortable with hugging. They hug readily—friends, children, and pets—whereas men need to learn the skill of hugging. He also said that most men need some instruction in how to become more affectionate.

The therapist presents a list of "touching" examples and asks each member of the couple to try at least two between then and the next session. The examples might be the following:

1. When a partner returns home, stop what you are doing and hug him or her for at least 15 seconds.
2. When out on a date, find and hold your partner's hand.
3. While watching TV, reading, or working on the computer in the evening, reach over and stroke your partner's arm.
4. While having dinner (at home or out), reach across the table and place your hand on top of your partner's.
5. When passing in the hallway, place your hand on your partner's back.
6. At night in bed, lie next to each other and cuddle for at least 10 minutes.

Reactions to these suggestions might go like this:

Husband: If I do those things, she's just going to think I want sex.
Wife: I don't really feel like doing any of that because I'm too mad at him.

Therapist:	I understand how you feel, but this is an experiment, and from my experience in asking couples to do this, it has been very beneficial. So, are you willing to do this to see the effect it has on your relationship? I would like you to pick two "touching" suggestions each. Will you do that?
Husband:	Okay, I guess so.
Wife:	All right, me, too.

Notice that it is not important to determine which came first—anger or lack of touching. Our job is to reintroduce touch into a couple's life, and when it comes to play, to encourage affectionate (nonsexual) touch as integral. Increased touch will yield positive interactions, balancing out the negatives, contributing to a healthy 5:1 ratio. It will also release the hormones oxytocin and viasporin. These hormones help lower blood pressure, reduce stress, and boost the immune system. We shape couples' behavior by moving them away from their stories and excuses, so that touching one another again begins to bring them closer both literally and figuratively.

Angela and Fred don't know who stopped touching first. "When I'm mad, I don't want to touch her," Fred explained. Angela added, "He rarely touches me, so I don't want to touch him either." The therapist asked what kind of touching they each missed most. For Angela, it was holding hands when they are walking in public. Fred missed his wife's head on his shoulder while watching TV. Over the next week, they each made a conscious effort to touch one another in those exact ways, and something interesting happened. From hand-holding, Fred started putting his arm around his wife while walking to the train in the morning. Angela moved closer on the couch in the evening so she could rest her head on Fred's shoulder, and by the end of the week, he was resting his arm on her knee. "I guess we just had to take the first step," Angela reported, smiling. Fred nodded and leaned over to squeeze his wife's arm.

A couple's nonsexual touch usually involves being in close physical proximity—sharing a restaurant booth, walking together, dancing, playing sports. Even a board game puts a couple within easy arm's reach. We want to encourage a couple to touch one another more frequently when engaging in play. We want them to experience how mutual physical touch will ramp up their emotional connection, increasing the likelihood of creating positive memories.

Couples in therapy are rarely satisfied with the amount of physical affection between them, and this can significantly disrupt a couple's ability to maintain a flow state. When a couple is in a flow state (Csikszentmihalyi, 1990), there is a spontaneous and organic interaction between the internal mental states of affection, love, and joy and the expression of those states through physical affection (as well as other communication). It is effortless and highly pleasurable. A couple creates this mutual "flow" of energy and communication largely through touch. Nowhere is this more palpable than in the areas of affection and sexuality (which we discuss in Chapter 8). Here, we want to use the fertile area of touch to explore the flow that actually stems from the improvisational maxim of accepting and building on "offers." Those offers are both intrapersonal and interpersonal.*

To gain a clear understanding of this flow during a therapy session, couples are asked to consider the following questions:

1. Would you say you touch your partner frequently or rarely?
2. Would you say your partner touches you frequently or rarely?
3. Are there times when you have an impulse to touch your partner and you act on it?

Follow this up by asking for more information about how and when this typically occurs:

4. How does your partner respond when you do follow that impulse to touch? Does he or she block you?
5. Are there times when you have an impulse to touch your partner and you *do not* act on it? (Follow up by asking for more information.)
6. How do you feel when you do not follow through on that impulse?
7. How do you respond when your partner touches you?

You are looking for whether there is a disconnection or connection between the feelings of affection and the impulse to act on it through physical touch. And, you are looking for whether there is a dampening or amplification to the offer of affection.

In other words, if Rebecca feels affection or love for Benjamin, does she think about reaching to caress his face or put her hand on his shoulder? If the impulse to reach out actually becomes conscious, does she act on it? Assuming she does act on it, how does Benjamin respond to the "offer"? Does he exhibit a *"yes, and"* response, for example, by taking a deep breath, looking her in the eye and saying, "I love when you touch me like that," or somehow acknowledge her gesture, perhaps by placing his hand over hers? Or, does he ignore her overture? In the former case, this completion of a flow circuit is usually rewarding to both parties, and the flow is maintained. In the latter, Rebecca probably does not get reinforced and will most likely drop out of her flow state. Eventually, she may begin to inhibit herself from acting on her affectionate impulses.

This brings us back to the other potential path that may occur, assuming that Rebecca is consciously aware of the impulse to reach toward Benjamin. In this other path, she inhibits herself from acting. This may be due to earlier rebuffs that now are coded in her brain as painful. Or, it may be due to her belief that

---

* These questions can actually be used in any content area: making plans, playing games, using humor. Does the person follow an impulse to make a joke? Does the partner find a way to accept the offer and play along, or does the person shut it down by some type of blocking comment?

Benjamin will misinterpret her affectionate gesture as an invitation for sex that will result in a fight. Or, perhaps her inhibited behavior is due to her fear of being rejected. The point is, she is inhibiting her own flow and consequently inhibiting the shared flow between them.

Obviously, the same dynamic can be occurring for Benjamin. By the time a couple shows up for some sort of treatment, there is usually some breakdown of this flow, either intermittent or widespread. This truncated, unsatisfying flow may be obvious to the couple, or it may be surprisingly out of their awareness. Either way, our job is fourfold:

1. Increase each partner's awareness of the issue.
2. Encourage the couple to increase the times they act on the impulse to touch.
3. Help the receiver of the action adopt an attitude that will yield a *yes, and* response.
4. Help the couple understand and let go of inhibitions that reduce the amount of physical touch.

FLIRTING, MYSTERY, SURPRISE, AND ROMANTIC ACTS

Flirting

Webster's New World College Dictionary (1988) defined the word *flirt* this way: "to touch lightly, move from flower to flower, to pay amorous attention to without serious intentions or emotional commitment, to trifle or toy (as in flirt with an idea); a person who plays at love." Flirting and wooing are special cues between partners that there is something special going on just between the two of them.

Here is a scene worth considering: At a party, in a corner, a man and woman lean toward each other. Both smile suggestively; they giggle. They gaze deeply into each other's eyes, laugh and tease and touch lightly. She leans forward and whispers in his ear. He touches her face gently. Chances are we are spotting the early stages of a romantic relationship—a budding sexual or romantic attraction. Chances are they are not married. But, what happens to couples after they marry? What happens to the fun and excitement of flirting, so predominant in the early stages of the courtship? Does marriage preclude flirting?

When their therapist asked Susan when she last flirted with her husband, Susan thought, then replied, "Probably when we were dating." Yet, within a marriage it can be magical and fun, so what is the reason our couples do not engage in it? Flirting says to each partner, "You should know now I am still attracted to you, still very interested in you." To be flirted with boosts a person's self-esteem. It says someone who knows me well still finds me attractive and still wants me. Most spouses need to know that they still excite their partner. Flirting is an investment in the relationship and, although it does not always have to be an overture for sex, it can be both encouraging and stimulating. When long-married couples do flirt with one another, often it is seen as an aberration.

> Francine and Guillermo, married 18 years, were dining out one evening. They were smiling, laughing, and gazing into each other's eyes. To their surprise, a friend who had been sitting a few tables away approached them and laughed with relief. He had recognized Francine, saw her flirting, and worried she was with another man. He, like so many others in our culture, did not expect to see a married couple still romancing—yet isn't that how their joint venture began?

In therapeutic practice, the therapist introduces the subject of flirting behaviors to the couple by asking each partner when he or she last flirted with his or her spouse, why this stopped, and whether the partner is now willing to practice and resume flirting. The approach here is to reintroduce a behavior that once worked so well: the fun, the games, the play, the joys that brought them together in the first place. Therapists must get consent from the couple, of course. If one or both partners do not feel ready, the therapist can help the couple engage in some of the other behaviors mentioned in this chapter. At the same time, the therapist can explore with the couple their resistances to flirting and how that relates to their difficulty in creating more love, joy, and fun in their relationship. When the therapist does so, one of two things usually occurs: either the couple starts flirting again and feels closer to each other, a step in the right direction, or there emerges a resistance or a difficulty in flirting, which provides useful grist for the therapy mill.

Finally, therapists must attend to the interactive aspect of these small behaviors. To borrow from improvisational comedy: Does each person initiate an offer or a behavior? Does each person accept and build on the offer or behavior of the other? Or, does the person on the receiving end kill or block the small behavior of the other?

Mystery and Surprise

Just as on the stage or screen or in a good book, surprise and mystery create excitement by introducing the unexpected. In a relationship, the unexpected surprise and mystery can intensify positive emotion, stimulate interest, and deliver instant, playful fun. Surprise is a good example of the kind of novelty we suggest (in Chapter 1) you encourage couples to include in their relationships to keep the spirit of play alive and improve the relationship quality.

Before encouraging surprise and mystery, however, it may be useful to test the waters first. Establish if one or both partners have a built-in aversion to being at the receiving end and if either or both partners lack confidence at planning to surprise the other. The good news is that encouraging individuals to go outside their comfort zone in this regard can itself be a helpful step in moving couples back into a mindset of embracing new activities that have the potential to revive a relationship that scores low on the play scale.

We cite these possibilities for couples and remind them that parents constantly surprise their children with fun activities and presents to alleviate boredom and routine. Yet, often these same parents rarely think about doing the same for each other. It is also helpful to point out for couples that a good surprise can be a small gesture as well as a grand one.

Some examples of small, surprising gestures might include the following:

1. Leaving a love note on the bathroom mirror for a spouse to find.
2. Performing secret random acts of kindness (slipping a pack of mints in a travel bag; taking a car to be washed).
3. Sending a partner a sexy or funny card (via e-mail or postal service).
4. Setting up a bath, complete with candles, music, oils, or bubbles.
5. Picking up a spouse from the train station on an especially cold day (when he or she normally walks home).
6. Bringing a partner breakfast in bed or a cool drink while working in the yard on a hot day; warming up the car on a cold morning.

Grander-scale surprises know no limits and are not dependent on a grand budget:

1. Inviting friends for a milestone birthday party for a mate.
2. Planning for a weekend away (including arranging for child care, if needed).
3. Buying a gift the partner has yearned for but has denied him- or herself.
4. Ordering tickets to a concert or a show.
5. Preparing (or bringing home) a nicer-than-usual dinner, complete with candlelight and flowers.

These examples, and others you may be able to suggest to couples based on your knowledge of their likes and tendencies, can help illustrate the value of surprise. They send the message that not only is one mate thinking about the other but also took the time and made the effort to arrange something for the purpose of giving the other pleasure, demonstrating love, and at the same time enriching the relationship. While marriages need certainty, stability, and security, they also need some good-spirited uncertainty, just enough to keep the relationship alive and fun.

The recipient of a surprise typically does not (or should not) know what is coming, which means the surprise has the potential to startle and excite. Mystery is related to surprise but is achieved as something unexplained or as a secret unfolding; the recipient senses that something is going on but is unsure of the eventual outcome. The process in mystery is just as important, maybe more so, than the end point.

Planning a mysterious adventure, or allowing oneself to be taken on one, is another great way for couples to keep the novelty going. When a partner detects a mystery is afoot, the intrigue is titillating and enticing. Routine can be alleviated with sporadic mysterious acts. (This is true especially with sex, as we point out in Chapter 8.)

Some ideas for staging a mystery include

1. Leaving a series of notes around the house that lead to a pleasant surprise.
2. Sending cards with clues to a planned upcoming activity.
3. Arriving home (or appearing for a night out) with a new look (hairstyle, clothing) that relates to an activity secretly planned.
4. Taking a mate on a mystery date (setting off without telling the destination, especially if it is something the two have never done before).
5. Sending texts over a few days with clues to something in the works for the weekend.

The following are questions to ask a couple to get the couple started:

How do you feel about giving and about receiving a surprise for your partner?

How do you feel about planning or receiving a mystery?

Can you recall a time in your marriage when your partner surprised or planned a mystery for you? If so, how did you feel about it?

Can you recall a time when you did the same for your partner? If so, what was your partner's response?

The following are questions to ask each spouse alone in your office:

What small surprises are you willing to do for your partner this week?

What large surprises are you willing to do for your mate within the next 2 months?

What are you willing to do this week to create mystery with or for your partner?

Spouses often plan surprises or mysteries based on romance, although romance does not always have to be the most important basis for these novel acts. It is more important to focus the couple's attention on the idea, and the act, of thinking of what will please the other and delivering that in a playful, exciting way. Romance, of course, does have its place when it comes to couple play.

Romance

The definition of *romance* from *Webster's New World College Dictionary* (1988) is to seek to gain favor of, as by flattery; court, to woo. But, this kind of intentional romantic behavior frequently stops after marriage. We include this because many women tell us they miss the romance of their earlier days, and yet men often say, "I'm just not romantic." Yet, it is clear these same couples were romantic at one time, most notably during the courting phase of the relationship. Women like to be wooed. It allows them to feel special, wanted, and attractive. So, we encourage men to have at least a small repertoire of romantic acts, employ them frequently, and see what happens. Romance is not really such an old-fashioned idea, although its importance seems to fade over time; most of your couples will remember it fondly and be eager to see more romance in their current lives. Reintroduce it into their lives by reminding them it might have been what brought them together in the first place. Ask them about the last time they shared a romantic moment. Ask them if they would like to share in its glow again. Ask them if they think it would change things.

We do this in our work with couples, and it produces the most marvelous results. Here is an example:

> Helen and John were married 15 years, and their lives had turned into a balancing act. There were the demanding jobs necessary to keep the bank account in the black, work commutes, a house always in need of repair, children's homework and afterschool activities, teacher conferences, a refrigerator that seemed to keep emptying itself, meals to be made ... the list continued. They always felt exhausted and were coming to the conclusion that their married life amounted to little more than planning sessions on how best to divide the list of chores.

Think about it: What did Helen and John's marriage need most?

    A. A strategic planner?
    B. A personal shopper?
    C. A tutor?
    D. A chauffeur?
    E. A shrink?
    F. A cook?
    G. None of the above?

The answer is G, none of the above. What Helen and John needed in their marriage was a little romance. Romance, if properly applied, could greatly raise their spirits and lighten their loads, even though nothing else may change; the same tasks still need to be accomplished, yet with a little romance in the background, those responsibilities can come to feel less burdensome. They began by closing their minds to the minutia of daily living. Instead, they looked deeply into each other's eyes and recalled for themselves some of the special qualities that attracted them to each other in the first place, their first impressions of one another.

On the way home from dropping the couple's two teenagers at a dance on a Saturday evening, Francisco decided to do something romantic. First, he went to the market and bought candles, wine, and flowers, then stopped in at a local gourmet shop and bought dinner for two. Then, he returned home, set the table, put the food on plates, and called his wife, Phyllis, into the kitchen. When she walked in she shouted, "Wow, this is amazing," grabbed him and gave him a big kiss. Francisco knew he had been successful at romancing his wife, and Phyllis got back that heady feeling of being desired.

Acts of Romance That Build Energy Over Time

A man can give a woman a lovely card telling her how much he loves her. A man can look into his wife's eyes and say he loves her, or a man can take a woman out to a nice restaurant that she likes. All these acts might be considered romantic. The problem may be that they do not build enough energy toward sexuality. But, if a man takes his wife out to dinner, looks her in the eyes and says he loves her, and arranges for the waiter to bring the card to his wife with the coffee, he is building romantic energy waves. There are two interesting secrets here. The first is doing things in threes. One and two just do not cut it—three, that is the ticket. Second, the little extra flourish and planning that goes into the waiter bringing the card is the essence of romance. It is the extra effort that is not necessary but done for the delight and pleasure of the beloved that creates the romance.

ACKNOWLEDGMENT, ENTHUSIASM, AND DELIGHT

The ratio of positive to negative interactions in a marital relationship can never be too high. In daily living, partners are involved in performing a plentitude of activities simply to get things done, including cooking, yard work, cleaning, laundry, auto maintenance, homework, driving, paying bills, and so on. These mundane but time-consuming tasks provide an almost unlimited opportunity either to take things for granted or to exchange compliments, gratitude, and appreciation. Is it required? No, but that is exactly the point. Active giving and active receiving of strokes create a great deal of positive emotion. If you want to be having fun, excitement, and joy, it helps to have an abundance of these positive behaviors floating around.

For a person to give heartfelt compliments, gratitude, and appreciation actively, he or she must be mindful of (a) all the things that others do to make one's life easier, richer, and more enjoyable; (b) an empathic connection of the special uniqueness of the other; and (c) the desire to give a gift of love to the other. What we explain to couples is that allowing yourself to notice and enjoy what your partner does for you actually makes you happier. It helps you remember and revel in the feeling that your partner loves you and cares for you. Communicating these "kudos" to your partner often makes you feel as good as, or even better than, the partner who receives them.

Of course, there are some people who have a difficult time accepting compliments. Usually, this stems from low self-esteem. If a person does not feel good about him- or herself, then the person will not let positive strokes in and instead will find a way to block them. It helps to point this out if you see it on display in one or both partners.

We encourage couples to increase the kudos they give to each other. We do this in many different ways, depending on the needs of the couple. We directly or indirectly communicate the idea that they are like teammates in a sport: They need to cheer each other on, "psych each other up." We remind them about the learning principle that positive reinforcement is the only training that really works. With some couples, we do this in a more conversational, informal manner, while with other couples, we do it more formally by asking them to make a list of the things that their partner does for them and the family and all the things that they feel that they do for their partner and the family. We have them discuss how they can give more compliments, thank yous, and so on.

For a client to give compliments, say thank you, and issue pats on the back sometimes requires a little encouragement. A therapist can help oil the wheels by asking the following:

- When did you last compliment your spouse?
- Have you shown appreciation for, and verbally acknowledged, any of your partner's contributions to your daily life today?
- When your spouse lets you know that he or she recognizes and appreciates something you have done or when you give a compliment, do you wave it off or take a moment to let it sink in that what you do has brought your partner some good?
- When and how would you like your mate to acknowledge you?
- What are some things you would like your partner to appreciate about you?
- From now on, would you be willing to commit to showing your partner some appreciation for actions that make your life a bit better?

Everyone needs a cheerleader; in marriage, one's spouse usually makes the best one. Who would not appreciate someone in the wings or behind the scenes, boosting one's morale, reminding of his or her support? It is not only when we are trying to tackle a major problem or achieve an important goal that human beings need enthusiastic interest from our loved ones: We need it every day.

If a spouse shows the other that what he or she is saying, doing, or planning is going to be met with a show of interest and enthusiasm, the possibility of keeping the play in the situation increases. It is much more fun to play with cooperative, enthusiastic people. By showing enthusiasm, we mean everything a partner can do to signal that he or she is engaged with the other—from a simple thumbs-up to a grander gesture, like a husband making a banner for a wife who is running her first marathon. In the courting stage, couples do not need reminders to show their enthusiasm for one another and for each other's interests; it comes naturally. They lean across the dinner table to hear every word our date says, and they usually find a way to respond enthusiastically. They show interest and let that interest show on their faces and in their body language. They are excited to be learning new things about their partner, who in fact is their playmate. Later in marriage, however, spouses often forget that they can greatly increase their mate's happiness with a show of enthusiasm, which then generates reciprocation, smiles, and additional caring behaviors.

> One night while they are cooking dinner together, Geraldo tells Kerry about wanting to join the new gym in town. She stops mixing the salad, turns toward him, and responds with a hearty, enthusiastic "Sure, why not! In fact, let's both do it!" which opens the door to the possibility of their sharing a fun new experience. Who knows, before long they may be laughing at how out of shape they both are after their first attempts at racquetball. But, even if Kerry is not interested in joining the gym, by stopping what she is doing, looking at her husband, smiling, and reassuring him with a supportive response, such as "Sure, you should join! You've always loved working out, and I know how much you miss it," it paves the way for Geraldo to increase his personal happiness, which in the long run will always contribute to their ability to share ideas and play together in the future.

To help couples think about ways they can show enthusiasm for their partner, we might introduce the following points:

- When your spouse tells you about something he or she is excited about, do you stop what you are doing, listen, and say something upbeat and positive in return?
- What fun way have you shown enthusiasm for something that excited your partner and in which your partner was involved?
- Even if you are not really thrilled with your partner's idea or story, is there a way you can think of to still be genuinely interested and enthusiastic for him or her (such as saying something like, "Well, I think it sounds wacky, but that's one of the reasons I love you so much!")?

"How delightful!" sounds like an old-fashioned phrase these days, something perhaps one's grandmother might say. Yet, *delight* is a terrific word to describe how people feel when someone they care about says or does something that delivers warm feelings of wonder, excitement, and love. Partners who want to make one another happy often seek to delight their mate, although we do not often hear the word much anymore. Delight is wrapped up in a bit of surprise with some pure joy tossed in as well. When a wife delights her husband, or vice versa, the partner is not only happy but also unabashedly giddy: The partner revels in the idea that someone he or she loves has purposely done something, said something, or caused something to happen that perhaps only he or she knew would thrill the partner.

When Mario and Sabrina, both amateur musicians who each worked two jobs, were newly engaged, he surprised her on a rare Saturday they both had off by telling her they were going on a secret date. He then drove to a park in a nearby town they had never visited, spread a blanket, laid out a home-made lunch of turkey sandwiches, and asked if it reminded her of anything? It did—the two had met 5 years before at a picnic given by mutual friends on the lawn at the site of a music festival three states away. They had both reached for the last turkey sandwich and began talking. Next, Mario took out the portable CD player he had brought along and popped in a disc he had burned—of the sonata that was playing in the background at that long-ago picnic. Sabrina was, well, delighted. Only Mario could know how much a simple picnic of turkey sandwiches and Bach meant to her.

Certainly, Mario's gesture also embodied other elements that contribute to a playful marriage: surprise, romance, shared activities. But, delight can also occur in much smaller ways: On a night when their budget was tight, had Sabrina put out a platter of turkey sandwiches and switched on Bach in the background, the delight would have been the same; it is not the sweep of the gesture, but the intention with which the act is tendered that causes the delight. A fabulous perk of bringing delight to a mate is that it is often repaid in—you guessed it—enthusiasm, smiles, flirting, acknowledgment, laughter, or silliness.

To illustrate this with couples, we might ask the following:

- When was the last time you purposely set out to delight your spouse? Did the reaction prompt you to want to delight him or her again, or were you rebuffed?
- If your mate delights you with words, actions, or even just a physical gesture, is your reaction one of joy and acknowledgment, or do you hold back?
- What are some small ways you can bring delight to your spouse each week?

An effective therapist makes decisions regarding which areas of a client-couple's relationship need the most work. This chapter was designed to help therapists consider addressing their clients' underlying behaviors regarding fun and play in their relationship. The components and principles described here, if applied therapeutically, become essential in our work of nurturing and developing play states within the marriage. By spending increased time in the play state, couples get closer to the 5:1 or even the 10:1 ratio of positive to negative interactions that is so vital to healthy and happy marriages.

We have described a number of exercises and practices you can do with couples to strengthen these underlying attitudes, and we describe more as we pro-
ceed through the book. Consider the idea that when individuals and couples
engage in playful behaviors, the nerves that fire together wire together (conversely, nerves that do not fire together unwire together). For couples who are
not at all playful, the way to cultivate necessary shifts in brain-based attitudes is
to engage them slowly in such behaviors—over time, those nerves will begin to
wire together.

For these approaches to be successful, practice is essential. Just as humans need
vitamins and food each day to maintain themselves physically, they also need to
engage in those types of experiences and behaviors that will maintain their emotional well-being and provide them with the neuropeptides of joy and love.

6

Promoting Paired Play
A Play Inventory for Couples

INTRODUCTION

"We are all faced with the same choice: to explore life's mystery. Deciding to set out as a playmate is a crucial event. Life becomes a playground offering unimagined possibilities for kindness. To accept the cosmic invitation to 'come out and play' is only the beginning" (Donaldson, 1993, p. 132). Unfortunately, putting the emphasis on play sounds so simple but is actually hard for couples to accept. Many couples do not make play a priority in their busy lives.

Lauer and Lauer (2002) came up with three rules to define couples' play, which succinctly sum up the ease and lack of obligation a couple should associate with the idea of play. The Lauers give three rules for couples play: "Rule one: If it's work, it isn't couples' play. Rule two: If you're not both enjoying it, it isn't couples' play. Rule three: If you don't feel better about yourselves and your relationship afterward, it isn't couples' play." (pp. 8–11)

In Chapter 3, we discussed relational and intrapersonal barriers that keep couples from being more playful and from playing more together. We have also discussed the cultural, social, and economic pressures that distract and sidetrack people from taking time to play. Couples play much more frequently and with more intention when they are dating. After getting married, for too many couples, complacency frequently prevails. We hear complaints about scheduling and paying for babysitters, lack of time, other obligations, kids' activities, and the challenge (and sometimes guilt) of setting aside money for couple playtime. They often complain that they are overwhelmed with the regular business of home and work life and see the planning and scheduling of recreational activity as a burden rather than a joy.

They also add that they just do not know what to do. But, if you can teach couples that all areas in their lives are available for playful activities, and that they will both benefit as a couple, then they will begin to prioritize joint play activities. Even the simplest form of play can be a great time for bonding:

> Kristen and Trevor together juggle two careers, two small children, Trevor's marathon running schedule, helping to care for Kristen's ill mother, and household chores. While they admit that

their relationship as a couple is rarely fun anymore, they are stumped about how—and when—to address the problem. It is not simply a question of reorganizing their priorities. Their dilemma is real: Time, money, and energy are all in short supply in their lives, and it is unlikely they are going to find more of any of those precious commodities without making major rearrangements. The first thing their therapist, Gail, did was to ask them how they currently spent time together. Kristen replied that on weekdays after the children were in bed, they worked as a team to clean the kitchen, bathroom, and family room. Gail suggested ways that the couple could take some steps to transform these mundane, routine tasks into low-key playtime, such as putting on some favorite music in the background, using this time to tell one another stories about their day or to talk over upcoming weekend plans, or taking turns giving one another a 2-minute shoulder massage when the chores were over. Clearly, this was only a first step, but it was a powerful reminder to the couple about the value of seeing play as an integral part of their time together. It also showed how it could be incorporated into the couple's everyday life without a huge commitment of time or resources.

It is clear that many couples are perplexed in this area; they just do not see the opportunities in their lives for play. They become so creatively blocked that nothing comes to mind when they are asked what they would want to do for fun. If therapists give couples an assignment of playing together, it is sometimes almost like telling them to go home and talk when they do not currently have any effective conversation tools. With play, a couple also needs tools, ideas, and suggestions.

Playing together is like any other practice. It requires a certain discipline, focus, and planning. Often, couples report that they have difficulty finding ideas and play activities that are mutually enjoyable and affordable and that fit into their schedules.

In this chapter, we describe a simple exercise that makes it relatively easy for couples to reconnect with their own abilities to play. The inventory will help to determine the play preferences of both partners in the couple, and while individuals who have the most similarity with play preferences will have an easier time increasing their couple play than those who are not similar in this respect, the inventory is an enormously effective tool to help uncover where those preferences overlap.

The core of this procedure is an inventory of play activities. Completing this inventory will jog the couple's minds and help them discover which activities they find appealing and can mutually choose to do together. The act of completing the inventory itself also provides a real-time, forward-looking, shared activity that either leads to an improvement in the couple's situation or provides a microscopic peek into the resistances and blocks they each have to having fun. The inventory and its associated exercises are designed to be utilized in a number of ways depending on the needs and style of the clients as well as the approach of the therapist. The inventory can be done as a simplified, singular activity, or it can be broken down as a series. It is not a standardized test. It is meant to be both informative and evocative. Ideally, the entire inventory process is carried out over two to three sessions.

The inventory is generally presented to the couple as homework and given toward the last 10 to 15 minutes of a session. At home, each person fills out the inventory independently, choosing from more than 125 separate types of positive and playful activities. They individually check what they like, how often that activity currently happens in their lives, how much joy it brings, and how satisfied they are with the frequency of this activity. Most people find this first phase highly evocative and clarifying, reminding and reconnecting them to the playful activities they each enjoy. Sometimes, it shows each partner that some play does exist in the relationship; other times, it can lead to introspection about how one or the other has strayed so far from what he or she likes to do for fun. It can also spur a strong motivation to move toward reclaiming the playful self as well as play in the relationship.

The therapist tells the clients:

> "I am going to give you each an inventory of playful activities designed to help you evaluate and strengthen the positive experiences in your life as a couple. We are going to do this activity in several phases. The first part of filling out the inventory takes about 30 to 45 minutes. Each of you is to fill out your inventory alone. In addition to filling out the form, notice your own reactions. Write them down if possible. Then, in the next session we will discuss the results and talk about the next step. This is a very important process. Please give yourself the gift of taking your time. Schedule up to an hour with no sense of having to rush."

COUPLES PLAY INVENTORY*

The form that is the first part of the inventory is given next. It lists many different activities that adults find fun or playful. No one is expected to like all of these things or to have tried or even thought about engaging in all of these activities. It is our hope that by seeing all of these ideas listed, many husbands and wives will be inspired to consider some new activities as a way to increase the joy and fun in their life together.

Instructions

Each person should fill out his or her inventory separately. After it is filled out, you will have the opportunity to compare notes.

Step 1: Check the box if it is a form of play that you currently like to do or would like to do in the future. It is important that while filling this out you assume that you are getting along with your partner. If you are not currently getting along with your partner, then think back to when you were and respond as you would under those circumstances.

---

* You can order a PDF of this survey that gives you unlimited rights to reproduce it for your clients at our Web site: http://www.wearenofunanymore.com.

Go down the list vertically and check all the boxes that apply to you. Then, go back and do the rest of the steps for each box you checked.

Step 2: For every box that you checked, in the first column please rate the number of times per month (average it over the last 3 months). If you cannot do that, do it for the last 30 days. The exact number is not important. Just put down your best estimate.

0 = zero
1 = one
3–4 = three to four
5 = five
10+ = more than 10

Step 3: For every box that you checked, in the second column please rate (on a scale of 1–4) the degree of pleasure this behavior generates (or would generate if you did it). *Remember to mark this column for how much joy or fun this behavior would generate even if you are not doing it now.*

1 = a little fun or joy; mildly pleasant
2 = somewhat fun and pleasurable
3 = definitely fun; leaves a warm glow
4 = tons of fun; makes me happy for days

Step 4: For every box that you checked, in the third column please rate your satisfaction with the frequency of these behaviors

1 = not at all (I feel totally deprived of this)
2 = a little (I need want/need a lot more of this)
3 = some satisfaction (I could still use a significant increase in frequency)
4 = a lot of satisfaction (but a little more would be nice)
5 = completely satisfied (as much as I could ask for)

Section 1: Activities, Dates, and Outings That Are Outside the Home

In this section are various activities, dates, and outings that different people often enjoy. No one likes them all.

Cultural play	Times per Month	Degree of Pleasure	Satisfaction With Frequency
❑ Go to a museum or historic site			
❑ Go to a comedy performance			
❑ Participate in a book group			
❑ Go to a play			

Cultural play	Times per Month	Degree of Pleasure	Satisfaction With Frequency
❏ Go to the ballet or other dance event			
❏ Go to the opera			
❏ Go to an art gallery			
❏ Go to a movie			
❏ Read a book together			
❏ Take a class together			
❏ Be a tourist in your own city or town			
❏ Go to a lecture			
❏ Go to a poetry reading			
❏ Go to a concert			
❏ Other			

Entertainment play			
❏ Go to a sporting event (baseball, soccer, football, etc.)			
❏ Go bowling			
❏ Go to a restaurant you have never been to before			
❏ Go out for pizza, ice cream, etc.			
❏ Take a dance class together			
❏ Shop together			
❏ Go out and sing karaoke			
❏ Go to a craft fair			
❏ Go to a community function together			
❏ Go to the aquarium or zoo			

The great outdoors and sports			
❏ Go to the park, arboretum, or botanical garden			
❏ Go to the beach			
❏ Go the mountains			
❏ Have a picnic or barbeque			
❏ Go skiing or snowboarding			
❏ Go waterskiing			
❏ Go snorkeling or scuba diving			
❏ Go canoeing			

❑ Go kayaking			
❑ Go sailing			
❑ Go hiking			
❑ Go camping			
❑ Garden together			
❑ Go biking			
❑ Go jogging together			
❑ Walk the dog together			
❑ Go for a walk (on a sunny day, a foggy day, a rainy day, or at night)			
❑ Play tennis			
❑ Play golf			
❑ Go fishing			
❑ Go rock climbing			
❑ Go surfing			
❑ Go bird watching			
❑ Go jet skiing			
❑ Go motorboating			
❑ Other			

Section 2: Activities, Dates, and Events That Take Place in and Around the Home

	Times per Month	Degree of Pleasure	Satisfaction With Frequency
❑ Talk together about daily experiences in life			
❑ Talk together about big question issues (e.g., the meaning of life, spirituality)			
❑ Talk together about life goals in terms of vacation, finances, career, children			
❑ Plan a vacation together			
❑ Meditate together			
❑ Practice yoga or exercise together			
❑ Eat dinner together in a leisurely manner			
❑ Cook dinner together			
❑ Make a fire in your fireplace, sit together, and enjoy			

❏ Make a fire outside (in a chimera or outdoor fireplace)			
❏ Have a big party at your house			
❏ Have a small dinner party at your house			
❏ Have a wine tasting at your house			
❏ Have a talent show at your house			
❏ Play a board game (Scrabble, checkers, chess, Monopoly)			
❏ Play a card game			
❏ Do a puzzle together			
❏ Play a game with other people (charades, board games such as Balderdash, Cranium, Apples to Apples)			
❏ Play croquet			
❏ Play pool			
❏ Listen to music together			
❏ Play music together			
❏ Sing songs together			
❏ Make a snowman			
❏ Have a snowball fight			
❏ Have a water gun fight			
❏ Have a pillow fight			
❏ Other			
❏ Other			

Section 3: Small Playful Behaviors That Create Positive Emotion (Clowning Around)

Humor	Times per Month	Degree of Pleasure	Satisfaction With Frequency
❏ Make your partner laugh			
❏ Your partner makes you laugh			
❏ You laugh together			
❏ Tell jokes			
❏ Make fun of yourself			
❏ Speak in a funny accent			
❏ Do something silly			
❏ Make up a silly song			
❏ Share a funny experience from your day			
❏ Look at comics or joke books together			

❏ Mimic favorite comedy bits (e.g., from *Seinfeld, Monty Python, Saturday Night Live*)			
❏ Tell funny or engaging stories			
❏ Make rhymes or limericks			
❏ Engage in playful teasing (that partner likes)			
❏ Watch comedy on TV or online together			
❏ Listen to comedy CDs			
❏ Give your partner a gag gift			
❏ Put on a funny outfit			
❏ Keep playful objects around the house			
❏ Take a comedic improv class			
❏ Take a stand-up comedy class			

Small acts of love, kindness, and fun			
❏ Give a card			
❏ Write short sweet notes			
❏ Receive a short sweet note			
❏ Write a love poem			
❏ Receive a love poem			
❏ Give flowers			
❏ Give chocolate			
❏ Give a compliment			
❏ Give a thank you			
❏ Make a favorite dish for no particular reason			
❏ Say I love you			
❏ Make a brief phone call to say hello			
❏ Give a gift or do something unexpectedly for no reason whatsoever			
❏ Express gratitude for something, small or large			
❏ Make breakfast for your spouse			
❏ Other			
❏ Other			

Small acts of physical affection			
❑ Give hugs			
❑ Give kisses			
❑ Give gentle strokes			
❑ Scratching			
❑ Hold hands in private or public			
❑ Put arm around your partner			
❑ Give a nonsexual pat			
❑ Stroke partner's hair			
❑ Gently touch partner's face			
❑ Other			
❑ Other			

Section 4: Romance, Sensuality, and Sexuality

Romantic-sensual	Times Per Month	Degree of Pleasure	Satisfaction With Frequency
❑ Take a shower or bath together			
❑ Wash each other's hair			
❑ Give each other a massage (body, face, hands, or feet)			
❑ Go dancing together			
❑ Go to a bed and breakfast or hotel for a night or a weekend			
❑ Have breakfast in bed			
❑ Meet for lunch			
❑ Cuddle in bed			
❑ Both read books in bed, by a fire, or on a sofa together			
❑ Feed each other			
❑ Watch a sunset or sunrise together			
❑ Make a special candlelit dinner at home			
❑ Go out on a date			
❑ Go for a walk in a romantic setting (e.g., beach, lake, park, garden)			
❑ Watch a romantic movie together			
❑ Sing to each other			
❑ Look at wedding photos or video together			
❑ Give partner jewelry			
❑ Give a long kiss to partner when you come home			

❑ Leave love notes around the house			
❑ Dress up and go out for the evening			
❑ Play romantic music in the house or car			
❑ Read love poetry			
❑ Create a sensual mood in bedroom or other room (using candles, essential oils, plants, music, lighting, etc.)			

Sexual			
❑ Sexual intercourse in bed (in a variety of positions)			
❑ Sexual intercourse anywhere outside bed			
❑ Sexual pleasuring other than intercourse (oral)			
❑ Sexual pleasuring other than intercourse (manual)			
❑ Sexual pleasuring other than genital (e.g., breasts, back, neck, legs)			
❑ Sufficient foreplay (20–30 minutes)			
❑ Masturbate in front of each other			
❑ Talk during sex			
❑ Use erotica (movies, books)			
❑ Use sexual toys (e.g., vibrator)			
❑ Use feathers, silk, or similar things for pleasure			
❑ Use food products in sex (e.g., whipped cream, chocolate, ice)			
❑ Have sex in an unusual place (not in the home or hotel room)			
❑ Play strip poker			
❑ Wear sexy clothing (e.g., lingerie or loin cloth)			
❑ Practice tantric sex			
❑ Go to a sex shop together			
❑ Other			

Use of fantasy			
❑ Tell each other one fantasy and act it out			
❑ Pretend you are much younger			

❑ Pretend that this is the first time that you are making love and ask your partner what he or she likes			
❑ Have phone sex			
❑ Use food or fruit as a sensuous object during sex (see the movie *9½ Weeks*)			
❑ Buy a movie or book and try different positions or activities depicted			
❑ Wear a costume			
❑ Pretend you are someone else (e.g., use a French accent or pretend to be a Russian spy or movie star)			
❑ Other			
❑ Other			

Other ways to increase the romantic mood at home			
❑ Dress up a bit more than usual (newer jeans and a nice top instead of sweats)			
❑ Wear cologne or perfume			
❑ Play romantic or special music			
❑ Give extra-juicy compliments			
❑ Look into each other's eyes			
❑ Light a fire			
❑ Light candles			
❑ Use aromas or scented oils or candles			
❑ Bring flowers			
❑ Flirt with partner			
❑ Call each other by an endearing pet name			
Anything else			
❑			
❑			
❑			
❑			
❑			
❑			

Look Over Your Own List

1. For each category, look at the number of boxes you have checked. This reveals your interest in that category.
2. Now, for each category and each box that you checked, look at your frequency per month. If you see lots of zeros and ones, then you are most likely not doing what makes you happy or not doing it frequently enough.
3. You can easily confirm this by looking at the rightmost column "Satisfaction With Frequency." For some things, you may be satisfied with the frequency. Other things you may want to do more often.

Write down any thoughts, feelings, or realizations that occur to you for later discussion with your therapist. Bring this inventory and your notes with you to your next therapy session.

SESSION 1: PROCESSING THE PLAY INVENTORY PART 1

When the couple comes back for their next session, the first job is to debrief them about the experience of completing the first section of the inventory. Assuming that each person has done the homework, the therapist should be looking to emphasize the positive and the hopeful possibilities that have been raised. In addition to analyzing the responses, those partners who have brought in their notes about how the exercise made them feel should have an opportunity to read them aloud and discuss them with their partner and with the therapist.

Finally, the therapist needs to get the couple to focus on the next phase of the work. We ask that you have the couple sit in chairs facing each other with eye contact and preferably holding hands. We suggest that you take a moment with the couple and have them talk directly to one another and affirm that they are going to continue in a spirit of fun and cooperation, without assigning any blame, but with the goal of having more fun and joy in their lives together.

Step 1: Debriefing the Inventory (30 Minutes)

The therapist can read the following directions (or paraphrase in your own words):

"Let's start with the first two sections of the inventory that have to do with doing fun activities outside and inside the house. Take turns of up to 5 minutes to show your partner your list. First, focus on areas of strength. Point out to your partner the specific activities that you are satisfied with or relatively satisfied with in terms of how frequently they occur. Say a positive comment about this, such as "I am glad that we go to movies a lot." Notice areas of play that are currently your strengths and offer a positive comment about this. Once you have gone over what is going well, take some time to show your partner which activities you would enjoy but are currently not happening often enough and you would want to increase. Then, we will repeat this process for Sections 3 and 4. Okay?"

The therapist should try to let the couple do this on their own with the therapist drifting toward the background, saying as little as possible and letting the couple have their experience. The therapist may want to say a few things to keep the couple moving in the direction of building positive energy and positive feelings. Guide the couple so that they do not become too task oriented and forget to savor the good feelings. It can be useful to remind them gently to slow down and savor the areas where they do feel connected. In fact, by pointing out that a couple is enjoying the interplay of reviewing the inventory, you can even suggest to the couple that engaging in this very activity is an example of how they can transform a "chore" into a playful activity in itself.

Step 2: Reflecting on the Results and Their Implications (10 Minutes)

Based on our clinical work, we know that most couples find that completing the inventory is an eye-opening experience. They typically have known all along that they are no longer doing what they used to do for fun, but somehow seeing it on the page hits home. We want to maximize the motivational impact of this found moment. We also want to take advantage of the new knowledge about neuroplasticity, namely, the rule that nerves that fire together wire together. A shared "aha" moment is a powerful binding force. Sometimes, the couple can feel discouraged if they find little on the list that they currently do together. But, this knowledge is important and helpful; if utilized well, it can propel the couple to increase their efforts at future joint pleasurable activities. Therefore, in this part of the session, the goal is to create a positive and hopeful conversation between the couple about what they have learned.

Therapist:	Did you find this exercise useful?
Husband:	Yes, it really hits home how much we have let things go.
Wife:	What strikes me is how much we take each other for granted.
Husband:	Yeah. I sort of have always known that we spend so much time taking the kids to activities, work, and so on, but I just didn't really realize how much it affected our own happiness and took time away from the two of us.
Therapist:	So, this is a pretty big revelation?
Husband:	Yes.
Wife:	Oh, yes.
Therapist:	Okay, I want you to look each other in the eyes and talk about this revelation.
Wife:	I'm glad we're doing this. I'm seeing a lot of things I hadn't noticed.
Husband:	So am I.
Wife:	Maybe this is a good opportunity to break our pattern and start to have fun together. Do you agree?
Husband:	Sure. I want to have more fun with you like we did in the beginning.
Wife:	It's going to be a challenge to make the time and to get good coverage for the kids, but it will be worth it.
Husband:	I know. I'll help with the logistics. I'm excited about doing some of these things again.
Wife:	Me, too.

To this point, we have only identified all of the activities that people find playful and would like to participate in more often. We have tried to create awareness and motivation for the couple to be excited about creating more playful activities together. The next step is actually to plan which activities the couple wants to increase.

Step 3: What You Are Willing to Give? (10 Minutes)

In this step, each person needs to find three activities that the partner wants to do that he or she also likes and wants to engage in more frequently as well. The instructions are as follows:

"Cheryl and Alan, please give your inventory to your partner. Thank you. I would like you to look over what your partner has said he or she likes and would want to do more. Your job is to pick three activities that your partner likes and wants more of and that you also like and would want more to do. Cheryl, look over the activities that Alan has checked and find three things that you also want. I want you to write them down on List A. Alan, you do the same thing. Since we want to create as much positive energy as possible, try to pick things that you like to do that are high on your partner's pleasure scale (in the third column)."

Cheryl looks at all of the things that Alan would like to do more. She looks for three of those things that she also would like to do more. Some of the things he wants to do more include playing games like cards, going to comedy clubs, going out for pizza, playing tennis together, having sex in places other than the bed, her wearing perfume. Cheryl picks three of those things that she wants to do as well at this moment in time: playing cards, wearing perfume, and going to a comedy club. She writes them down on List A.

CHERYL'S LIST FOR ALAN

List A: What My Partner Wants—My Choice From His or Her List That I Will Initiate

1. Wear perfume
2. Go to a comedy club
3. Play cards

Then, Alan does the same. Now, each person has a list of what the partner wants and his or her choice from the partner's list that he or she will initiate. Each spouse now puts these activities in his or her daily calendar or activity scheduler. Cheryl shows Alan what she has chosen to do and vice versa. The therapist asks the partner, in this case Alan, to describe how he thinks he will feel when Cheryl does at least one of those things. Cheryl commits to initiating more of at least one of those activities each week for the next month (or whatever time period is chosen).

The therapist needs to manage the couple's expectations and guard against creating unnecessary feelings of disappointment. One way to accomplish this is by suggesting that they pick one activity to do between this session and the next. For instance, if Cheryl picks playing cards, the therapist can ask how many times and when does Cheryl think she can initiate playing it during the week.

The therapist wants to make sure that everyone understands the choices and is in fact feeling good about the lists. Any hesitancies or potential ambivalence should be explored. The goal is to keep the inventory exercise, and the actions it will spur between sessions, as positive experiences meant to deliver playfulness and togetherness, not point out past neglect or blame. With that in mind, keep the couple focused on deciding together what to do about what they have learned. The therapist should never be the person urging the couple to do more. When there is any doubt, it is better for the therapist to suggest that they do less for that week. You want to caution them not to overcommit and set themselves up for disappointment.

Step 4: Committing to Action (2 Minutes)

In this final fun action step, each person states out loud what he or she is going to do, and the therapist asks each to express this with as much fun and enthusiasm in the voice as possible; the idea is that the playfulness begins when a couple makes plans. The couple then should be asked to hug, shake, or kiss to seal the deal, with the session ending on that positive note. It helps if the therapist has pom-poms to shake or applauds rhythmically or chants "go, go, go, go" (like in a sporting arena) as they leave the room (just kidding—please read Chapter 7).

PLAY INVENTORY FOLLOW-UP SESSIONS

The shape and tenor of follow-up sessions to the inventory can vary widely depending on the couple and what they do together in the time between sessions. The first, and simplest, thing is to debrief the couple about the activities of the week, the false starts and unsuccessful attempts as well as the successful and satisfying ones. If the couple completed the assignment, the therapist's job is to reinforce and build on the movement and the positive behaviors, as well as the positive feelings and closeness that it is hoped resulted from those behaviors. It can be helpful to ask the couple how the changes they are making are affecting their ratio of positive to negative interactions. The goal, of course, is an increase on the positive side.

The remainder of the follow-up sessions might be more complicated.

If the couple has only partially completed the assignment, there are two important distinctions the therapist must make at the outset. The couple may not fall into complaining and blaming, and the couple must continue to remain in a positive frame as a team.

Wife: We only played cards once. I think we have to do a better job of scheduling time for it. We let too many things get in the way.

Husband: I wanted to play more but you got into bed with the girls and fell asleep. I think getting into bed and reading to them is not a good idea because then you're done

Wife: for the night. Would you be willing to sit in a chair next to the bed and then leave right after you finish reading the book?

Wife: Yes, I can try doing that even though it might be difficult to leave right afterward.

In this example, the husband has a small complaint but presents it in essentially a problem-solving frame, and his wife receives it this way and responds in kind. The therapist's goal is to facilitate the problem solving. The therapist might acknowledge the challenges of the bedtime routine and its hypnotic effects on the parent putting the children to bed. The therapist might ask the husband what he could do to help with the bedtime routine.

The other possibility is that the couple moves more into a mode of complaining, blaming, and defending.

Wife: We only played cards once. I think we have to do a better job of scheduling time for it. Too many things get in the way.

Husband: I wanted to play more often, but you kept getting into bed with the girls and falling asleep. It really annoys me.

Wife: I'm tired by that point. Maybe if you helped with bedtime, it would be different. Anyway, when you get like this, I don't even want to play cards with you.

It is important for the therapist to avoid falling into the same trap as the couple and focusing on what did not go well. It is far more important to build on what did go well. The therapist might intervene with the following:

Therapist: As we have discussed before, marriage is a team sport, and sometimes your teammate drops the ball. It ruins morale if the team members blame each other. The best question to ask is, "What didn't work, and how can we do better next time?" That is the question that will move this situation forward. Does this make sense?

Husband & Wife: (Both nod)

Therapist: Okay. So let's do something different. You said that you did play cards once. How did the two of you make that happen?

Husband: Well, that was Thursday night. I put the girls to bed that night. I guess I am less susceptible to falling asleep. And while I was doing that, Cheryl was shuffling the cards and getting us a snack ready.

Therapist: That was a good alternative, and it worked.

Husband: Okay, I get it. If we are going to play cards, I put the kids to bed, and Cheryl gets things prepared.

Therapist: Cheryl, will you be okay with that plan?

Wife: Yes, absolutely!

The other possible outcome is that the couple fails to do what they planned. In this circumstance, the therapist has two jobs. The first is to put a frame on the situation that increases the odds of future compliance. A good all-purpose frame that we have used borrows the externalization strategy of narrative therapy (White & Epston, 1990):

> *Therapist:*   You guys left here committed to doing something, and yet it did not happen. I see this fairly frequently. The meaning I make out of it is that there are often significant forces working against couples that rob them of the fun that they can have together. And, couples often underestimate those forces and what they need to do to overcome them. Can we talk about what forces you, together and separately, have to deal with and what you can do to overcome them?

The therapist then follows the couple's lead, exploring whatever comes next. They may mention social forces, or it may be internal individual blocks and so on. As in most therapeutic settings, the general rule is to use whatever comes up as grist for the mill, recognizing that the play inventory is not just a task. It is also diagnostic, pointing to the blocks and resistances of the couple and the individuals toward play and connection.

It can be interesting to see what couples do with the different sections of the inventory and their behavior in response to the commitments they make between sessions as a result of the inventory. Does the couple or one partner avoid or discount a section of the inventory? A common dynamic is that the man is pushing for more sexuality and undervaluing romance and the woman is doing the opposite. Does one or the other circumvent the plans they have made? A typical response is the woman making time for the planned playful activity, and the man pleading that he is either too tired from work or needs to watch an "important" sports event on TV.

While this dynamic can be discerned in other ways as well, it becomes concrete when couples look at the inventory. The small discrete actions within the inventory can make it easier for people to take "baby steps" toward increasing the positive interactions in the diminished area. It also helps people move from a negative blaming ("You never do X") stance to a positive supportive stance ("Let's build this up one step at a time").

All along the way, there can be rich opportunities for dealing with resistances and personal issues either in discussions during the session or after a debriefing during which the therapist discovers something that became a problem.

> Sherry and Kurt decided they would go dancing, so Kurt made a reservation at a nightclub. They got dressed up, ate dinner at a nearby restaurant, and while there, they ran into some friends. While conversing with the friends, Kurt said that they were on their way to a dance club because "Sherry got what she wanted." After they walked away from the friends' table, Sherry felt upset and embarrassed. She said she no longer wanted to go dancing because she thought Kurt really did not want to go, and she would rather go home. Although Kurt's comment may have been shortsighted, Sherry was the one to curtail their evening.

ADVANCED USE OF THE INVENTORY

Beyond those that have already been discussed, there are actually many additional ways in which you can use this inventory as a tool for helping couples build a better discipline or culture around giving, receiving, and amplifying fun in their lives. The following is one we have used with highly motivated couples.

Step 1: The therapist gives the following instructions:

"Now that you have been working with the play inventory, we are going to take it up a notch. It is hoped that the act of filling out this assessment will have reminded you that there are a number of activities that you know will bring more fun and play into your life with your partner. Last week, we focused on you doing something that your partner likes that you also like. This week we are going to focus on two things. The first is initiating more discussion and planning based on what you want; the second is increasing your ability to do a 'yes, and' and 'accept the offer' when your partner initiates. What I would like you to do now is for each person to go over the charts and highlight seven specific activities: (a) activities whose frequency you want to increase and (b) activities you think would really make a difference to you and to your relationship. These should be things that you are willing to initiate. Write them down on List B."

Each person fills in the following list:

List B: Playful, Joyful Activities I Want and Am Willing to Initiate

1._____
2._____
3._____
4._____
5._____
6._____
7._____

Step 2: Therapist Gives the Directions

"Now, give your List B to your partner and take his or her List B. Look at your partner's list of seven things. Pick three activities that you would be willing to do over the next month. For our purposes here, you are picking things that you are willing to embrace and have fun with when your partner initiates. In other words, your partner is going to initiate, and you are going to accept the offer (do a *yes, and*) and play along. Write them down on List C. Then, put a check mark on your partner's List B next to the three things you have chosen. Hand List B back to your partner."

List C: Playful, Joyful Activities That My Partner Wants That I Am Willing to Embrace When My Partner Initiates

1._____
2._____
3._____

Step 3: Consolidating, Cooperating, and Committing

In this final step, the therapist will go over everything with the couple, help them to create a master plan, and make sure that everyone is feeling good about the plan. The therapist should underscore that there are activities that each person will initiate, and there are activities that each person will respond to once the partner initiates. The entire point is to cooperate in creating more positive energy in the relationship. This involves both initiating and responding.

First, each person fills in the summary page of the three lists of activities:

Name _____

List A: Playful, Joyful Activities My Partner Wants That I Will Initiate

1._____

2._____

3._____

List B: Playful Joyful Activities I Want and Am Willing to Initiate

1._____

2._____

3._____

List C: Playful, Joyful Activities That My Partner Wants That I Am Willing to Embrace When My Partner Initiates

1._____

2._____

3._____

Finally, the couple needs to decide on how many activities per list to do for the next week, being mindful to manage expectations and guard against creating unnecessary feelings of disappointment. The therapist should almost always be the person saying less is more. If the couple says they want to do all nine activities between sessions, the therapist should say something like the following:

> "Wow, that is a lot of enthusiasm and commitment. I respect that. But, are you sure you can actually do that given your other work, family, and household obligations? I want to make sure that we do not raise expectations too high, which could lead to feelings of disappointment. I would rather you commit to doing less and succeeding at making your commitment, rather than saying you are going to do nine things and only doing six and feeling upset. Remember that "success" is having fun while doing the activities, not checking things off a list."

If one person wants to do more and one less, the therapist should almost always urge the smaller amount. If one partner is impatient, that also becomes a subject for therapy.

There is a great deal that a couple can learn about themselves and each other from using the inventory, even beyond its usefulness as a tool to spur increased play in their lives as a couple. We also know that couples fall into ruts, and that all people naturally resist change. When counseling couples who need to change their play lives to revitalize their marriages, having the inventory in your repertoire puts a powerful, concrete, demonstrative instrument at your disposal. When couples respond to your suggestions of increasing play in their lives with the standard, "Sure, but how?" you now have a road map to offer.

We believe that couples do want to have more fun together but lose sight of their commitment to their relationship, mistakenly expecting that it will flourish on its own. When the inventory is introduced, they are usually open to it, relieved, and grateful to have the encouragement and aid spelled out in black and white. The possibilities for fun and joy, seen in the lists, may now appear endless and, even more important, available to them.

Using the inventory is an effective way to guide the couple in discovering new, forgotten-but-still-loved, and unusual activities they might enjoy doing together. Following where the inventory experience leads—participating jointly in some of the activities—not only can improve the quality of the couple's relationship but also can bring them happiness and pleasure, a greater desire to be together, and ultimately more intimacy and love.

If playing together was something a couple enjoyed in the beginning of their relationship—and we would be hard pressed to find a couple who made the decision to marry who did *not* have fun, playful times together—then we will be more likely successful helping get them back to that mindset again. Using the inventory is a proven, concrete way to guide couples to a more loving, lasting relationship by increasing play, which of course increases the ratio of positive to negative (described in Chapter 2). Many couples who have used this inventory reported a positive shift in their relationship. They are having more fun, and that is not only a wonderful outcome for the couple but also a satisfying result for the therapist.

7

Protecting the Play Zone
Dating in Captivity*

INTRODUCTION

It has almost become a cliché for marriage therapists and educators to suggest that couples need to continue to go out on dates after the wedding. On the other hand, clichés exist for a reason. Markman et al. (2010) found the average couple only goes out on a date about once almost every 2 months. We see this as an indication that most couples are not having a satisfactory amount of fun together. Many therapists have discovered that when it is suggested to couples that they need to have "date night" or some other similar activity on a weekly basis, the typical response is that the couple sighs, shakes their heads, and rolls their eyes. The couple sees the suggestion as one more chore in an overburdened life.

The fact of the matter is that dating is to a relationship as exercise is to physical fitness. Of course two thirds of Americans are overweight, so perhaps this is not the most motivating analogy. Nevertheless, the couple needs to buy into the possibility that going out together and having fun will enliven the relationship. Not unlike many people who finally start going to the gym, the motivation will begin (and build) *after* they start to date and have some success. Like getting physically fit, the key to keeping the romance and love alive is to make their relationship their number one priority, putting the marital relationship before anything else.

THE SECRET TO GETTING COUPLES DATING AGAIN AND LOVING IT

When you read the heading, did you notice an increase in interest or excitement? That was probably an increase in dopamine and norepinephrine in your brain. The word *secret* is a bit mysterious and dangerous. It connotes the possibility of novelty. These meanings help to stimulate the production of these neuropeptides,

---

* This title is a shout-out to Ester Perel (2006). Imitation is the highest form of compliment.

the very same ones that are associated with the feelings of passionate love (Fisher, 2001). Staying home watching reruns of *CSI* just does not cut it. Nor does the same old rerun of the dinner and a movie, all the while talking about how Samantha is doing in school. "Zzzzzzzz" ... [snore].

This is a book about how to help couples have more fun in a relationship. But, even fun requires some ground rules, so there also are rules and guidelines about how to do this. As therapists who are helping couples with this matter, it is important that you approach the entire enterprise with some energy, a healthy sense of humor, and of course some compassion for the couple who have dug a rut or even a giant hole for themselves. If you are successful, the path to playfulness will begin right in your office. Your goal then is to help the couple transfer the light atmosphere, playful attitude, smiles, fun, and laughter that they are able to engage in during sessions or classes to the rest of their lives.

The couple may also be scared and anxious about becoming open and vulnerable again. They may have disengaged emotionally from each other, and it may have been a long time since they have attempted to reengage. In the back of their minds, they are worried:

> "Will my partner still think I am interesting or funny? My God, I don't even think I am interesting or funny myself."
> "Will we have anything to talk about?"
> "Will I say something wrong? Are we going to have a fight?"
> "I am so anxious. What is wrong with me? Maybe that means I don't really love my partner or my partner is not right for me?"
> "What do we do if we don't enjoy the same activities?"

We use the safe atmosphere of therapy and the associations of laughing, positive mood, memories of better times, novelty, and excitement to combine with the prospect of reengaging with each other. This begins to shift the brain chemistry and unconscious mind of each person.

MARRIED DATING MOOD KILLERS

There are many mistakes couples make that can ruin a married date even before it starts. In fact, one of the reasons couples do not go out with each other as much as they used to, beyond benign neglect, is that they have attempted to date before and the dates went badly. Then, they began to engage in avoidance behavior consciously or unconsciously. At some point in the process, you need to explain these things to your clients. Preferably, you should do it sooner rather than later so they do not bungle their first steps back into dating. These should be explained as general guidelines that are applicable to everyone. Let us get the negatives out of the way first.

Mood Killer 1: Indecision That Leads to No Decision

One reason couples do not have regular dates is that they argue about what to do or simply cannot decide on an activity or how to spend their time. Often, a typical dialogue between a couple attempting to decide what to do on a date goes like this:

Cindy:	What do you want to do tonight, Frank?
Frank:	I don't know. What do you want to do?
Cindy:	You make the decision; I don't care.
Frank:	I'll do whatever you want.
Cindy:	Why don't we just stay home then?

This kind of conversation is neither uplifting nor enticing, and the worst part is that it leaves the couple exactly where they started—at home, probably not interacting with each other. Even if the couple does go out, the fun is often deeply dampened; they cannot get going. However, since the couple has filled out the fun inventory, there really is enough information at their disposal to make decisions and plans. The issue is one of getting them to act on the information. Typically, this type of dialogue occurs as a function either of the man not taking the lead or the woman not saying what she really wants.

Mood Killer 2: Date Planning Is Just Another Wifely Chore

Gray (2000) has said, "If a woman does it, it's domestic. If a man does it it's romantic." We have heard women complain that they have to set up all of the arrangements for dates or nights out. For the same amount of time, we have listened to the laments of wives wishing that their husbands were more romantic. The more successful the woman is in the work world, the more we hear this complaint. For women, the experience of romance comes from an increase in the hormone oxytocin, which creates the warm rush of letting go. The husband needs to take charge for these things to happen, just as when he was dating and pursuing her; he was in action, and biochemically, dopamine and testosterone were at work. Of course, a woman can arrange a date, and that can be romantic as well. For a married couple, the key here is that the couple shares in the date planning so it does not become a burden.

The real mood killer is if she has to plan the entire outing every time, adding to her perceived list of domestic chores and obligations. An example of shared planning is the wife expressing her desire for Chinese food, and the husband jumping right in with a suggestion of a Chinese restaurant they both like. But, if she mentions that their favorite local band is performing at an outdoor evening concert that encourages picnicking and then she is the one who has to buy the tickets; hire the sitter; feed the kids; then select, shop for, prepare, and pack the picnic food; carry the food to the car; and meet him there on his way home from work—that is a mood killer for her.

Mood Killer 3: The Bathroom as Date Staging Area

The saying, "Absence makes the heart grow fonder," reflects the truth that having some space as individuals is important. There is another saying, this one from the music world, "Music happens between the notes." Perel (2006) emphasized the importance of couples creating sufficient space for passion, desire, and longing to flourish. She pointed out that need for security, safety, and dependency pulls couples closely together. While this may be comfortable, it does little for excitement, mystery, and fun. This brings us to an almost iconic scene that couples should avoid in all of its forms. Just describing the scene to couples usually leads to fits of smirking and laughter, followed by knowing head nods of recognition.

Once upon a time, a man and a woman met and found each other attractive. They would look forward to each date. He would shower and shave and put on his coolest clothes and sexiest cologne in the confines of his own bathroom. She would shower and put lotion on her skin in her own bathroom. She would carefully select which dress and jewelry to wear that would make her look attractive to her partner. Oh, the exquisite anticipation of it all. When they finally met for the evening, he would do small acts of kindness to show his affection. She would appreciate his every word.

A few years later, they are married and have a child. They hardly go out any more. If they do go out, the ritual is somewhat different. She walks around in her robe (stained with baby spit-up) while rubbing antifrizz gel in her hair. They both walk into the bathroom. He sits in his underwear clipping his toenails and farts while she shaves her legs. Ahhh … there is romance in the air tonight.

Couples need to create space and anticipation, even mystery ("What is she going to wear tonight?"). Instead of getting ready in their shared bathroom together, we suggest they get ready for the date separately, or at staggered times, and surprise each other with their attractive appearance right before leaving.

Mood Killer 4: Talking About "the Relationship" and Other Hot Button Issues

Once upon a time, Hector and Elana were on their way from their Connecticut home into New York City for a night out on the town. It was a 1-hour drive into the city, and Elana had wanted to talk to Hector about a financial problem that had been bothering her. They had been very busy over the last week but now seemed like the perfect opportunity; she had Hector all alone for 60 minutes. She reasoned that they could talk about the problem, and then they could have a good time. Meanwhile, Hector was looking forward to a great time on the town with Elana; he could leave the stress of the week behind. She started to bring up the financial problem subject. He immediately became tense and snapped, "I don't want to talk about this now." She replied, "We need to resolve this issue; don't try to avoid it." Both were upset, and the last thing they felt like doing was spending the rest of the night together.

There is some disagreement in the literature about the point underlying this modern fable. Markman et al. (2010) suggested that fun times together must be protected from conflict. This means that the date should not include discussions about money, children, or household chores or expenses. The date starts once you are out the door, not when you have arrived at the destination. On the other hand, Gottman (1994, 1999) suggested that a weekly date could also be used as a low-pressure release valve, a way for the couple to stay connected even during conflict. He advised that a couple might purposely use the date time to discuss sticky issues or talk over an argument they may have had earlier that week. Doherty (2001) also noted that a date might be a good time for couples to talk about their relationship, as separate from the usual conversations about money, children, the house, or career. We believe that doing that is risky unless the couple has become expert at handling conflict.

We agree with Markman et al. (2010) that playful outings—that is what married dates are—exist for the purpose of creating positive connection, fun, and even passion. Conversations should be free from daily problems and heated topics, especially ones that have caused conflict for the couple in the past. Therefore, we suggest that couples avoid flashpoints and known hot topics that inevitably lead to arguments and steer away from discussing money, the in-laws, the kids and any of their problems, career difficulties, and other major issues.

The partner who wants to talk about the relationship needs to contain this wish for the moment. Those kinds of conversations should be scheduled for other times. If need be, that can be negotiated in the session. Frankly, we strongly recommend that couples do not make the mistake that Hector and Elana made. We tell them the story, and we encourage them not do this on the way to the date destination. Do not do it during the main activity. Do not do it on the way home. We tell them some couples even think that if they promise not to get upset that they can at least have part of the "relationship conversation." We discourage them from even trying it. Things can get hot in an instant. Protect your good times together.

The therapist's suggestion to avoid contentious issues usually yields one of three different responses. The most common is that the couple agrees to follow the "doctor's orders" and winds up happier for it. Then, there are those who will not be told what to do and ignore the order. Finally, there are couples who do try to follow this mandate but fall into a hot topic or an argument anyway. Occasionally, a couple will report that with the awareness that they had gained through therapy, they were able to break our rule, have a civil discussion, and not have it escalate into a fight. But, this is the exception, not the rule. In anticipation of the possibility that a hot topic will flare up, we tell couples in advance that if this occurs on a date, they will agree to take a time-out and then schedule the discussion for a future time: "Honey, let's enjoy tonight. Can we talk about this on Saturday morning when the kids are at swimming lessons?"

The more stressed out the couple is, the more they need to follow these rules. The idea is to keep the date light, focused on mutual satisfaction and contentment, and for it to be fun and playful.

We also ask some couples to write out three lists: verboten subjects, desirable subjects, and borderline subjects.

Verboten Subjects

Verboten subjects for conversation on married dates include any topic that has the potential to cause conflicts or arguments or has repeatedly caused them in the past. The entries on this list will vary greatly from couple to couple. One couple cannot seem to discuss career shifts without arguing, while another enjoys that topic and finds it gratifying to help one another with career strategies. One husband might put finances on the list; his wife might list vacation planning. It does not matter who puts what on the list; once it is a verboten subject, both are encouraged to respect the list and find something else to talk about.

Desirable Subjects

Usually, there is more agreement on this list than on the verboten list. Often, the date activity itself provides a desirable topic of conversation: the plot of the play a couple has just watched, the musical genius of the jazz band they are listening to, his bowling three strikes in a row, her serving him six aces in a tennis match. Beyond that, we suggest couples use the date time the way they used to long ago—ask each other questions, especially those that create an opportunity to think about positive experiences; bring up positive emotions; and learn something about one another. These might include discussing dreams or fantasies, reminiscing about good times, sharing pleasant memories and positive experiences, telling jokes and recalling funny experiences, or exchanging thoughts about books, articles, or current events.

If the couple needs a nudge in this direction, here are questions and conversation starters to suggest they try. It might be helpful to give them this list.

1. What is the best thing that has happened to you lately?
2. Tell me about that book you have been reading (or would like to read).
3. That was such a great TV show we saw the other night, don't you think?
4. I was thinking lately about when we dated and how much I loved X. What was the best part of our courtship for you?
5. My friend X and her husband recently tried Y (some new activity). I think that sounds like fun. What about you?
6. What have you always wanted to do but never did?
7. Let's think up a few more fun ideas for next month's dates.
8. What could we do if we won the lottery?
9. If you could live anywhere, where would you live?
10. If we get a chance to take a trip, just the two of us, where would you like to go?

Borderline Subjects

Some borderline subjects may start on the verboten list, then migrate to the borderline list, and as the couple gains some tools during therapy to better handle their conflicts, the subject may no longer pose as much of a risk as before.

Depending on the couple, any of the following might also fall on the borderline list: moving, career plans, retirement, savings, holiday/vacation plans. Here, a couple needs not only to listen to what one another has to say, but also to keep an open mind.

Mood Killer 5: Cell Phones, Texting, and Other Electronic Intrusions

Perhaps we are deeply influenced by both our baby boomer status and the fact that we have spent the bulk of our married years without the blessings—and curses—of modern technology. Yes, we do understand that the integration of technology into the lives of younger adults is probably permanent and in many ways a plus. Yet, as parents and as therapists, we have also seen the downside and the threat to the relationship success for those younger adults whose fingers seem to be permanently attached to a keyboard or cell phone and whose eyes are constantly focused on screens.

Technology can be both harmful and enhancing to intimate relationships, depending on its use (Henline, 2006). Moderation and timing are key. If one partner is away on a business trip and uses e-mail, texting, cell phone calls, or instant messages (IMs) to keep in touch, that is great. Using technology together to have some fun time during an at-home evening—playing tennis on the Wii or challenging one another to a computer game—is fine.

But, when couples are on a date, they need to clear some space for face-to-face interaction. If she is a doctor and is "on call," of course the pager needs to stay on. A cell phone is a help if the couple has a young child and a new babysitter at home. Beyond that, however, we say ignore the outside world and focus on one another. A spouse who takes a call or answers a text from a friend or colleague while on a date sends a powerful negative message to the other: "You don't hold my attention. I'd rather be in touch with others and not with you."

Mood Killer 6: Too Much Drinking and Beyond

Dining or visiting a bar or a dance club can be part of a great date night. But, too much drinking can negatively affect a couple's time together. As part of the date planning, partners can agree to limit their alcohol consumption and the use of mind-altering substances. (We are not taking a stand on the use of consciousness-altering substances; humans have been doing this for thousands of years.) The question we ask couples is, "To what extent does the use of outside substances help or hinder your having fun together?" More than a few times, couples have told us that a small-to-moderate use of alcohol "loosens me up" or "puts me in the mood." But more often, we hear that drug or alcohol use has created problems and serious fights. It is our view that couples need to protect their date, keep it conflict free, and thus increase the odds that both will have a pleasurable, satisfying time. Depending on the couple, some of the ways to protect the date can vary from, say, having a drinking limit to not consuming any alcohol at all.

GUIDELINES FOR SUCCESS AT THE MARRIED DATING GAME

It takes skill, intention, and practice to be successful at dating in marriage, regardless of how wonderful a couple's dating life was for a few months or even a couple of years before the wedding (or before children). We are talking about a lifetime of dating in a long-term marriage. Children, household upkeep, work, bills, all scrape away at the once-carefree experience dating was during a couple's courtship. Much more preparation, planning, time, energy, and thought have to be spent on married dating. Logistics, time management, child care, and budgets all must be considered.

It seems like a big "job." We tell couples it *is* a job, but one worth working at, because the benefits are enormous. Yet, even for the most dedicated couples who believe us and want to date actively again, their dating skills are often rusty. If we can help couples dust up these skills and again view dating as a game, it will go a long way toward their success.

We urge couples to set a weekly date night, no matter what. No matter how bad a relationship is, we can almost guarantee this will positively enhance the relationship. In the beginning of the chapter, we mentioned that Markman et al., 2010) maintained that the average amount of time a couple goes on a date is almost every 2 months. An interesting finding is that the women reported that the length of time was twice as long as the men. Markman et al. (2010) surmised that men and women have different definitions of a date. So, we suggest that the couples are asked to define what they think a date is so that there is no ambiguity.

We explain the benefits of having consistently scheduled dates and give couples techniques, guidelines, and ideas within the context of playfulness.

Mood Enhancer 1: Try Something New

Banish the routine, get out of the rut. Break up the monotony and be creative. Research has shown that sharing novel adventures increases marital satisfaction (Aron et al., 2000). New activities do carry some risk, but the payoff is great, reigniting the spark of love and romance. The rule is to choose an activity that interests both spouses—or at least one that they are not opposed to trying. Novel activities help release dopamine in the brain, which increases positive feelings, a natural high (and safer than alcohol or drugs). The Couples Play Inventory in Chapter 6 is a wonderful resource for couples to find new ideas for dates that are a little bit outside the comfort zone. For example, invite couples to go to a new restaurant that they have never visited before, suggest that they learn a new sport together, or perhaps they can take a course on a subject both know nothing about or take dance lessons. Help your couples take those steps to shake things up a little bit.

Mood Enhancer 2: A Playful, Positive, and Entertaining Agenda

Some married couples have unconsciously jettisoned the idea of keeping their mate engaged, enchanted, and entertained while on a date. The thinking goes, "That's the beauty of marriage; we can just relax and be ourselves, let it all hang out." Yet, this same couple completely understands the unspoken social code of keeping friends or business associates sufficiently engaged during a work or social event—making sure the other person is having a satisfying experience. As mentioned in Chapter 5, parents are always looking to entertain their children, keeping them surprised or at least not bored. We charge the couple to have the same attitude when on a date. In Chapter 4, we talked about the importance of cultivating a playful attitude and playful behaviors. A date is a perfect opportunity to practice using "yes, and," smiling, laughing, flirting, touching, being humorous, sharing funny stories, having give-and-take conversations, and generally being lighthearted, optimistic, joyful, and present—all the qualities and behaviors that one would bring to any social situation.

In premarriage dating, couples put their best foot forward: dressing up and looking attractive, using their best manners, conversing in ways to please their date. Then, the chase is over, the wedding fades to a memory, and all bets are off. Couples get lax. We say turn back the clock, which takes mindfulness and commitment. We advise couples to make the date the best experience possible by being positive, appreciative, generous, agreeable, patient, accepting, flexible, happy, and kind. Good manners are appreciated no matter how long a couple is married. Most women still like it when men open doors for them, carry the umbrella, pour a glass of water, let them order their food first, and listen without interrupting (this one is vital). The therapist encourages the couple to look their best, dress up, and act as if what happens on this date will determine if the other wants to go out again.

Mood Enhancer 3: Admitting You Do Not Know Everything About Your Mate

One of the major mistakes spouses make after being married for a while is assuming that they know everything there is to know about their partner. As therapists, we know that not only are they mistaken (it could take an entire lifetime to really know a person), but also this attitude precludes the fun in learning more about one's spouse. We tell the couple to become reinterested in their partner; to be inquisitive and ask questions; to find new questions to ask about old stories; and to pretend it is early in the dating process, which can be fun and exciting and yield surprising thoughts and feelings.

To demonstrate how this might work and to get an idea of how effective the couple is at listening to one another, the therapist shows the couple the questions that they have previously listed under *desirable subjects* for date conversation. He or she asks each partner to ask two of the questions of the other and to listen to each other with curiosity, with an open heart and open mind, and to come from not knowing his or her mate in that moment. This brief exercise usually shows the couple the possibilities of seeing one another as dynamic rather than static.

Mood Enhancer 4: Be Pals

Gottman (1994, 1999) talked about the importance of developing a close friendship with a partner. He stated:

> At the heart of my program is the simple truth that happy marriages are based on a deep friendship. By this I mean a mutual respect for and enjoyment of each other's company.
>
> These couples tend to know each other intimately—they are well versed on each other's likes and dislikes, personality quirks, hopes, and dreams. They have an abiding regard for each other and express this fondness not just in the big ways, but in little ways day in and day out. (Gottman, 1994, pp. 19–20)

A date is the perfect time to cultivate a close friendship. After all, what are good friends but folks who want to spend time around one another, folks who choose one another as "playmates"? Not everything on a date has to be planned around, or lead to, romance and sex. According to Markman et al. (2010) and Markman, Jenkins, and Whiteley (2004), being friends is among the top expectations that partners have for marriage. They explain that when people marry, however, they frequently shift their thinking to relating as spouses and parents rather than as friends. The point is to help couples remember that they can be all three. Markman, Stanley, Blumberg, Jenkins, and Whiteley (2004) contended that on dates couples should talk as friends, sharing common passions and beliefs, and not compete in negative ways. The idea is to separate spouse talk, which is more about solving problems and often seeing the other as the enemy, from friend talk, which is relaxing and pleasurable.

Sometimes, it is helpful to ask the wife, "What do you talk about with your women friends?" and then ask the husband, "What do you talk about with your male friends?" Once each hears the other's answer, the couple can begin to readjust their thinking and find ways to converse with one another about the things each cares about that are separate from the household and family, such as hobbies, sports, current events, and so on. The idea is to bond and connect intentionally through conversation, with a special emphasis on exchanging confidences.

On the other hand, men often consider talking overrated. Instead, they prefer shared activity. According to marriage expert Willard Harley (2007, p. 82),

"Among the five basic male needs, spending recreational time with his wife is second only to sex for the typical husband." (p. 82)

Mood Enhancer 5: Be Fully Present

We continually come back to the concept of being fully present throughout the book because it is so crucial to a satisfying human interaction. If a mate is worried, guilty, or resentful, if his or her attention is diverted, it will be impossible for both to enjoy the time spent together. On the other hand, when a person uses all his or her senses, whatever experience they are having is heightened and enhanced. To be fully present requires both a purposeful mental outlook as well as physical or logistical screening of distractions. We discuss with couples the importance of mentally focusing on the date and spouse, and not job, household, or other worries, and shutting out TV, cell phones, computers, reading materials, and background activities.

To help couples be more present on their date, we make the following recommendations:

1. Look into your partner's eyes.
2. Look at your partner and notice something attractive and then tell your partner what you see.
3. Hold your partner's hand, touch his or her face, experience your warm feelings and thoughts about your partner and share them with him or her.
4. Listen with all your senses.
5. Breath deeply, get in touch with your body sensations, and share your appreciation.

Mood Enhancer 6: What a Little Romance Can Do!

When women are asked how their husbands can be more romantic, they reply: "I would like him to plan dates, to compliment me, and to be more affectionate. I would like him to be more attentive, the way he was when we were dating." This isn't surprising, as romance is often defined in the dictionary as to make love, court, and to woo, as in making amorous advances. Such amorous advances might include giving compliments, touching a partner's hand, talking softly, putting an arm around her waist, saying "I love you," planning an elaborate evening out, and gazing into a partner's eyes while on their date.

When a husband initiates the date, this typically sets the mood for romance. To help the couple explore their romantic behavior relating to dates, it is often helpful for the therapist to ask each partner: "Do you see yourself as romantic?" and "How are you romantic toward your spouse on a date?" "When you go out together, what could your spouse do that would be romantic or a turn on for you?" The answers often reveal a lot about where the gap may be between the level of romance each craves or expects and that which is actually in play during dates. Based on the answers to these questions, the therapist helps the couple understand what may be in the way of being more romantic with one another and how to implement more playful, romantic behaviors into their dates. This includes lots of affectionate gestures, like hugging, kissing, and flirting, which stand out among the key behaviors in the romance category. We encourage these behaviors on dates for married couples. Some playful behaviors, like flirting, can even be overdone because that will have such a positive effect on enhancing the mood of a date and adding sizzle.

Mood Enhancer 7: Whatever Turns You On

Getting ready for a date can start before wardrobe and makeup. We suggest couples begin to prepare mentally a few hours ahead of time by thinking positively about one another, anticipating a smooth time, and perhaps recalling memorable past dates. This can be an effective tool for building desire for a partner and a great way to ignite a spark and motivate the individual to want to please his or her mate.

After a while, every couple has a pretty good sense of knowing what each other likes, from foods to music, and this usually extends to understanding what may enhance the mood of a date. We encourage the couple to think of augmenting the atmosphere of a date by incorporating what they know appeals to their spouse. This can include tuning to a spouse's favorite radio station or playing CDs he or she enjoys, planning meals around his or her favorite cuisines, splashing on that perfume or cologne the other likes, or wearing undergarments in the spouse's favorite color.

Dating During Difficult Times

There are life circumstances that present real-world concerns that require creative thinking to continue spending quality couple time. Here are some examples to share with couples:

The arrival of a first child. Dating is often the last thing on this couple's priority list and understandably so. The emotional, logistical, financial, and physical adjustments are huge. In the first few months, this couple needs a list of "at home dates" they can commit to engaging in on a regular basis, ideally when the baby is asleep (either at night or during weekend naps). These might include board games, movies, Wii Sports, romantic or sexy movies, food-based fun (fondue, baking), and so on. Once some equilibrium is established in the household, we firmly recommend resuming an out-of-the-house dating regimen.

Money is incredibly tight. Understand that free and very-low-cost dates abound in just about every locale. We ask couples to consider activities they may have once dismissed as too corny or not exciting enough, such as high school plays, free concerts by community bands or choirs, going on a picnic at a neighborhood park, and the like. Some more money-saving tips include arranging for free "babysitting" by swapping nights out with another couple who has children, joining a babysitting coop, or inviting grandparents to spend the weekend with the understanding that the couple will go out one evening.

One partner must take frequent business trips. Few things disrupt the rhythm of a marriage more than when a spouse is required to take frequent business trips. Logistics, time constraints, and the emotional toll of separation all conspire against both spontaneous playful moments and scheduling dates on a regular basis. Yet, ironically those in this situation probably need couple playtime more than others. Some suggestions include adopting a formula of "one trip = one date on return"; a phone or online video "date" banning all talk about kids or work; making the airport drop-off/pickup into a minidate, with a meal or walk on the way to or from; and, if possible, joining the spouse on an occasional trip.

Clearly, many couples have forgotten how to date or are not aware of the huge benefits playful dating can bring to their marriage. Other couples simply do not know the dos and don'ts of married dating, so they often make attempts that go awry, with ensuing hurt and frustration. In this chapter, we have provided specific tools to help guide those couples to successful long-term dating. The material that is presented is meant to arm the therapist with plenty of ammunition when getting agreement from a couple to put dating back on their radar.

In this chapter, we described mood killers such as indecision that leads to no decision; date planning as just another wifely chore; the bathroom as a date staging area; talking about "the relationship" and other hot button issues; cell phones, texting, and other electronic intrusions; too much drinking and beyond. These are described to help avoid pitfalls and discouragement. We also discussed mood enhancers such as trying something new; having a playful, positive, and entertaining agenda; admitting you do not know everything about your mate; being pals; being fully present; adding a little romance; enjoying whatever turns you on. These were presented to help the couple succeed in their dating.

We hope that passing along these guidelines will facilitate the playful dating process for your clients and help you to inspire them to again treat alone time together as a fun, playful game. They can feel successful in their own ability to create positive experiences with each other right now and into the future. By successful, we mean that after the date, both partners feel more playful and positive about themselves, their mate, and their marriage: They experience more closeness. By successful, we mean that each person will say (or at least feel), "That was fun!" or "Let's do that again." Successful dating will enable couples to renew, reconnect, and grow continually. Successful dating opens, maintains, and expands the space and possibility for joy and is a key factor to reigniting and maintaining the spark in marriage.

8

Sex and Sexuality and Marital Play Deficiency "Disorder"

INTRODUCTION

The nature of sexuality in a couple can be expressed through three levels of what we like to call marital play deficiency "disorder" (MPDD). The first level is characterized by a strong loving relationship without much resentment toward each other. Sex is still enjoyed and enjoyable, but it is somewhat routine and unexciting, like eating at a decent chain restaurant. You know it is clean, and it is always the same no matter where you are in the world. It is reasonably tasty and satisfying, but far from memorable, special, or inspiring. But, it is also predictable; surprises are few and far between. In the second phase of MPDD, a couple's sex life has declined to the point at which couples are having sex as little as twice a month. Sex has lost much of its playful character. The amount of sexual energy that runs through the larger relationship is increasingly diminished. There is less and less flirting as well as decreased romance. Sex is viewed more as a chore or a necessity. What is typically present in this phase are growing resentments and a resistance to communicating about them. Intimacy is impaired, and playfulness is missing in sex and in other areas of life. Sex has become like eating bread and water just to sustain oneself.

In the third phase of MPDD, the couple's sex life has deteriorated to a point that there is little-to-no sex happening. The common definition of a *sexless marriage* indicates couples who have sex 10 times per year or less (McCarthy & McCarthy, 2003). In these relationships, the sexual energy between the couple is almost completely diminished and depleted of any vitality. In some relationships, one partner continues to push for sex while the other has low desire, and there is considerable overt conflict about the topic. For other couples, the conflict goes underground and on the surface is hostile distance and negativity. There is a strong probability that the ratio of positive to negative interactions is reversed, with the negative interactions far outweighing the positive. There is a great deal of resentment or hopelessness in the couple.

In this chapter, we describe many different aspects of how couples can re-create a fulfilling sex life. Not all ideas are for everyone, of course. The last thing we want is to make someone feel that he or she has to conform to some ideal. We want to reiterate that this is not a book on sex therapy. We are focusing on how to help couples have a more playful, joyous, free, satisfying sex life as part of the overall contribution playfulness will make to a more satisfying marriage. What we cover in this chapter on playful sex are general principles to teach couples.

SEX FOLLOWS THE SAME RULES AS ALL OTHER FORMS OF PLAY

Since in a committed marriage sex is another form of adult play, it follows the same rules as other forms of play. Sex is often an expression of love between two married people, and is something done in partnership. A couple who has a good sex life is usually a couple who is cooperating, communicating, being creative, trusting of each other, being flexible, improvising, being in the moment, and having fun. They are enjoying each other as well as their sexual experience. They are in sync. In fact, sex and sexual play, as we see it, is the ultimate form of "team play" that bonds couples together in joy and pleasure. For many couples, it is difficult to maintain a healthy sex life if the couple is not cultivating a playful attitude in everyday life. Conversely, it is sometimes difficult to maintain a playful attitude in everyday married life if a couple is not having a sufficiently satisfying sex life. It is like the old saying, "When sex is good, it is ten percent of the relationship. When it is bad it is 90%" (Schnarch, 2002, p. 133).

Sex is the one and only thing that is exclusive between marital partners. Any number of other activities can be done with someone else, but a commitment to marriage implicates a commitment to monogamy. During the courtship period, when monogamy has not yet been declared, each partner makes an effort to look as attractive as possible, to flirt, smile, laugh, and listen attentively to the other. Those behaviors and that mindset, which often go missing after marriage, are equally vital to the health and success of a couple's married life and to their sex life.

A person's sexuality is expressed in everything he or she does. It affects how he or she functions in life and behaves within intimate relationships and is reflective of the general tenor of the relationship. Previously, we talked about the importance of maintaining a high ratio of positive to negative interactions, which contributes to the ability of the couple to be playful together. Since sex is a form of play, a couple cannot create a satisfying sex life if the ratio of positives to negatives in their relationship slips below 5:1. A low ratio indicates that a couple is not at ease and playful with one another in other areas of life and therefore probably cannot be lighthearted and playful in bed.

Another factor that plays a major role in a couple being able to sustain a well-functioning sex life is a level of emotional maturity. Emotional maturity is measured by our ability to identify our emotions—both positive and negative—to be able to regulate and feel them, and to express them honestly and appropriately. It is also measured by the ability to be relatively secure in oneself without the need for a partner's approval. Difficulties regulating affect or the need for approval can be a significant source of sexual difficulty (Schnarch, 2002). Emotionally mature people are more comfortable with play because they are relatively secure in their identity; they do not take their own foibles or the foibles of others so seriously.

Developing this playful outlook surrounding sex is a key step because couples who lack play in their lives often need to expand their understanding about sex being much more than orgasm and intercourse. Seeing that sex offers a much larger "playing field" will help a couple connect and view sex as a "dance" that, when orchestrated with care, play, and love can be enormously satisfying even without an orgasm or even intercourse.

GENERAL PRINCIPLES OF SATISFYING, PLAYFUL, JOYFUL SEX

From our perspective, there are eight principles that make sex an excellent source of pleasure and play. The eight principles are (1) being present, (2) creating bridges from nonsex to sex, (3) giving and receiving, (4) good timing, (5) romance, (6) novelty, (7) appropriate expectations, and (8) recovering well from episodes of less-than-satisfying sex.

All eight principles do not have to be present at the same time every time a couple engages in a sexual experience. Your couples will find that they are good at some of these principles and not as adept at others. As we have stated throughout the book, encourage couples to approach these new and possibly scary ideas with a playful and pleasant attitude. As a therapist and educator, you need to coach couples not to expect so much from themselves in every sexual encounter and not to be overly critical of themselves or their partner. The key is to take small steps toward a fulfilling sex life—and to understand that a fulfilling sex life means the couple will actually have completely satisfying sex only some of the time, not all of the time.

Principle 1: Being Present

Being present is the ability of a person to be fully aware, fully available, and fully living in the moment. Siegel (2010) pointed out that "rather than being consumed by worries about the future or preoccupations with the past, living fully is an art form that liberates the mind to relieve mental suffering." It is often more helpful to convey this concept to clients by describing the *lack* of presence. Here are a few examples:

Sally tries to engage Jim in romantic kissing, but Jim is worrying about the taxes that are due in 3 days.

Juan lights a fire and begins telling Miranda how attractive she is, but she is thinking about how annoyed she is at Juan for coming home 20 minutes late that night.

Dan is taking off Adrienne's clothes, but instead of being excited, she thinks, "I've gained so much weight. Dan can't really still be interested in my body."

Andrew is in the middle of intercourse and starts to worry that he may lose his erection.

Martha and Gary are making love, but Martha's anxiety is raging as she wonders, "What if I can't have an orgasm again?"

In all of these examples, one person is in some way not present. To understand how this affects play, think about a tennis match in which one competitor's mind is not on the ball but on an argument with a coach or a brother's upcoming surgery. Not only will the player underperform, but also the player is robbing his or her opponent of the chance for a well-matched game. In sex play, one of the partners cannot be present when also worrying about the future, regretting something in the past, or focusing on other obligations.

For each half of the couple, there are three key aspects of being present: The first is to be present with oneself, the second is to be present with one's partner, and third is to be present with what is transpiring between partners. When people are not present with themselves, it will not be possible to be present with a partner. To achieve being present with oneself, a person exhibits a keen sense of self-awareness, is cognizant of personal actions and feelings, and is able to experience all the senses in the moment. Surely, the relevance to sex is obvious.

This brings us to the second part of presence, namely, being connected to one's partner. If a person is present with one's partner, there is an awareness of what the partner is most likely feeling, what is going on with body language, and what the needs of the partner are. So, if a man kisses his wife's neck and hears her sigh and feels the pressure of her moving toward him slightly, he knows she likes what he is doing. He can feel confident that he is pleasing her. She can then respond to his confidence and her own pleasure by reciprocating. They are playing together, not separately.

This segues to the third aspect; when one is fully present to this interaction, there is a magical ebb and flow, comparable to when musicians are "tight" or when members of a sports team are all "in the zone" together. This moves a couple from "you did that/I did this" to "Wow, that was fun." Presence creates this ineffable quality because presence ensures that the couple is connected and allows a flow between them. Each person effortlessly responds to the other's energy, sounds, and movement and vice versa.

Principle 2: Creating Bridges From Nonsex to Sex

Many people can relate to the cartoon in Figure 8.1, especially couples who have at least one child. The problem is not so much that they cannot have good sex when they get there. It is that couples have no bridges to get from where they are in their rush-rush lives to the place where they can set aside the time and both be emotionally present for a satisfying sexual encounter. In the real world,

Figure 8.1   The bridge not taken.

the experience is more likely that a person wants to have sex but just cannot shake off the other parts of life, the demands and worries. Or, if the situation has gotten even worse, he or she does not even want to have sex because it has become routine and boring, there is so much other stuff to do, or the couple's sex life is no longer playful but burdened with pressure, unfulfilled expectations, or judgment.

These couples need a bridge, a way to get from there to here, from sex as a joyless sporadic act to sex as the most fun a couple can have together. However, there is not a one-size-fits-all bridge but many different kinds of bridges. Each person and each couple has to discover or rediscover what bridges will work, how to find the right exit ramp from the highway to get onto the bridge, or if there are several different bridges that will work for them, depending on the circumstances. In some cases, the bridge has been so neglected that it needs repair. In still other cases, couples may need to build a brand new bridge they have never ridden over before.

The Bridge From Exhaustion and a Tiring Routine to Energy and Variety

Teaching couples to create a time and space for sex to happen when they are neither preoccupied nor exhausted is crucial. It is always helpful to check the obvious. Most couples think about sex happening only at the very end of the wake cycle, before going to sleep for the night, so they need a different way to cross to sex that does not involve this old routine. The bridge might be having them take turns turning off the TV before the late news begins, a signal to the other that what is left of the evening belongs to the couple, not the TV. Or perhaps, a couple turns in earlier than usual to get up for a morning roll in the sheets. Another bridge might be marking a day on the calendar to go into work an hour late, meet home for lunch, or send the kids to a friend's house and stay in for the evening instead of heading for a restaurant.

The Bridge From Work Life or Child Care to Couple Time

Even in dicey economic times, a couple can learn that work will still be on the desk, and the household chores and family obligations will still be there the next day. We encourage couples to do 90 minutes less of their usual daily work over the course of a week, or to arrange for at least that amount of child care time, and use those found hours to get in the mood and to have sex. Even when that is not possible, on any given day partners can lay a few feet of bridge by expressing their love and sexual energy for their spouse in between actual sexual encounters. Some ideas are the following:

1. Calling a partner (even if one has to leave a message) to express whatever thoughts and feelings the person is having, such as, "I'm thinking how good you looked this morning and am looking forward to doing something about it when we arrive home."

2a. Writing a short note either by e-mail or, for a memorable gesture, an old-fashioned note on real paper. The act of writing the note is almost as important as whether it is actually sent and received. Either way, the person has created the beginnings of a bridge.

2b. An interesting variation on the note is to write a note to oneself. Individuals can tell themselves what they are feeling about their partner in their own words and in complete confidentiality. Often, it is easier to be expressive when assured that no other eyes will read the words. Options include mailing the note to oneself and reading it when it arrives, keeping it in a place where it can be visited repeatedly, or carrying it around as a reminder of the thoughts expressed and the hoped-for actions.

3. Stopping to savor a feeling for 2 to 5 minutes. Instruct the person that should he or she feel a romantic or sexual thought, feeling, or memory, this is a good sign that playfulness is returning to the couple's sexual relationship, and that the relationship deserves at least 2 to 5 minutes of uninterrupted attention. Tell the person, "Allow yourself to savor the thoughts, whether that means recalling a past episode or letting the mind wander into a fantasy that involves your spouse. You might be thinking

of a past vacation in the Bahamas or a simple moment in your backyard. Allow the feelings of love and sexual energy to be present and for your body to react. Even if part of your mind says that it is not a good time because you are at work or doing something that requires concentration, just tell that part of yourself that a short break is deserved. You might be more productive afterward, and the important thing is that this interlude serves as a bridge to getting into a more sex-play-togetherness mindset, which can be more easily recalled when reunited with your mate."

More advanced instructions a therapist might give a client include the following:

"Go back to your 2- to 5-minute interlude, which is really serving as an emotional and image bridge. After you have allowed yourself to be saturated with good feelings, imagine taking these feelings with you forward in time to later in the day when you are with your spouse. Spend the last minute or two of this time imagining yourself acting on these feelings with your spouse and your spouse responding favorably. It may help if you really do picture an image of a bridge transporting you from those feelings to the future imagined (planned?) experience. Or, you can create a cue word for yourself to help remember these loving and sexual feelings. To do this, when you are at the most intense part of the imagery, say the cue word in your mind. It could be your spouse's nickname, a phrase, or maybe the name of a song that is a turn on. Say it several times to yourself silently while you imagine acting on these feelings in the future. Then, later when you get home, say the cue word to yourself when you want to act on and recall those feelings again."

Bridge From Supermom to Sensuous Woman

Loving mother and turned-on wife are two radically different states of mind. Some women get so wrapped in the role of mother they lose connection with their sexual selves. Still others believe (often unconsciously) that motherhood precludes being a sexually active creature. Nevertheless, it *is* possible to be both a virtuous mother and a wife who is interested in her role as sexually playful and active wife. Here is where you as a therapist can help women create transitions between the two very different states of mind. The following are exact instructions for two techniques you can use with female clients.

1. "Take some time by yourself to connect with yourself and your body as a sensual or sexual being, using any of the following methods or your own: (a) take a sensual bubble bath; (b) put on clothes or underwear that make you feel sexy (c) reread love notes your husband has sent you; (d) engage in a physical activity that connects you to the good feelings and sensuous feelings of your body, such as yoga, massage, or a Jacuzzi soak; (e) dab on perfume that smells good to you or listen to music that makes you want to dance or evokes a sensual mood."

2. "Find a physical object or article of clothing that represents the mother state of mind for you and another that represents the sexual wife."

April had a silver chain that her mother had given her that represented motherhood for her. She also had a pair of gold dangly earrings that she got as a gift from her husband on their second anniversary. She decided these would be her sexual wife symbol. She wore the silver necklace during the day when she was doing mothering tasks, but when the children went to bed, she removed it, and did so consciously, thinking about letting go of the mother role. Sometimes, especially on date nights, she then put on the earrings, but other times, she stopped there. Either way, she discovered that once she relinquished the silver necklace, she thought less about her "job" as mother, a good way to transition to the role of wife. She felt more affectionate and emotionally available, wanting to cuddle more and even be romantic.

Principle 3: Giving and Receiving

As an activity, sex is about giving and receiving pleasure, love, and erotic energy. It is this mutual and unreserved exchange between the partners that is so important in a relationship. Satisfying sex involves a partner being willing to give what his or her partner desires and being open to receiving what his or her partner gives. The partners are in sync with one another, in the way musicians in jam sessions or actors doing improvisational work are—there is a give-and-take, sharing the spotlight, then backing off one at a time for the other to shine, then swapping roles, all apparently done without any outward discussion. The "rules" of this game are actually simple: (a) Accept what the other person offers then (b) build on what they have done and "answer" with your own contribution. To continue to do this over time requires attention, cooperation, risk taking, supporting the other's risk taking, and sharing in giving and taking. It is a deeply satisfying experience that cannot be done alone. Engaging in the playful dance of give-and-take, and doing all of this while naked and touching private areas in the context of love, brings the game to a different level.

Principle 4: Good Timing

When teaching couples about sex, good timing means that one partner is aware of the needs of the other and reacts in accordance with that awareness. When you think of playing music or playing sports, timing is the thing that usually separates the greats from the average. When it comes to "sexual playing," timing is everything and is important on three levels:

1. Knowing differences in arousal patterns of men and women.
2. Catching the wave: building sexual energy.
3. Realizing the space between the notes is as important as the notes.

Differences in Arousal Patterns of Men and Women

The most important thing to help your clients understand about the difference between male and female arousal patterns is that women physiologically have a much slower buildup to becoming sexually aroused than do men. In terms of timing, this means that a man needs to take considerably more time during foreplay, allowing the gap to close between when he first becomes aroused and when his wife has more or less caught up. While most men can get turned on in about 1.25 seconds with a rush of testosterone, from there it is pretty much "Mission Control, we are ready for blast off."

But for women, these things take longer; there is, metaphorically, an entire precountdown checklist:

> "Husband greeted me with a kiss and a hug and 'How was your day?' on returning home at night." Check
> "Husband has helped clean all the dinner dishes and helped with the kids." Check
> "Husband did it with a smile on his face." Check
> "Husband has refrained from prematurely groping my breasts." Check
> "Husband has made me feel special by prioritizing me and listening to me." Check
> "Oxytocin beginning to flow." Check
> "Stress of the day beginning to fade." Check
> "Husband continuing to be affectionate during the precountdown checklist." Check
> "Mission Control, we are ready to go to sexual turn on initiation phase."
> "Roger that. Proceed to sexual turn on initiation."

If, while his wife is moving through the prelaunch sequence, a man does something too sexual too soon—in other words, gets the timing wrong—instead of "check," it is "abort." That same move later on during sex leads to "booster rockets ignited." The point is, timing matters.

Catching the Wave: Building Sexual Energy

One of the most important aspects of timing for married couples is catching and amplifying the sexual energy wave. The actual act of sex is only the final segment of the buildup of sexual energy between the couple. One of the big changes from dating to married life is that when couples are dating they pay much more attention to the playful dynamic of building sexual energy, noticing every small nuance along the way. However, it is done without much actual thought. When couples get married, they tend to get complacent. Ask each partner: "How many times have you had a sexual thought or impulse and instead of acting on it, you decided to go back to work, the dishes, or the yard?" We are a very scheduled culture. We force ourselves to ignore our own rhythms. Married men often do not engage in the step-by-step process of building romantic energy as they did while dating. Married women typically ignore their own sexual energy and do not catch or build on the wave in anticipation of sexual play.

If couples want to sustain a good sexual life throughout the life of their marriage, they need to pay close attention to nurturing and cultivating their individual and shared sexual energy. By cultivating their ability to be playful, the couple creates a state of mind that is conducive to responding to that sexual energy. Romance, affection, caring behaviors, dating, and togetherness are all potential builders of sexual energy. Doing something different sparks the brain and adds excitement.

Here is an example to illustrate:

Alice and Jim usually watch television at night after their 12-year-old son goes to bed. Jim often wants to have sex, but Alice is never in the mood. Their therapist recommended they take a 20- to 30-minute walk in the neighborhood a few nights a week instead of watching TV nonstop. The therapist suggested that on the walk, they could be silent, talk, or hold hands. They were also encouraged to take walks no matter the weather. As luck would have it, the first night they decide to walk, it was misting, damp, and foggy. They almost bail but go for the walk. Alice finds walking in the mist very romantic. She tells Jim it reminds her of the movie *Casablanca*. Jim is a Humphrey Bogart fan and immediately puts on his best Bogey voice. She laughs, they hold hands more tightly, and both are feeling amorous. Suddenly, it feels like fun, like play. She suggests they walk a little faster so they can get home sooner.

One of the problems couples have is focusing too much on the sexual act itself without including the more playful elements that take place during the buildup. In other words, couples spend too little time constructing a conducive field or a playground as a setting for their sex experience. The other problem is that there is little sexual energy harnessed during early phases of the wave to build toward sustaining sex once it gets under way. When Alice and Jim were watching TV, he was focusing too much on the idea of wanting sex and not having it. She was on guard about possible sexual advances she was unlikely to reciprocate while on the couch watching crime shows. TV was the focus, not conversation, eye contact, touching, or a shared activity. Neither of them was able to infuse the TV-watching situation with any nascent sexuality, which is understandable. On the walk, however, they were focused on the shared experience, in tune with one another's strides, holding hands, and talking, all of which helped build a shared playing field. Alice played with Jim by mentioning the fog and *Casablanca*. He played back and upped the sexual energy by impersonating Bogart.

Flirting

Here, we are discussing flirting in the context of the energetic buildup of sexual energy. It really is so simple. When people are single, they flirt because they are trying to attract people of the opposite sex. It is fun, a way to build up sexual energy. Great flirting is all about sending a packet of sexual energy to the other and seeing what happens in return. It may be subtle or blatant, but either way the sexual energy amalgamates toward romance, indicates sexual interest in the other person, and sometimes reveals one's heart. Is it playful? Absolutely. As the therapist, you can ask your couples if they recall how they each played with flirting during their dating and courtship days. Then, ask if they still do it. Chances are the answer is no or seldom. One of the most common reasons is that the flirting is directly linked to initiating sexual activity, but when there is no buildup of energy or the idea of following through with sex feels like too much of a demand, rather than being playful, flirting is dropped from the couple's repertoire of ways to play together. One approach to reintroducing flirting is to instruct couples to go ahead and flirt but ask them not to follow it up by engaging in touching any erotic areas. The goal here is to help the couple get back to using flirting as play, a way to build a wave of sexual energy, but without the pressure or expectation that it will always lead directly to sex. Sometimes, sexual tension without the follow-through is a terrific turn on and can help heighten sexual desire the next time around.

Of course, one or the other partner may be poorly skilled at flirting behavior, and this may fall under the category of one of their blocks. Now that they are married and there is no real fear of not getting the girl or the guy, flirting can fall into the category of things that one no longer needs to be bothered about employing. Flirting takes practice, and once rusty, a couple will need to have some fun while relearning the skill.

The Space Between the Notes Is as Important as the Notes

In the cult film *The Rocky Horror Picture Show*, there is a scene in which Dr. Frank-N-Furter is singing a song: Although the audience knows it word for word, they await a single key moment at the end of the line, when the doctor stops short, and as a body, the audience shouts out the missing syllable into the silence, exhausted with delight and anticipation.

Pausing, stopping, changing tempo, changing direction, and releasing pressure are all part of great sex and represent the spaces between the bigger, louder "notes." Silence is also part of great flirting as well as great moments of intimacy. Being able to be silent at the right time (there is that timing thing again) can be a powerful and intimate act. When one is talking, he or she is not listening, and if one's partner is saying something loving, passionate, or vulnerable, one needs to listen. Staying quiet also allows someone to notice and feel the impact of the words on a partner and to consider one's own internal feelings in response. Silence also affords one or both the opportunity to bask in the moment. It is a little like keeping your head down while taking a golf swing. Sure, you want to look where the ball went, and you will, but it is not yet the right time.

Foreplay That Is Guaranteed to Build Sexual Energy

For the most part, advice on foreplay that is guaranteed to build sexual energy is given to men on how to make sure a wife is really turned on. But, it also works the other way. Counsel couples in these ways:

1. Savor foreplay like a great appetizer. There is a great deal of fun and play that can be had before the main course. Women love a man with confidence. Be willing to be playful if that is what is happening. Have the confidence not to rush ahead. Plan on spending 15–30 minutes on foreplay. Count on at least 10 minutes (and this is fast) before engaging in genital stimulation.

2. John Gray (1995) rightly pointed out that men always want to get right to the point, whereas most women rarely want to get right to the point, especially in sex. In foreplay, the man should never go straight for an erogenous zone. Spend time on every other part first. There are the neck, the shoulder, the back, the arms, the legs, the feet. Even if he is going to head for her breast (after spending time elsewhere), he should not head straight for the nipple. Kiss the outside of her breast, then the underside. Only glance at the nipple for a quarter second on the way to the top of her breast. Take a long time to get to any point. Then, do not stay on that point forever. Move away and then come back.

3. Refrain from using the same old routine all the time. The secret to really turning a woman on is that she does not know what you are going to do next. It does not mean that he needs an unlimited number of techniques. It means that he needs to mix things up. Change hands. Move from hands to lips, change speed, change direction. As we mentioned in Chapter 5, the element of mystery is effective in sex.

4. We know long conversation is not going to be happening during intercourse. So, now would be a good time to look her in the eyes, say how beautiful she is, how much he loves her.

5. He must pay attention to what his partner likes. When does she moan? When does her breathing change? He should consider himself a musician of pleasure, and she is the instrument. Do more of what works. Just remember to keep teasing and backing off. Both partners sharing sexual likes and dislikes when not engaging in the sex act is helpful.

6. He should balance the previous points with doing what turns him on as well. If he has an urge to run his fingernails down her arm, he should do it. Notice how (if) she likes it. When we are really in sync with our partner, we can become unconsciously connected so that we get urges to do things that are exactly what our partner wants. You cannot force this, but you can allow yourself to get in sync with it.

7. He should allow space for his partner to do things to him as well. Remember that this is a mutual playful adventure. It is also fun for his partner to turn him on. Especially as men get older, they need more stimulation. When a man is 20, a single thought could keep him turned on for hours. It is just different when he is 55 or 60.

8. When he finally gets to more consistent genital stimulation, apply everything we have said up to now during genital stimulation. Do not stay in that one spot all the time. Keep her guessing about what he is going to do next. Again, keep the mystery going. Whatever happens, have a playful, light attitude about it. Stay present in the moment and have fun. It will never be the same twice, so do not try to make it the same.

Principle 5: Romance

Once upon a time in a land far, far away, Jack meets Lorena at a party. He asks her out on a date. She agrees to go. He thinks to himself, "She is beautiful. I really like her. What can I do to let her know I think she is special? A movie and dinner is okay but will probably be uninspired and uninspiring. What did she talk about at the party? Hmm ... she likes music. I can take her to see live music. But what music?" He looks through the paper and there it is! She is from New Orleans and the Radiators, a great band from New Orleans, are on the schedule at a local club.

Meanwhile, in another land far, far away, Russell wants to have a romantic evening with his wife, Theresa. She is an overworked doctor. She comes home exhausted much of the time and complains of how hard it is to get back to feeling like herself. Russ knows that she always feels so much better after they have sex, but it is so hard for her to get in the mood. Russ puzzles over the dilemma. What would do the trick? He remembers that once she told him about how romantic it was when her friend Jessica's husband lit 100 candles in their house one evening. He remembered the look in Theresa's eyes when she told him the story. He also remembered how Theresa used to take long baths before she got this new job, which is draining her energy. A plan began to form. He arranged to have their 6-year-old son sleep over at a friend's house, then got a friend to drop him off at the hospital before his wife's shift was over. When Theresa walked out of the hospital, she found her husband waiting with flowers and a note that said, "Sit back and relax. I have taken care of everything. I love you." In her car was a bottle of champagne on ice. Theresa was surprised and a bit confused, but to her credit, she just allowed events to unfold. She was too tired to resist anyway. When she got home, Russ poured her some champagne and asked her to wait 10 minutes while he took care of something. When he returned, they had a toast together, and then he led her upstairs and into the bathroom that was lit with as many candles as possible, and the tub was filled with hot water and scented. For years, she would tell the story of that night.

These are two examples of large acts of romance. We will also describe smaller acts of romance. But, what is romance? Why is it so important, especially for women as part of satisfying sex? A romantic act displays or expresses love or strong affection. A romantic gesture is one that is imbued with idealism or a desire for adventure or chivalry, the idealizing of one's beloved. We are talking about romance here as a form of play, a positive game; like all games, it has rules, but only two major ones.

The one rule that is clearly evident in the two examples is that the person doing the romancing has spent considerable thought and taken action with the intention of making the other person feel special. The other rule is that the person being romanced gives themselves permission to receive the gift. Generally, in the Western Hemisphere, it is the man's role to do the romancing and the woman's job to receive. This actually follows the ancient ideas of yin and yang, masculine and feminine. The masculine energy is involved in action, and the feminine energy is involved in receiving. Energy works just like positive and negative poles, with sexuality flowing along these energetic pathways. It is reported that 33% of women feel they have lost their sexual drive (McCarthy & McCarthy, 2003). We suspect that as Western women have taken on increasing masculine roles in terms of work, it has disrupted the polarity between yin and yang.

At the same time, women want to be cherished, be adored, made to feel special, and be a priority in their husband's mind. A woman's sexuality blossoms in the context of feeling cherished. Gray's (2003) latest work suggests that for men sexuality is driven more by the neurotransmitter dopamine and the hormone testosterone. Women's sexuality, on the other hand, is driven more by the neurotransmitter serotonin and the hormone oxytocin. How do you get oxytocin flowing through a woman's system? One major pathway is to let her talk while the man listens and demonstrates that he understands her. This is a highly romantic act. It is not the candlelight at the dinner table that does the trick. It is the talking, listening, and sharing in the glow of the candlelight. The other major pathway is by performing large and small acts that demonstrate she is special in his eyes.

A question that is often asked is, "So, is romance designed mostly for the woman?" One answer to that would be yes, in the sense that romance is more of a necessity for women, particularly as it intersects with the lead-up to sex. But, here is the surprise: Romance also does something for the man because he is the one taking action. What does taking action do? It stimulates (you guessed it) dopamine and testosterone, the keys to male sexuality. That is probably why guys like action films.

In his workshop on marriages, comedian and Reverend Mark Gungor (2009) pointed out that in every action film the guy always goes back into harm's way for one reason: to get the girl. The act of being in action to stimulate romance, then, is good for guys. "Going back and getting the girl" is a real turn on. Gungor advised that when people at the office say they need to work late, a man ought to say, "You guys go on without me, there is something I've got to do!" And then go back and get the girl. When a man is in action, you can be sure he is engaged in the game, having fun, playing with the romantic buildup.

And yet, therapists so often hear men say, "Well, I am just not romantic," so we need to reinterpret this by telling them that we understand they are not well practiced at the game, but they can learn, just as couples can learn to be flirtatious again. We also explain that they probably just do not really understand the importance of romance for their wives or themselves, but once they do understand, we show them that a new mindset can help them to focus on and practice romance.

So, the general rule is the man does things for the woman (including listening without solving problems) to make her feel special, which reads as romantic to the woman. The one stumbling block is that each woman has different things that make her feel special, so we suggest two courses of action for every couple. First, the wife should create a list of things that she considers romantic—everything from a grand act (hot air balloon ride) to the smallest gesture (one rose). We have already given couples a head start on this in Chapter 6 with the play inventory, which has a section on romance. You can build from that. You might find other activities elsewhere in the inventory under another heading that also might be romantic depending on the context and the couple. Have them include these in their list.

Principle 6: Novelty

Even partners who love each other deeply can get into a rut. Even if they are intensely present with each other, they may become aware that they are just bored, bored, bored when it comes to sex. They are doing the same old sexual moves in the same order, the same location, the same time of day. This can be particularly problematic for the feminine psyche, which requires a certain amount of mystery to be fully turned on. The answer to these issues is novelty. Since marriage precludes changing partners as in single life, it is essential that the couple use conscious intention to create the novelty that was so much a part of their initial excitement and the early phases of the relationship. During courtship, simple hormones and brain chemistry of lust kept the two people going. Now, each partner needs to trigger those mechanisms consciously and intentionally.

Novelty does not mean that every week the couple has to come up with a new sexual position; they would have to spend so much time on research they would not have time for sex. It does require employing enough variety in their sex play that the different combinations end up lending a thrilling variety to their sex life. Novelty is all about playing with new activities, trying on a new hat, so to speak, to see how it fits. The novelty can begin long before the actual sexual act, with the first hints of flirting, suggestive behavior, or language. New and different activities in all areas of the couple's life, not only on dates, will keep the dopamine and oxytocin flowing.

Principle 7: Appropriate Expectations

Approximately 2,500 years ago, Buddha pointed out that one of the major sources of suffering is disappointment. We are disappointed when our expectations are not met. Having too high expectations of self or a partner or about sex in general is the surest road to killing the playfulness and togetherness sex can offer. For today's couples, there are some pretty strange expectations from the media and entertainment industry about what we should expect from a sex life.

Here is a news flash:

James Bond is not real.
Porn is not real.
Hollywood is not real.
Music videos are not real.
Everything on YouTube is not real.
Romance novels are not real.
Disney is not real.
Second Life is not real.
Reality television is not real.

We are not saying it is not all right for couples to fantasize and pretend. In fact, if your clients want to act out a James Bond fantasy, we encourage you to support that, even to suggest it when appropriate (see further discussion in this chapter). They just need to realize that real men have feelings, are flawed, and are sensitive. A real woman, on the other hand, does not feel all hot and passionate all the time or melt in her man's arms if he looks at her a certain way, even if he says her name in a deep, swarthy voice.

Creating new levels of intimacy or sexuality is inherently anxiety provoking. Any time one moves into new territory, it is at least mildly anxious. When this is accepted, it is often experienced as excitement. When a couple first dated, their first kiss was anxiety producing. Will he be a good kisser? Will she kiss back? What is going to happen next? Each person expected this anxiety and knew it was normal in that context—the delicious excitement of anticipation mixed with trepidation.

When a couple has been married for 5, 10, 15 years or more, they probably think, "We're an established couple. There's no anxiety, and if there is, something is wrong with me or with us." Nothing could be further from the truth. If a couple is breaking into new sexual territory, trying to reintroduce play into their sexual lives, they are likely to feel anxious. We urge you to teach couples to reinterpret this as a sign they are heading in the right direction.

Appropriate Expectations Through the Life Cycle

Couples need to adjust their expectations to the realities of changes in the normal course of life; an inability to account for these changes guarantees not making appropriate adjustments in how the couple approaches sex. This leads to increasingly less-satisfying experiences, more anxiety and upset, and increasingly worse sex.

There are three areas in the life cycle for which we can easily predict the need to shift expectations: (a) from dating to marriage; (b) from childless to being parents; (c) from a younger to an older adult.

Shift From Dating to Marriage

The biggest issue at the phase from dating to marriage is the transition from unintentional reactions based on infatuation (or some have called it the "drug-induced state") that makes it easy to be turned on without even thinking about it, to a more intentional sexuality as reported by Love and Robinson (1994). The infatuation phase or illusion stage typically lasts 2 years. After that, reality sets in, routines become entrenched, and complacency rules. The haze of lust lifts, and one sees a partner for who he or she really is. There is the risk of becoming disappointed and dispirited. Now is the time when a couple needs to continue intentionally doing the things that they used to do (flirting, romantic behaviors, etc.), even when they might not feel as motivated to do it.

Children

Children change everything. Those who do not have them can only guess about what happens. Those who are parents know the major upheaval parenthood causes in a couple's relationship. It is reasonable and normal to expect a drop in sexuality for a year or so after the first child is born, and statistically it is also reasonable to expect sex to drop until after the last child leaves home. If couples want to beat the odds, they need to use intention again to practice the ideas we described throughout the book. They need to remember to preserve and cultivate their sexual relationship as husband and wife separate from their relationship as mother and father.

Aging

In the area of aging, appropriate expectations are vital. Human bodies change as we age each year. This natural process, which begins long before "old age," has an effect on our ability to live as vigorously as we did just a few years before. Even when a couple is relatively young, their bodies continue to evolve, from the 20s to 30s, and then into the 40s, 50s, and beyond, changing in both subtle and significant ways during each decade. These changes affect a couple's ability to continue to enjoy the same kind of sex lives they once did. The natural aging process includes changes in libido and physical changes involving sexual stamina, desire, and competence. Aging may also mean illness, weight fluctuations, injury, medications, restricted agility, and physical limitations. Any of these can become a barrier to a couple's sex life. It is up to the therapist to help the couple accept any new parameters and to rethink and reimagine ways to have a satisfying sex life despite either individual's aging challenges. Suggesting options in lovemaking positions, frequency, and style, like experimenting with fun and novel sensual experiences, is a tool a therapist can offer for a more satisfying and playful sex life.

A few positive aspects of aging include the end of active parenting and retirement. With age, the responsibilities of child rearing lessen; an empty nest offers a great deal of free time to be sexual. Retirement can also be a boon to a more spontaneous sex life. Reinforcing the importance of continuing to cultivate a positive playful attitude is key, so that behaviors, like romance, dating, flirting, laughter, and affectionate touch can bridge any barriers.

Principle 8: Recovering Well From Episodes of Less-Than-Satisfying Sex

A sex life that is satisfying, playful, and joyful means that some sex will be great, some will be average, some below average. The trick is to accept what is and enjoy it anyway. The couple tries a new position, a new fantasy, or whatever. It turns out to be mediocre, or it does not work at all. So what? They learn to laugh at their own foibles, which is what any two people do when playing and enjoying an activity instead of worrying about who wins. At least they tried something together. Maybe they stayed out too late or had too much to drink. Maybe they wanted to have sex in a new place, but they were just so tired they were out of ideas. It is okay.

However, if a couple wants to kill their sex life faster than a speeding bullet, they should follow these easy rules:

1. Focus all of their energy and intensity on analyzing an episode of bad sex and put a negative spin on it.
2. Blame themselves or their partner.
3. Take it all very, very seriously. They should be sure to think that this is the end of their sex lives.
4. Discount all of the good sex they have had in the past.

If they are trying to rebuild their sex life and they want to guarantee failure, they should follow Steps 1–4 and then add Step 5:

5. Do not count any small steps made in making things better. Decide it is only the final result that matters.

In sports and in acting, excellence is measured by how well one can regain composure when things do not go so well. The same is true throughout life. Sex is no exception. A client whose ego says that he or she must perform well to be okay is setting him- or herself up for failure.

When advising a couple with a negative sexual experience, emphasize the following:

- Do not be self-critical.
- Do not get down on your partner.
- Do not take it so seriously and do not attach meaning to it.
- Stay connected as a team and laugh and cuddle in the aftermath.
- Problem solve as a team. Ask, "What can we do next time that would make things more fun or better?"

PERSONAL BLOCKS TO SATISFYING SEX

If sex, like play, is so important for relationships, then why is it such a problem? As we discussed in Chapter 3, we need to become aware of the blocks we have that stop us from going "directly to Go and collecting $200." As we also discussed, spouses cannot simply blame their partners. They each need to look at themselves first because any individual block will be brought into the relationship. One does not necessarily need to invest 5 years in analysis to resolve these blocks. Many times, simple awareness and a bit of intentional action can get a couple to "Go."

When partners become aware of their personal blocks and work to overcome them, one of two things happens: Either he or she gets to "Go" or he or she does not. If a person has a clear focus on wanting to overcome blocks to good sex or have more play in general to have a better relationship, this makes any therapeutic endeavor more cost effective and, dare we say it, even more "fun."

Fun here is meant in the same sense that it is fun or satisfying to work on improving a golf swing or playing a musical instrument. Yes, there is work involved, but there is a deep sense of purpose and reward as one makes progress. So, we suggest partners look at these blocks for themselves and remember to do so with compassion and kindness, knowing that they can be overcome without undue hardship. The work of doing so actually can be fun for a couple trying to overcome sexual blocks.

The following list is of situations, thoughts, beliefs, or attitudes that can act as blocks. Make a copy and give this to each partner and ask them to check off those that apply to them. It helps to remind the couple that it takes courage to look at oneself truthfully.

- ❑ Blocks to play in general (see Chapter 3) that also affect sex.
- ❑ Sex is not that important in a relationship.
- ❑ If I do not feel turned on, then there is no point in even starting down the road toward sex.
- ❑ If there is any conflict or tension in my relationship, sex is pointless, meaningless, or will not help anything.
- ❑ I do not enjoy sex with my partner.
- ❑ My partner is boring in bed, and you cannot teach an old dog new tricks.
- ❑ Sex is dirty, sinful, or wrong.
- ❑ I make little time or give little priority to having sex.
- ❑ I make little time or give little priority to flirting, kissing, hugging, and other sexual/sensual activities that often lead to sex.
- ❑ My partner ought to know what I like sexually without my explaining.
- ❑ I have memories or experiences associated with sex that are traumatic or negative (painful, awkward, or shaming experiences during adolescence; rape, or sexual abuse; emotionally painful experiences around sex from prior relationships).
- ❑ Sex is only a duty to be performed.
- ❑ Sex is only for procreation.
- ❑ Sex is the only form of affection that counts.
- ❑ I am into sex, but not romance.
- ❑ I have a lot of anxiety and worry about "failure" or difficulties with the act because of previous difficulties.
- ❑ The only thing that counts in sex is orgasm.
- ❑ I do not think of myself as a sexual being.
- ❑ I do not feel good about my body.
- ❑ It is too late to get our sex life back.
- ❑ I have low desire.

❑   I don't feel emotionally connected to my partner.
❑   We each like to have sex at different times of the day.

Remind the couple that now that they are more aware of their blocks, they are well on their way to making changes.

There are four levels of intervention that can be applied to these blocks: increased awareness, awareness about hidden motivations (asking why), cost-benefit/return-on-investment analysis, and making a commitment to do something different to overcome the block (especially as a team).

Level 1: Increased Awareness

When we have led workshops on the power of play in relationships, many people say, "Wow, it was really helpful to recognize my blocks; now I can focus my attention on dealing with this." That is exactly what this first level of change is about. When spouses become aware of their individual blocks, each partner has the possibility of simply changing his or her mind.

Level 2: Awareness About Hidden Motivations (Asking Why)

A workshop participant, Gail, became aware that she thought sex was basically wrong. When asked where this idea come from, she immediately cited Catholic school teachings. She explained that for the years she was taught premarital sex was bad, a sin, and so on. She had then engaged in premarital sex, about which she felt guilty. We playfully kept asking her to repeat the teaching she had learned. She said, "Premarital sex is wrong." We kept asking her to say it repeatedly. She kept saying, "Premarital sex is wrong. Premarital sex is wrong." After about 3 minutes of this, which seemed like an eternity to Gail, she was getting pretty frustrated and complained, "You obviously are trying to make a point. I don't get it. I thought I never listened to those priests and nuns, but apparently I did listen because now I feel sex is wrong." Then, her eyes opened wide, and she gasped. "That is not what they said, is it?" She let out a small laugh, "'They said premarital sex is wrong. I am now married!" With a gleam in her eye she exclaimed, "Wait until Frank gets home tonight!" The entire group applauded.

It is helpful to think about the source of blocks. Couples need to ask themselves, "Are the issues then still relevant today? Have I really brought all of the learning I've had as an adult to bear on these thoughts or beliefs?"

Level 3: Cost-Benefit/Return-on-Investment Analysis

This is a book on play, not business, but sometimes we have to get serious to help clients deal with blocks to make their lives better. Here is an example:

Mary checked off that she believed "sex is not that important." She wanted her husband to love her even if they did not have that much sex. She was asked to draw a line down the middle of the page and on the left side write down the costs of this belief and on the right side write down the benefits of the belief. Figure 8.2 shows what she wrote.

Costs	Benefits
Lots of fights with my husband	Don't have to use contraception as much
Lots of bitterness toward my husband	Less anxious about pleasing my husband
Husband not as happy as he used to be	sexually
Feel less loved by my husband	Can continue to hang on to my point of view
Play less with my husband	and feel right
Fewer orgasms	Feel like I get to win an argument for once
Don't feel as close with my husband	Don't have to confront my husband about
Don't get to find out if we could have	how he does not take enough time with
better sex if he would take more time	foreplay for me to really enjoy sex

Figure 8.2   Costs and benefits/return-on-investment approach with "not having sex" as an example.

Just looking at this list, it became crystal clear to her that the costs far outweighed the benefits. It also became clear to her that one of the problems was that she was not assertive enough. This is one of the most interesting things about focusing on play. If a spouse has issues in any area of the relationship and how the couple communicates (as Mary did with assertiveness), those issues are going to show up surrounding play as well. When Mary became assertive enough to let her husband know how she felt, he said something like, "You mean if I slow down and increase foreplay, you will want to have more sex with me? Baby, I will be as slow as molasses on a cold winter morning."

Ask each person in the couple to take a piece of paper and do the same thing for one of his or her blocks. The instructions are as follows:

"Do not prejudge anything. Simply write the list of costs and benefits regardless of how irrational they may seem. Once they are written, look at them. You may be amazed at what you read and what this will have you thinking or doing next."

An example of the return-on-investment approach is that of Tony.

Tony was one of the men who said he just was not romantic, but he also did not like the fact that his wife was not that turned on by him. He was convinced to try the following experiment: He was asked to create a specific romantic evening. It was acknowledged that it would require a considerable investment of his time and energy. In fact, he was instructed to pay close attention to how much effort he put into the task. He was also asked to pay attention to the return on his investment of energy. In other words, he should pay attention to his wife's reactions and how valuable it was to him. He put in a good effort, and his wife was quite moved by his efforts. She responded in a very amorous fashion. Tony was asked to evaluate the return on investment of his efforts. He said it was high. He happened to be a stockbroker, so this was a perfect analogy. If being a romantic were a stock, would he invest in it? You could just see the puzzle click into place in his eyes. He said, "Doc, I would invest a fortune in that stock." Tony became a romantic.

The fact is it often requires work and energy to play, to be romantic, or to listen or engage in any number of behaviors people know are good for improving their sexual relationship but that takes them outside their current comfort zone. But, it also takes just as much considerable work and energy to fight, be depressed, or even be bored. So, the only question is, What is the return on one's investment of energy?

Level 4: Making a Commitment to Do Something Different to Overcome the Block (Especially as a Team)

It really is as simple as making a commitment to do something different to overcome the block, especially working as a team. Some people will take on this challenge as an experiment for a month. Others will take it on in smaller increments. It does not matter. It is only important that a person do *something* different in the direction of overcoming the block.

> Both Kathy and Jacques had the same block: that a partner ought to know automatically what the other likes sexually. When they both saw this, they were of course halfway home. They decided that for the next month they would confront the idea that the other ought to know anything about their partner, not just involving sex. They decided they would make this the number one thing in their lives for the month. They asked each other questions about anything: What is your favorite color? Do you like salmon or tuna better? It did not matter if they already really did know the answer. They asked anyway. During sex and even during affection, he would ask her if she liked what he was doing. Did she like it more when he stroked her slower or softer? She would answer. She asked him the same kind of questions. Then, each wrote out a vivid description of a great sexual experience they wanted to have together.

Years ago, miners brought canaries down into the coal mines as early warning detectors. If the canary keeled over from breathing in leaking gases, everybody knew it was time to get out. The state of a couple's sexual relationship is the canary in the life of a modern couple. Decreases in the quality and quantity of sex are signs of a dying canary. Many books have been written about this topic, all of which deal with the lack of desire and decreased libido in marriage and ways to deal with it. In *The Sex Starved Marriage*, Weiner-Davis (2003) explained that couples with a discrepancy in sexual desire can find solutions to this problem and rebuild their intimate connection. *Rekindling Desire*, by McCarthy and

McCarthy (2003), explored the complex problem of inhibited sexual desire by focusing on low-sex and no-sex marriages and by offering practical solutions to both of these states. *Hot Monogamy* by Love and Robinson (1994) addressed the issue of how monogamous partners can maintain the excitement and passion they experienced at the beginning of their relationship. In *Mating in Captivity*, Perel (2006) pointed out that more erotic, playful, exciting sex can be possible in monogamous long-term relationships. In *Resurrecting Sex*, Schnarch (2002) guided couples with severe or chronic sexual difficulties or boredom in creating deeper erotic sexual connections.

Different couples have different issues, and there is a variety of different approaches that can help. Of course, in this book, our focus is on helping therapists help their client couples to improve their relationships by bringing playfulness and fun back into them, and we believe that this should naturally include bringing play and fun back into their sexual relationships. If approached in a spirit of play, sex can then become a pleasure and a joy rather than an obligation or chore. The goal is to help couples find their way back to fun and playful sex with specific behavioral tools and new mindsets.

Throughout this book, we have been advocating for therapists to take seriously the idea of encouraging couples to play together more. Certainly for a married couple, sex is an important playground, and cultivating a richer sex life should be one of the priorities when counseling couples who are no longer having fun. It is hoped you now have enough tools to use with the couples with which you work to help them take their sex lives to a new level and have enormous fun while doing it.

9

The Playful Therapist
Personifying Play in Your Practice

PART 1: THE PERSON OF THE THERAPIST

As we have established, a client's capacity to engage in play is closely linked to his or her personal history and inner world. Therapists are no different. Gerald Corey (2009) has noted, "As therapists we serve as models for our clients." (p. 17) The extent to which you, as a therapist, engage in play and fun in your own life—with a partner, if you have one; by yourself; or with close friends and family members—will naturally influence your ability to empower your clients to engage in play in their lives. We believe that therapists who hope to encourage their married clients to adopt play as a key behavior for renewing their relationship must be playful themselves.

Playful therapists model comfort with their inner creativity and playfulness through demeanor, attitudes, words, and actions. It is hoped they do this in both their personal and professional lives. It is likely that we have our own inhibitions; therefore, we should seek opportunities for growth in this area. More than one therapist has commented to us that he struggles with a professional superego that tells him in a deep, booming voice, "You should not act that way. Be professional. Be serious. Be proper." Other therapists longingly lament, "Oh, having more fun in my life and even with my clients sounds so appealing! Somehow, I just don't do it. I am so busy. I get so bogged down."

Perhaps clinicians are very much like their client couples who, because of the weight of their perceived responsibilities, are "no fun any more." We assert that because clinicians feel so restricted, stuck in repetition, and frustrated with the results of their efforts, many get burned out. A clinician who is excited, creative, spontaneous, and experiencing the rewards of successful results with clients usually feels more happy and alive in his or her work.

Therapists often find it difficult to bring their playful selves and play-like techniques with them into the therapeutic context because they are subject to the same social and cultural attitudes as well as personal limitations that we discussed in

Chapter 3. However, because of the nature of the profession, they may have some additional constraints. These include

- A strict professional superego
- The doctor/scientist persona
- Lack of training
- Theoretical resistance
- Fear of doing it wrong
- Personal problems with playfulness

A STRICT PROFESSIONAL SUPEREGO

Under the influence of their strict professional superegos, many therapists approach their work with such concentrated levels of seriousness that the use of play would be like attempting to mix oil and water. The source of a strict professional superego or controlling parent ego state is often an amalgam of memories and tapes of relatively strict dos and don'ts from professors in graduate school blended with an internal model of what it means to be a "professional" therapist, often patterned from earlier childhood scripts and messages. The therapist under the influence of the professional superego is concerned about what he or she *should* do. The professional thinks thoughts such as the following:

> After all, my clients arrive heavily laden with serious problems. Doesn't this dictate absolute seriousness on my part? Wouldn't incorporating a playful attitude, or even play-based therapeutic techniques, be inappropriate given the gravity of the situation in which my clients find themselves? Wouldn't it be taking too great a risk? Might it not give my clients the impression that their problems were not being treated with the gravitas demanded?

The seriousness of the therapist can actually be a detriment to the therapeutic process. Just like a child who falls down and scrapes a knee, who then looks at the face of the parent, people often unconsciously look to others to pick up minimal cues to assess the significance and meaning of specific events (Erickson, 1980; Seigel, 2010).

> In an attempt to create an atmosphere of sympathy for the genuine suffering of patients, the realm of fun is often ignored or avoided. A grave, concerned expression on the therapist's face may be appropriate at some points in the work, but if it becomes habitual it tends to suggest the problem is more insoluble than it is. This, in turn, creates an undue dependency on the part of the patient who comes to rely on the therapist's indications of when things have improved. (Blatner & Blatner, 1988/1997, p. 135)

THE DOCTOR/SCIENTIST PERSONA: "DAMN IT JIM, I'M A DOCTOR/SCIENTIST, NOT A COMEDIAN"*

The field of psychology in the early 21st century is deeply concerned about "evidenced-based therapy." There is a deep worry that therapists do not pay enough attention to science. Increasing numbers of graduate schools and textbooks want to see the "scientific evidence." While there are many beneficial aspects to this development in the field, it becomes problematic that many therapists have been trained in an atmosphere that eschews intuition and improvisation. The professional injunction is to focus heavily on science and fact to the exclusion of all else. It is not that we are against science or fact. The problem is the neglect of integration and use of the entire personality of the therapist. It is the overreliance on the adult ego state and the cutting off of information from the child ego state. Therapists who already have intrapsychic patterns that restrict access to intuition and creativity can be both vulnerable and drawn to this narrative.

LACK OF TRAINING

Except for expressive therapists, psychodrama therapists, movement therapists, art therapists, and play therapists, there is little in most clinician's education and training that exposes them to the powerful opportunities available using play within the therapeutic context. Furthermore, they are often concerned that since they do not know how to do it, they may harm their clients. Frankly, this is one of the reasons for this book. It is often accurate that many therapists who might otherwise be more playful with clients are inhibited because doing so is out of their comfort zone. It is completely normal to have a certain amount of discomfort and anxiety when you try something new; of course, this is the exact issue that many couples have.

THEORETICAL RESISTANCE

Some therapists resist the idea of introducing a playful atmosphere into the therapy room, ostensibly because they do not believe that play could have any possible value in their work with their clients. Little in their education, training, or clinical experience has exposed them to the powerful benefits of helping clients learn to increase positive emotions and experiences through play. There is an inherent bias to "fixing what is wrong or broken" rather than restoring resiliency and the conditions for optimal health. Perhaps the thought is that increasing the positive interactions in a relationship is akin to taking vitamins. It is a good thing to do, but it is not serious medicine.

---

* For the Star Trek impaired, this is a reference to one of the classic lines of the show, said repeatedly by Dr. McCoy.

FEAR OF DOING IT WRONG

With more than 30 years of experience training therapists in active forms of therapy, we know what the most dreaded words in training workshops are: "It is time to practice." This is not unique to therapists. Most adults are afraid to get it wrong. It is safe to listen to an expert speak and take notes. But, when it comes time to actually practice something new, just watch the resistances emerge. Of course, this is exactly parallel to the couples with whom you are working. The fear of making mistakes is one of the great killers of creativity. It stunts growth and change.

If a person is asked to stretch out of that comfort zone, the person is not comfortable. The only question is, will the person do it anyway? The answer needs to be, "Yes." A story about Gandhi comes to mind here:

> A woman brought her son to see Gandhi. She walked a week to get there. She went into the tent and told Gandhi her son was diabetic, but he would not stop eating sugar. Gandhi told her to come back in 2 months. She walked home with her son and then walked back at the appointed time. She brought her son in to see Gandhi. Gandhi looked into the boy's eyes and said, "Sugar is very, very bad for you. I want you to stop eating it." The boy agreed. While the mother was happy about the outcome, she asked him, "You could have told him that when we first came to see you. Why did you make me go home and then walk all the way back?" Gandhi answered, "Because first I had to stop eating sugar myself!"

The challenge for clinicians is to practice what they preach and to grow along with their clients. Integrity and authenticity are far more impactful when encouraging change.

PERSONAL PROBLEMS WITH PLAYFULNESS

Many times, counselors are willing to admit that the problem of using this approach is their own personal lack of playfulness. Saying it is his or her own personal limitation speaks to the person's self-awareness and willingness to change. Again, this is a close parallel to the situation of many couples who walk into counseling. Educators, counselors, and therapists are also people. They have families, often with two income earners, children, aging parents, and so on. They grew up with the same injunctions and issues that we discussed in Chapter 3. The fact of the matter is that we believe that many of the other resistances mentioned actually boil down to this problem. In other words, professionals often unconsciously justify and rationalize their personal issues by relying on professional narratives that support their own psychological defenses.*

---

* The professional narratives themselves may in fact have intellectual and scientific merit. But, that does not mean that the deeper motivation is a psychological defense.

PERHAPS IT ALL COMES DOWN TO FEAR

In discussing this with many colleagues, therapists in workshops over the last few years, what becomes clear is that "fear" is often at the heart of the resistance to play. The fear takes the classic forms: There are the "what ifs" or fear of negative consequences: "What if I upset a client?" "What if I hurt a client?" There are the fears of acting unprofessional or of getting sued. The fear of harming clients is part of the professional ethical standards and is so instilled in most therapists by professors and supervisors that it can become like a psychological straitjacket that inhibits experimenting with new, creative techniques. Instead of it being an aid to the therapist, it becomes the opposite: a threat to his or her professional standing.

Perhaps the most revealing concern is the knee-jerk reaction that some therapists have had surrounding the issue of trauma. When we discuss the *general use* of humor and play in couples work, they almost immediately react negatively to the use of humor or playfulness and instantly bring up the objection that it is not appropriate to use humor or playfulness if a couple has just had a traumatic incident or is in the middle of some horrific and painful experience. Of course, such an admonishment is technically accurate since playfulness is not always the appropriate therapy tool. The deeper question is why this objection is raised so rapidly and with such intensity when the topic of trauma is not even on the table. Often, this type of response is a measure of the deep-seated reactions that occur around the issues of play and humor. These reactions seem to reflect some fear of either the shaming, belittling nature of humor or a fear that somehow a clinician who uses playfulness or humor would not be able to have the ability to know when it is appropriate or inappropriate to use. Or even more deeply, the fear may reflect a concern that the practitioner who espouses the use of playfulness and humor is somehow emotionally avoiding the intensity and pain that often is concomitant with trauma. Certainly, these can be valid concerns, but they do not prevent the therapeutic use of play and humor throughout clinical practice.

Skillful clinicians are creative and flexible. They do not themselves get stuck in the lethargy of clients' problems. Their emotional differentiation gives their client couples the opportunity to lighten up, to shift gears, to see and understand their problems in a new light. The therapist's approach, we maintain, can and should be empathetic, neutral, unbiased, and, of course, equally supportive of both partners. Yet, it can also be playful. We ask, then, that if you are open to play as a new and exciting therapeutic opportunity, that you also consider the impact of your own values and personal patterns in your therapeutic work. We invite you to reconsider and rethink rigid theoretical orientations that may have the effect of stifling the opportunity for play in clinical and educational settings.

IS A PLAYFUL THERAPIST BORN OR MADE?

Whether a playful therapist is born or made is a trick question designed to heighten drama and increase involvement. There is a deeper concern behind this question, however. Some people who have jobs as therapists, counselors, or marriage educators will make an identity statement such as, "I am just not funny," "I don't know how to be more playful," and so on. This type of self-limiting talk creates a self-fulfilling prophecy. We have no doubt that there are temperamental differences that may account for a certain percentage of this characteristic. We suspect it is correlated with genetic loading for happiness. But, remember that genetic predisposition only accounts for 50% of a person's happiness, yet 40% of happiness is modifiable through intentional activity (Lyubomirsky, 2007). Forty percent is more than enough to "make a playful therapist."

> The story of Alexa is a good example. Her two clients, Shandra and Kurt, were making slow progress in their couples therapy. At the end of each session, Alexa suggested activities the couple could engage in that might spark a renewed interest in one another and begin to restore the feeling of closeness that had eroded over the course of the couple's 12-year marriage. Alexa began each new session by asking the couple what they had done for fun during the intervening week. She noted that her clients rarely smiled or laughed when they shared these experiences. Neither related nor mentioned any fun, funny, or exciting thing that had happened. Alexa knew it could not be that nothing enjoyable had occurred and concluded that the couple simply did not feel comfortable sharing such experiences with her during the session.
>
> Alexa then reflected that she also rarely smiled, laughed, or mentioned anything during the session that might indicate that she had had some enjoyable "playtime" during the week. It is not that she did not have fun, she realized, but that in therapy, she did not come across as a person who had fun, who was playful. How, then, could she expect her clients to believe her endorsement of play was authentic when she seemed not to embrace or model the idea herself? She thought about her relationship with her husband and realized that they also did not laugh a lot together or do enough novel play activities. She shared this understanding with her partner and asked that they start to incorporate more fun into their relationship. She suggested that they play a game together at night and that they look in the newspaper and magazines for ideas of activities in which to engage. Alexa began to practice what she was preaching in therapy. Little by little, she began to make changes.
>
> Her new orientation found first expression in the décor of her office. Before her next session with Shandra and Kurt, Alexa took a look at the mix of serious and dull magazines in her waiting room. She added titles that suggested a more well-rounded life, a travel magazine, a yoga journal, a book with humorous jokes and sayings. She put a statue of a kitten wearing sunglasses and reading a comic book table in the therapy room. These changes brought conversation and chuckles from her clients in response.
>
> Once Alexa became aware of play as a possibility in her own life, she recognized that she had stopped playing tennis, was not socializing with her friends nearly as much as she used to, had no hobbies, and had few interests. Slowly, she incorporated tennis back into her life, started doing scrapbooks with old pictures, and began to meet with friends for lunch once a week. Alexa also began to use examples of her own activities during counseling sessions. One time, she mentioned the following to her clients: "You two might enjoy learning how to play tennis together.

This is something I do, and it has been great fun." Another time, she mentioned a comedy film she had seen, and an upcoming concert she was hoping to attend. At yet another point, she had her clients come up with some novel date ideas that they never did before.

Over time, Kurt and Shandra began to relax more in her company. They smiled more frequently and even began to ask follow-up questions, such as, "Did you get to that concert?" "How was that movie?" They began to tell Alexa about their own adventures more frequently and with greater detail and humor. By making these changes in her own life, Alexa managed not only to show the couple her own human needs for play, but also to open up the counseling room to the possibility of playfulness as an essential component of day-to-day living and interaction.

WHAT IS A "PLAYFUL THERAPIST"?

If playful therapists are cultivated, what are the steps? How does a therapist become more playful? There is an infinite number of creative pathways one can take to become a playful therapist, and as we have seen in our work, the playful therapist can operate within most therapeutic modalities. Let us look at the general characteristics of therapists who are playful.

The playful therapist recognizes that the goal of effective living is not to eliminate arousal and conflict. He understands that the goal has much more to do with developing the ability to encounter life in a creative and positive manner. As Gottman has pointed out, conflict is not a predictor of divorce. Hayes et al. (2003) concurred by suggesting that emotional avoidance of an issue or challenge is a much bigger part of dysfunction than the issue or challenge itself. The playful therapist will have many of the following characteristics:

- Models a playful, positive, and joyful approach to living
- Values improvisation and mindfulness
- Is creative and generates novel events and experience that increase the potential for change and healing
- Embraces humor
- Recognizes the evocative, entrancing, and dramatic use of play

Modeling a Playful, Positive, and Joyful Approach to Living

Playful therapists attempt to practice what they preach in their personal lives and in the therapy room. They follow the example depicted in the story about Gandhi, nurturing courage, authenticity, creativity, humor, play, and positive emotions in their personal lives and relationships. How this manifests will vary from person to person and will tend to be expressed by engaging in activities and hobbies that are fun and nurturing in areas outside the therapy room. The playful therapist emphasizes building resourceful and positive experience. Given a choice, this therapist will see life through a comic perspective rather than a tragic one, knowing that all of us go through trials and tribulations, yet maintaining hope and possibility for a good ending. They try to live out the dictum, "It is not what happens to you, it is what you do with what happens to you." When these therapists fail to live up to this standard, they see it as a chance for growth rather than an opportunity for self-flagellation.

In the therapy room, the playful therapist looks for opportunities to create a positive and warm atmosphere in which teamwork, togetherness, and laughter can naturally occur even in the face of conflict and negative life events, using frames of reference that undermine positions of victimhood. This therapist sees possibility and promise in clients rather than sickness and pathology, viewing people as whole and complete and as having barriers to living fully. This therapist embraces the maxim of the 1-minute manager (Blanchard & Johnson, 1982) and solution-oriented therapy (de Shazer, 1985, 1988) with the idea of catching people doing something right and building on that.

Improvisation and Mindfulness

Improvisation and mindfulness are two words that you do not usually see together; yet, it is precisely the pairing of these two ways of being that can yield such creative and powerful results. Mindfulness usually refers to the practice of attending to what is happening in the moment. It often involves a stance of "watching" the aspects of experience unfold in real time and the ability to notice different sensory modalities both internally and externally. For instance, a person who is scared might attend to the lion standing in front of him or her; this person's heart is pounding, the voice in the head is saying the words, "You are going to die," and so on. Another example would be a clinician listening to a couple talking, attending to their voice tones, noticing increasing tension in their bodies, noticing the husband interrupting the wife more quickly, noticing a mental picture showing up from last night's football game of a referee saying "offside."

Generally, mindfulness as a practice does not include taking action. Action happens. Of course, the quality of the action will be influenced by the information that is discerned in the mindfulness practice. Improvisation, on the other hand, is all about taking action in the moment, followed by attending to what happens next. Whereas mindfulness is more of a ready-aim-fire approach, improvisation is more of a ready-fire-aim approach. Mindfulness is intrapersonal. Improvisation is interpersonal. Together, there can be a synergy. The mindful clinician attends to as much of the in-the-moment data as he or she can notice. The playful and mindful clinician takes that data and looks for opportunities to help couples improvise away from their limiting routines.

The playful therapist is not interested in watching a couple engage in the same fight or interaction that they have repeated many times. If all the world is a stage, and if neurotic and unsatisfying lives spring from living through limiting or destructive life scripts (Berne, 1973; Steiner, 1974), then the solution is to let go of the script and be in the moment with the other people on your stage. What is going to happen next? You do not know. This can be both exhilarating and anxiety provoking. A deeply playful therapist comes to love these moments. This therapist embraces the intimacy that springs forth from such encounters. He or she trusts that what shows up is exactly perfect for that moment. It may be funny, or it may be poignant. Mindfulness alone would lead one only to attend to whatever is happening. Improvisation allows for the possibility of action that can sometimes allow for the possibility for humor and healing to emerge. So, if we return to our previous example of the therapist who just attended to the memory of the football referee saying "offside," this therapist also remembers that the husband is a football fanatic. So, the therapist stands up, points to the husband, makes the appropriate gesture, and says, "Offside: 5 yards." The husband is briefly startled. Then, he smiles and says, "Oh, so that is what you have been trying to get me to understand." A little later in the session, the therapist teaches the wife the offside signal, and they rehearse the husband cutting her off and her saying and gesturing "offside." Everybody is laughing.

Action is an important aspect of improvisational acting. Being mindful of the action in the consulting room can lead to great therapeutic moments.

> During one session, Janet became furious at her husband Arlo because he had been late coming home for the umpteenth time. She stamped her foot and said, "You are always late. I'm just sick of it." Arlo shook his head from side to side. His mouth was twisted. He sighed in exasperation. They both looked deeply unhappy. What should the therapist do here? For the playful therapist, there are, in fact, many choices. In the case in question, the therapist creatively improvised a blend of mindfulness with a sculpting intervention (Satir, 1983). He asked that they both stand up and instructed Janet to keep stamping her foot and to say, repeatedly, "You are always late. I'm just sick of it." Arlo was told to keep shaking his head, to keep his mouth twisted, and to keep sighing. Both asked for how long. The therapist said that he did not know, but it might be for a while. They followed instructions.
>
> After about a minute of these repeated behaviors, both Janet and Arlo looked at the therapist, who indicated they should keep at it but added that they should try to note what they were experiencing. After another 30 seconds or so, they began to lose enthusiasm for the task. At this point, the therapist suggested that they now needed to really throw themselves into it and to do exactly what they were doing but with even greater gusto. This they did. After another minute or so, Janet began to smile and laugh. Then, Arlo joined Janet in her humorous epiphany. Arlo turned to the therapist, "Are we really that childish?" Janet smiled and nodded her head as if to say, "Yes, Arlo, we are." A lovely therapeutic conversation followed, peppered with smiles and laughter and suddenly emergent goodwill. This atmosphere of fun and play helped Arlo and Janet shift their energy and allowed them to open the possibility of a positive emotional connection that enabled them to move forward and resolve their issue.

Generating Novel Events and Experiences That Increase the Potential for Change and Healing

The playful therapist embraces the idea that couples who want to grow need to experience novel ways of relating to each other inside and outside the consulting room. Doing and thinking the same old thing leads to more of the same. Here, the importance of educating couples about misconceptions and expectations needs to be stressed. In many cases, the information is so novel that simple imparting of information can be transformational. Even in those cases, the therapist wants to move beyond just sitting and talking and help couples enact those revelations in the therapy room and in their lives.

A variety of interventions is available to the therapist. That used with Arlo and Janet is just one example. Others might include using techniques from psychodrama (Blatner & Blatner, 1988/1997), family sculpting (Satir, 1983), symbolic tasks (Lankton & Lankton, 1983, 1987), or even asking couples to touch and hold each other.

> In a session, when Sam and Bernadette were asked whether they physically greeted each other when one of them returned home from work, they simultaneously said, "No." So, the therapist invited them to greet each other with a hug and kiss as though they were doing it at home and to do it enthusiastically. They did it tentatively at first, so the therapist asked them to increase the intensity. They followed the instruction and began to laugh. They were asked to do it at least three nights for the next week. They agreed to do it and returned to the next session agreeing that they felt closer.

Whether they are aware of the new data coming from brain research and psychotherapy (Doidge, 2009; Hanson, 2009), playful therapists intuitively understand the dictum that the more neurons fire together the more they wire together. They also understand that creating a context for intense and novel experience facilitates the creation of neural connections, which leads to far better learning. This is never truer than when clients experience a better way to relate to each other for the *first time*.

> Lakesha and Charles are both trial attorneys. It is their second session. Lakesha is complaining to Charles that she does not like it when he comes home late and does not even call her. He immediately becomes defensive. She then launches into proving her case. The therapist stops the action. He asks them to please hand him their work ID badges. They look at him quizzically. He says he is serious. As they are fumbling for their IDs, the therapist explains that arguing and counterarguing as if they are in court will be highly counterproductive in their relating to one another. It might work well in court, but not at home. He asks them to talk about what is underneath the argument. Lakesha says she feels that when Charles is late, it shows a lack of respect. And, when he defends himself he is disrespecting her feelings. Charles says at first he thinks that she is criticizing him, and then when she gets more upset, he thinks that she is not trusting him.
>
> The therapist takes their IDs and says, "I know that as lawyers you have been trained to argue about anything. You will try to make a case for the fact that the moon is made of cheese. But for right now, we are going to do an experiment, something completely different than you have ever done before. We are going to see what happens. For now, you are no longer trial attorneys. Lakesha, you are going to tell Charles again what you are feeling, but you are not allowed to prove your case. You can say that you do not like him being late, and you can say how you feel. You can repeat yourself, but you cannot say anything else, okay?" (She agrees.) "Charles, do you

in fact arrive home later than you say you will?" He starts to say, "But." "Charles, please answer yes or no. Do you come home later than you anticipate?" He nods yes. "Great, during this conversation you are allowed to do two things: You can apologize for being late. And you can agree that Lakesha is right to have her feelings. That is all you are allowed to do. It does not matter what happens. Remember this is just an experiment. Can you do it?" Charles agrees and is able to do what he agrees to do.

As you might expect, Lakesha first states her complaint. Charles apologizes. She then talks about her feelings, and he listens and then agrees that he is not being thoughtful to her needs. Lakesha then says, "Wow, that was great. I feel so close to you right now." Charles looks a little stunned and says, "You have just criticized me and told me how thoughtless I am, and you feel closer to me?" The therapist says, "Okay, you two. I want you to remember this moment. Just stay exactly in the moment now and allow your minds to absorb this new learning. You now have a reference point for this type of interaction for the rest of your lives." The couple and the therapist discuss what happened and its implications for the next 20 minutes. This first-time experience becomes a reference that they can use for the future.

The more a couple's patterns are entrenched and defended, the more likely the therapist needs to nurture opportunities for novel experiences to melt the mutual entrainment. These couples usually have significant problems regulating affect. Like Goldilocks, the affect is either too hot or too cold. It is rarely just right. By embracing opportunities for shifting clients out of this negative loop and by inserting comments or perspectives that increase the degree of humor and playfulness and decrease self-absorbed seriousness, the playful therapist is able to modulate the therapy room intensity and increase client emotional safety.

Humor

Playful therapists love to smile and laugh. They nurture those personal experiences or those of others, tell jokes or stories, or like listening to others' jokes and stories. They value surprise and unusual twists that are part of humor. Humor is a major food group of the positive experience diet. In the therapy room, the playful therapist uses humor to help maintain a positive emotional tone. He or she will use the comic perspective as a powerful technique for creating a normalizing and positive therapeutic environment. This has consistently had the effect of counteracting client perceptions that they are an isolated tragedy awaiting inevitable doom. It helps people face aspects of themselves that may be less than desirable.

Comedy is a profoundly healing device, especially when it is used to serve as commentary on relationships and human affairs. At its best, it establishes rapport and builds an understanding that comes from a place of compassion. When it is made a part of the therapeutic discourse, couples not only feel safer but also feel better understood. Bear in mind, however, that there are two clients present in the room, each with different levels of humor. One partner may have a positive reaction to a humorous intervention, while the other has a negative one. As we all know, women are often angry with their husbands because the husbands cannot seem to listen to problems without jumping in and trying to fix them. Men, on the other hand, handle stress by going into their cave of choice (the computer, the television, a book). Their goal is to forget their problems instead of talking about them. As a result, women feel shut out (Gray, 1992). Sharing the differences between gender-based behaviors brings healing levity, humor, and context to the therapist's office.

> After explaining some of the gender differences at work in the relationship dynamic, Tim, as a male therapist, often finds an opportunity to draw on the experience of his own marriage. He shares the following exchange with his wife as a model:

> Tim: (to the female client) I need to explain something to you so you know what to expect from Carlos here. We men (points to Carlos, the male client, and himself) are a little slow on the uptake. (Laura, the female client, breaks into laughter.). But when my wife comes to me with a problem, there are still times when every bone in my body screams, "Fix the problem, Tim. Tim, fix that problem!" (Turns to Laura) Men are just wired that way, and I'm no different. (Turns to Carlos) So Carlos, when Laura comes home and starts to tell you how she is upset about this or that, and when all the control panels light up with signs that flash, "Fix the problem, Carlos. Carlos, fix that problem," your job, at that moment, is to hit the override button and ignore those signals and tell yourself "Just listen, Carlos, just listen!"

The Evocative, Entrancing, and Dramatic Use of Play

We have discussed the importance of generating novel experiences. Novel experiences that open the door for new ways of being in the world are naturally trance inducing and entrancing. The work of Milton Erickson, arguably the most creative and playful therapist of all time, evokes that of a director in a play. Erickson used hypnosis, metaphor, stories, and tasks to fully engage the client. In many cases cognitive insight was not the goal. The director works to evoke and maintain the proper mood and creative tension of the play. In the language we have been using, the director raises and lowers the emotional temperature of the room in a manner that is hoped will create suitable conditions for learning and change. Furthermore, the director uses dramatic devices to evoke and bring into the room different aspects of the psyche. Lankton and Lankton (1983, 1987) further described the importance of the therapist using dramatic tools to heighten client involvement to maximize change. Psychodrama techniques (Blatner & Blatner, 1988/1997) and sculpting approaches (Satir, 1983) all involve the use of the body, movement, and interpersonal space to deepen the therapeutic connections. These are but a few of the experiential techniques that exist in the field.

The playful therapist may have learned or may want to learn some of these formal experiential techniques. Use of story, symbol, or metaphor can be powerful in bringing something more than just the conscious mind into the therapy room.

Each person can do it in a personal way. The therapist may focus on literature or mythology or might relate better to music, television, or movies. Poetry, movement, and visual arts may also provide endless material for the evocative nature of therapy. The playful therapist will be willing to engage clients in the room with the quotations, references, and stories to help evoke the appropriate resource needed for the therapy. Therapists need to be willing to reveal themselves and reach clients through personal choices. For instance, the therapist would be comfortable quoting from an appropriate poem to make a point.

BEING PLAYFUL INVOLVES MOTION/MOVING ENERGY

Traditional therapy involves the therapist and clients sitting on chairs or on a sofa and talking. Instead of the therapist as a talking head, being a playful therapist can include the possibility of actual movement. We are offering you an opportunity to stretch yourself, to take a risk and use creative tools that will generate novelty, fun, positive emotions, empathy within the couple's unconscious thoughts, self-expression, a cooling down of the room or heating it up, authentic communication, self-understanding, healing, and ultimately growth. The use of expressive therapy offers a variety of modalities to the therapist, such as art, play, movement, and music therapy; poetry; psychodrama; role playing; improvisation; sculpting; and photography. These are therapeutic techniques that have the potential to help couples stop negative behavioral patterns.

Role reversal can be a powerful, often fun, exercise to help a couple get unstuck from a negative pattern of behavior by being able to empathize with a partner. Asking the couple to get up out of their chairs and move alters the energy and lightens the mood:

In a therapy session, Serena complained that Jose did not give her any space. She said that when she was busy cleaning the house with the children, Jose would follow her when he wanted to be with her, and Serena would walk away from him. He felt rejected. She felt angry and disrespected. This was a constant source of frustration for both of them. The therapist invited them to do a role reversal in which Serena would become Jose and Jose would become Serena. They were asked to do the very behavior they both did but to play each other. They agreed, and Jose started to pretend he was cleaning the house while Serena followed Jose. They started to giggle. The therapist asked them to exaggerate their movements, so Jose started to run around the room while Serena chased him. All of a sudden, they broke into laughter, and the therapist asked them to stop, close their eyes, and get in touch with what they were feeling. After a minute, the therapist asked them each to share their feelings. Jose said he could understand how annoying it was for Serena when he followed her, and Serena said she could understand how rejected Jose must feel when she kept walking away from him.

The therapist asked how they could use this awareness to help them change their behavior. Jose said he would stop following Serena around the house, and he would instead ask her to schedule time to be together at night. She agreed to do that. Serena said she would make sure that she would sometimes let her housework go and be with Jose. A primary goal of this exercise is to allow each partner to experience empathy for the other.

A playful therapist incorporates playful activities into therapeutic sessions not only to help encourage a couple to play together outside the therapy room but also as a means to gather useful information about a couple's typical play attitudes. Weiner, in his book, *Rehearsals for Growth: Theater Improvisation for Psychotherapists* (1994), offered tug-of-war using an imaginary rope as "one of the most useful improv exercises" a therapist can use in "assessing several qualities of connection between relationship partners." (p. 121)

Weiner described having couples in stocking feet facing one another with some clearance behind their backs. They are asked to pick up an imaginary rope and enact a tugging match, with the requisite that there must be a clear "winner" within 30 seconds. They are be asked to enact it twice with each partner getting this an opportunity to win. The therapist watches for clues to each individual's "assumptions, judgments, and attitudes, especially toward power issues" and then in a supportive and nonjudgmental way, offers "feedback and suggestions in a way that conveys that all concerned are here to learn and play together." (p. 122)

The primary issue of clinical interest is whether the couple is involved with co-creating the reality of the rope and of the struggle. The activity itself often leaves couples feeling more enthused about playing together, but more important, casts them in shared roles of having to be convincing actors in a miniplay about play, which increases connection.

THE COUPLE'S FUTURE PLAY COLLAGE

Another useful, playful activity to introduce during a therapy session is the couple's future play collage, which allows each partner to indicate interests, desires, and dreams for the kind of play he or she wishes to engage in together. To begin the 10-minute exercise, the therapist presents the couple with two glue sticks, one piece of poster board, and a stack of magazines. The magazines need to be rich in photos of adults engaged in a variety of activities, magazines that cover, for example, travel, leisure time, regional events, the outdoors, sports, cultural life, and the like. For 5 minutes, working in silence, each partner flips through any magazines of interest and quickly tears out any photos that represent something of interest from any of these three categories: (a) activities I used to enjoy, do not do any longer, but hope to do with my partner in the future; (b) activities I have never done but want to do with my partner; and (c) activities we currently do together that I want to do more. Over the second 5 minutes, the couple works together, again without speaking, to assemble the torn-out pictures onto the poster board.

They are then asked to take the collage poster home, leave it someplace where they will see it over the next week or so, and casually talk about what each other has put on it. They return to the next session with the poster, ready to discuss what they have learned about the other's interests, desires, and dreams.

If it is not obvious by now, the development of playfulness and the affect and demeanor of the therapist during sessions about play is, ironically, serious business. We are not simply advocating that therapists should teach couples how to play more in their relationship. We are also suggesting that you, the therapist, must walk the talk. We have used the word *cultivate* many times throughout this book because it refers both to an ongoing incremental movement toward a goal as well as ongoing maintenance of a desired state. Wherever you are in your own personal journey, you can cultivate your ability to be more playful and positive. The more you do it in your life, the more you can do it in your therapy room; conversely, the more you do it in your therapy room, the more you do it in your life.

THE PLAYFUL THERAPIST MAKEOVER

Many colleagues have asked us, "How do I make myself over to be more playful? Where do I start?" In this section, we give you some guidance on this matter. As we begin, let us remind ourselves that this is an incremental process. We begin with a light-and-accepting heart, build with positive reinforcement, and are quick to notice and reward any positive steps the couple takes.

Part 1: Assess Your Present State

1. How often do you and your clients laugh? For 1 week, keep a pad of paper next to you and make a hash mark every time you or your clients smile or laugh. At the end of the week, add these and divide by the number of sessions. Do this before you make any other changes so that you have a base rate measure of how much play is present in your current therapy. Then, after making other changes, reassess this variable.
2. Look around your office. Is there anything in your waiting room or office that is fun, playful, or humorous? Is there anything you can change in the environment and physical space to suggest an appreciation or celebration of play?
3. Look around your house or apartment. Is there anything there that is fun, playful, or humorous? Look at the artwork on your walls. Is every other picture by Edward Munch? Is every wall white or off-white? What can you do to create some color, novelty, or playfulness?
4. Outside the therapy room, how often do you laugh? Do you read anything that is funny? Do you watch anything that is funny?

5. Outside therapy, what do you do on a regular basis that brings you joy or connects you to yourself? How often do you do this? How often do you not do this because you have work to do?

6. Examine your own relationship and apply the ideas we have been putting forward to your own life. Complete the couples play inventory yourself. Reflect on the outcome of the assessment to determine how things are going in your own life.

Part 2: Making Changes

Based on your answers to Suggestions 2–5 in Part 1, make some appropriate changes. After filling out the play inventory, assess which areas need attention in your own life. Remember, the word is *cultivate*. We like to think that we are playful therapists and people, and we regularly have to take stock of where we are. There simply are intense forces that pull us back toward work, chores, and responsibilities. No matter where you are on the curve, it always helps to ask, Am I creating enough play, joy, and positive energy in my life and relationships? In prioritizing which changes to make in your own life, it is suggested that you begin with small changes (i.e., putting up one funny cartoon on your wall or taking a walk in nature for 10 minutes each week). Watch a half hour of stand-up on the comedy channel. Take an improv class or a painting class. Learn a new sport or take an art class. Instead of going to the same restaurant, go to one with food you have never tasted. Discover what type of play makes your heart soar.

We cannot emphasize enough the importance of assessing your relationship with a significant other. If together you are no fun anymore, create and implement a plan based on the ideas in this book. Assess how things change in your own life as a result. Consider the value of being able to speak from experience.

Part 3: Going Deeper—Becoming Mindful About
Your Own Reactions to Play and Humor

1. Reflect on and analyze your reaction to the suggestions we have made in this chapter and elsewhere. You are looking for any strong emotional reaction. Did they appeal to you, or did they create anxiety? Did you scoff at them? As we have been maintaining, an individual's reaction to the possibilities of play is as significant as his or her reactions to sex, power, and money. Consider what these emotional reactions represent. Be mindful of those reactions. What comes up? What would your mother or father say about the idea presented? What would your graduate school professors say? What did it remind you of?

2. For another week, pay attention to moments in your consulting sessions when you have an impulse to say something playful or humorous. What

was happening in the moment prior to the impulse surfacing? Did you take the risk and respond? Examine the motivation. How did (or would) your clients have responded to your choice at that moment?

3. Begin to experiment a bit at pushing the envelope that you have been exploring. We discuss specific techniques in the next section. The best way to do this is with your healthiest clients. As soon as you do the slightly different intervention, pay close attention to what happens next. Does the couple reveal more personal information? Do they relax? Do they go deeper? Do they shut down? If the couple moves in a therapeutically desirable direction, the intervention was probably successful. Of course, if the opposite occurs, your attempt at being more playful and humorous was not successful. Do not let that stop you. While you are tracking their response, be sure to track your response. How do you feel? How does interaction with the couple feel?

Part 4: The Theory and Practice of Using Play and Humor in Sessions With Couples

Creating and Maintaining Safety and Comfort Through Humor and Play

Many clients have never been to a therapist before and therefore can be justifiably anxious about the prospect. They have not been able to solve their problems on their own, and they are likely uncertain about how to solve them with someone else's help. Other clients have worked with therapists but have had poor results. Common complaints we hear about previous couples therapy from our clients are that "We ended up fighting more in the therapist's office," and, "We left feeling more upset than when we went in." It is often the case that a couple's hesitation and resistance to therapy is rooted in a previous and negative experience. Even with a new therapist, they fear more of the same.

The therapist who is a conduit for change needs to create a safe environment in which taking risks is both suggested and encouraged, positive outcomes occur, and making mistakes is acceptable. It is up to the therapist to facilitate sufficient positive and playful interchanges between the couple so that, in the session at least, the 5-to-1 rule is achieved. The couple coming into your office is already well under that ratio. There is little chance that left to their own devices they will begin to create a better ratio once in your office. When therapists are not sufficiently active in protecting the therapeutic space, the therapeutic environment is likely to become contaminated by increased "negative energy." When this happens, the couple is reenacting what they have come to excel in at home. This is not therapeutic.

Although the use of play and humor may seem counterintuitive as the means of tackling difficult and complex issues, research about the reaction of the brain to pleasurable activity has established that the positive feelings that can arise from play and humor help to override negative feelings (Hanson, 2009). Nobody was making jokes on 9/11 or the day after, of course. At that point, the United States was deeply traumatized. But, it was not long after that the first jokes began to circulate. The trauma demanded a release, and humor delivered it. Diffusing tension, stress, fear, and grief is the sociological function of jokes, humor, comedy, comedians, and late-night talk show hosts. What is comic can be, more often than not, immensely healing.

Of course, there is nothing funny or hopeful to someone in the midst of significant trauma or someone suffering an insult to his or her ego or narcissism. In the midst of a storm, things can appear unremittingly bleak. Since meaning is ultimately a construction, the perception of the seriousness of a situation engenders an amplified set of dire predictions and responses. In other words, seriousness breeds seriousness, which in turn produces anxiety and fear. Negative affect and dysfunction escalate in turn (Hayes & Strosahl, 2004; Johnson, 2008). Within the marital dynamic, interpersonal wounding ricochets and reverberates.

The playful therapist is able to monitor both the affective intensity and the negative meaning making going on in the room. Typically, when things get too negatively intense, clients either shut down or spin out of control (Levine, 1997). The playful therapist will often use different forms of play and humor to lower the emotional temperature in the room. Humor in the therapeutic context can break the ever-escalating cycle of negativity. It can also bring with it unexpected shifts of perspective. This is the true significance of its positive therapeutic influence. When one or both individuals in the couple are able to take the step back that occurs after an injection of humor takes place and are able to detach from the overwhelming sense of the "seriousness" of the situation, a more positive, hopeful, and even comic set of perceptions often arises.

"Lights, Action, Therapy!" The Playful Therapist as Director:
Cultivating Novel Adventures in Intimacy for Couples

As we have seen, the creative therapist can more effectively manage the therapeutic environment by using play and humor to cool things down and to reduce intensity when it is useful to do so. Sometimes, however, the room needs to be heated up, its intensity increased. A number of authors have described how to create therapeutic openings and memorable experiences through intensive play (Weiner, 1994), humor (Whitaker, 1982), surprise (Erickson, 1980; O'Hanlon, 1987), and metaphor and drama (Lankton & Lankton, 1983, 1987). As we know, it is sometimes the case that clients come in stifled by negative thinking, not the least bit open to new learning and new approaches. A novel and intriguing event in the therapy room can change everything by helping clients to overcome habitual thinking (with its emotional intensity) and by stimulating the brain to be receptive to new learning.

To create such catalyzing therapeutic events, the therapist needs to move beyond mere talk of the problem to getting creative and increasing the intensity in the room. Incorporating movement, touch, and feeling and by working to direct the scene, the playful therapist can facilitate new approaches and fresh responses to old feelings and patterns of reaction.

Another highly effective intervention is to ask the couple to jointly and non-verbally draw a picture of themselves doing something fun and different together or to have them sing a favorite song together. Or, the couple can be encouraged to bring in photos of activities, places, and events from magazines or Web sites that they find intriguing. Further still, they can be "assigned" the task of writing love letters to each other and taking turns reading them aloud in the session or of developing a joint vision statement that declares a commitment to enriching the time they spend together through new and novel activities and interests.

Will the couple resist such engagements as silly and frivolous? Probably. Yet, the playful therapist is almost counting on this resistance because it opens up an opportunity to focus on why they are avoiding having more fun and joy in their life. Of course, if they do not resist, the couple will move that much more quickly toward the positive experience of fun and play. Either way, it is a win.

Creating and Enlarging Therapeutic Openings

Therapeutic opportunities are a bit like improvisational doors that open and close throughout the therapy session. It is up to the therapist to be alert to emergent possibilities by grabbing the handle, opening the door fully, and inviting the couple to step through it. One way to do this is to gather what Schaefer (2003) called "humor tools," which include things like cartoons, props, jokes, anecdotes, puns, and signs to illustrate events that clients might be facing in their lives or to provide a poignant learning opportunity.

Here is an example:

Adrienne and John were working on lightening up in their marriage. Both had come from very strict homes. They tended to judge the other as silly or out of control when he or she did something spontaneous. During one particular session, they earnestly attempted to engage the therapist into playing the role of judge to settle the matter, once and for all. The playful therapist instructed the couple to stand up, hold hands, walk over to a desk, look at the objects on the desk, and together decide which object was the most appropriate solution to their problem. On the desk was a candle, a crystal, a statuette, a framed picture of two candy bars with a saying, and several other objects.

Adrienne and John resisted at first, but then began to follow the instructions. They went to the desk and began looking at the objects and talking about them. The therapist kept reminding them that they needed to be holding hands the entire time, and that they needed to reach an agreement together. After a couple of minutes, they started chuckling and brought back one of the objects. Their serious and restricted attitude had been replaced by playfulness and even a kind of giddiness. They handed the therapist the object and asked, "This is the one that you wanted us to pick, isn't it?" The therapist responded, "Why did you decide on this one?" Adrienne said, "Well, we were worried whether or not what we think or want to do is wrong or out of control.

And this just turns the entire thing on its head." "It made us laugh," John added. The therapist asked, "So the next time you are faced with this dilemma and one of you is tempted to get judgmental about being weird or crazy or out of control, what are you going to do?" The couple looked at each other and started to laugh. John said, "Well, that's easy, we are going to do and say what the sign says, 'Sometimes you feel like a nut. Some times you don't.'"

The object that Adrienne and John had picked up was a small folding photo frame with a picture of a Mounds bar on one side and a picture of an Almond Joy on the other along with the advertising phrase: "Sometimes you feel like a nut. Sometimes you don't." A previous client who had been struggling with similar issues had given this object to the therapist after he had suggested that she go buy these two candy bars and reflect on them whenever she started to worry if she was going crazy. The simplest and strangest props can become useful tools to such a creative therapist. We suggest that you begin with one or two and then slowly build your inventory of such tools. You will soon see how handy they can be.

THE PLAYFUL THERAPIST'S TOOL KIT

Where do you start to develop a tool kit as a playful therapist? How do you find and collect such humor and play tools? Once you understand that these are simply physical means of communication, you will begin to find them everywhere. A therapist might consider bringing in humorous articles from newspapers or magazines; a large ball; a printout of something funny from the Internet; masks; sand trays with miniature figures of people, houses, and objects; a cartoon from the *New Yorker*; a copy of a silly typo or a ridiculous advertisement from a church or temple bulletin; a clown nose; a magic wand; or different hats, balloons, or puppets. Sharing with clients about a humorous video from the Internet (YouTube is a great source), a film in the theaters, and a television show that speaks to a playful marriage are other ways of incorporating humor and play into therapy and encouraging clients to seek it out in their own lives. Art materials, markers, paper, crayons, paint, and clay are good for playful self-expression. Songs are another rich source of therapeutic humor. As we have discussed, useful points can be made about relationship expectations through the use of the absurd sentiments expressed by popular love songs. We particularly like some of the songs of folk singer David Roth, including, "Don't Should on Me and I Won't Should on You" and "We Don't Have Issues, We Have Subscriptions." Bring the song into a session, change the feeling in the room, and share your own responses in the moment (check out http://www.DavidRothMusic.com).

Creating Catchy Hooks

As any good musician knows, a good musical hook makes a song memorable. And, it is short (Beethoven's most famous hook (from the *Fifth Symphony*) had only eight notes), simple, and catchy. It is also evocative and easy to remember. In therapy, a hook can serve several functions: (a) It marks something as a "reference experience," (b) it creates drama, and (c) it has the potential to lay down a lasting therapeutic memory and response. Let us use the example of Adrienne and John to illustrate: They were given the task of finding the "proper object." This was not easy and created drama. Their difficulties in finding and agreeing on that object ("Sometimes you feel like a nut. Sometimes you don't") included dialogue, tension, and finally resolving laughter. Finally, the therapist ensured that the event was imprinted to create a long-lasting memory by challenging the couple to think about how they would use this experience in the future (Erickson, 1980).

The playful therapist should approach hooks as therapeutic motifs that can be accessed and referenced repeatedly. As a creative therapist, you need to look for those humor tools that can be usefully linked to the most common problems faced by your clients. These may include a story you like to tell, a contextually appropriate joke, a piece of art in your office that you have clients view. Whatever you use, make it relevant, engaging, and memorable.

The song "Don't Should on Me and I Won't Should on You" is a brilliant hook. Our couples have reported back that they have frequently used it in their own "should wars."* Here is how this typically goes: Just past the point at which the should battle begins, one or the other or even both clients recognize the pattern they have returned to and, in response, begin to sing the hook from the song. The war abruptly ends, shared laughter emerges, peace prevails again. This out-of-therapy event was able to happen because the therapist facilitated it in session. The therapist had the song cued up on the desktop, and when the couple started to get into the shoulds, the therapist said, "Hold that thought, will you?" Then, he hit "play."

Out of the Mouths of Clients …

Sometimes, it is the clients who write the hooks. When this happens, the playful therapist seizes on the opportunity and works with the couple to transform the memorably negative into the positively therapeutic. As an example, not too long ago Claire, one of our clients, said in a burst of sarcastic holiday frustration, "Great, it's Christmas Eve, and Mom is manic." Claire was a long-standing client who knew her therapist well. Client and therapist looked at each other. Both smiled. The therapist said, "That really would make a great song, Claire. Why don't you write it? Use a Christmas jingle and add your own words." They both laughed at the possibilities. Several days later, an e-mail arrived. Here are the chorus and two verses:

CHRISTMAS EVE AND MOM IS MANIC

(To the tune of "Winter Wonderland")
(Chorus)

---

* In a should war, each member of the couple tells the other what they should or should not do. It just goes round and round.

Christmas Eve and Mom is manic
but let's not get in a panic
Hopefully she'll see,
there're more people here besides me.
And she'll put on her little show.
(Verse)
Later on, she will prattle,
and our nerves will be frazzled.
She'll go on and on
ignoring our yawns
Talkin' 'bout herself incessantly
(Verse)
"Where's my drink, guess who called me last week"
"Oh my legs, my heart, my back, my head"
"Why don't you come visit me more often"
"What was it that you just said?"

Talk about a therapeutic hook; here was a whole song that Claire was able to use to save her sanity during times of crisis and holiday duress. Therapists can always be on the lookout for catching clients using their own sense of humor. Whenever that happens, the therapist needs to reinforce this development. Perhaps the best way to do that is simply to enjoy it and let the client see that you are enjoying it.

WALKING THE TALK: THE POWER OF MODELING
CREATIVITY, PLAY, AND JOY IN COUPLES THERAPY

We believe that modeling behavior is one of the most powerful ways to teach and influence our clients since couples look to us as experts and as examples. As we have shown, the inhibitions of our clients are learned. Eros, creativity, and spontaneity are heavily repressed in the modern American culture. There is considerable pressure on therapists to do what is "right," to do what one should do, and above all, to avoid making mistakes. In such a cultural environment, following one's own unique inner voice is often contrary to expected norms. Through his or her own demeanor, words, and actions, through what he or she does as a person and a professional, the therapist is also a player in this behavioral drama. As we have pointed out, he or she may have inhibitions and therefore opportunities for growth. Therapists have often shared with us that they struggle with their professional superegos and that they grapple with inner voices urging caution, propriety, and, most important, seriousness.

When as therapists we allow these voices to have the day, our professional work suffers. When we do not engage our playful selves because we are wary of appearing unprofessional, we invite client suspicion. As Corey put it, " If we hide behind the safety of our professional role, our clients will likely keep themselves hidden from us." (p. 17) By modeling an embrace of the fundamental role of play in his or her own life, the therapist can help a couple to see that although it might seem "extracurricular," play is, on the contrary, a vital part of his or her overall development and life satisfaction.

Playfulness and humor must be used appropriately and only in the service of the client to help move the conversation forward, of course. But, it has been our consistent experience that clients are relieved when they find out that we also are human and that we live rich, full, and imperfect lives. The beauty of the profession is the difference we can make when we incorporate the example of our own life experience in the service of normalizing behavior, being inspiring, helping clients see possibilities they could not see before, and by offering fresh and healing perspectives on problems that once seemed daunting and impossible.

Above and beyond the specific techniques and tools we have been advocating, the playful therapist engages the couple with a twinkle in his or her eye. The therapist looks beyond the evident "seriousness" of their problems toward the nascent joyful possibilities that invariably lie within them. By doing so, he or she facilitates their manifestation. The creative therapist has fun in the room with the couple. The therapist laughs with the couple and coaxes and cajoles them into trying new things and stretching themselves by taking playful risks. These can be, of course, delicate maneuvers. A therapist has to be strategic about what, when, and how he or she interjects lightness. Schaefer (2003, p. 126) described therapy as "planned spontaneity—the therapist spontaneously responding in the moment based on planning reflected by the therapist's training and expertise."

A THERAPIST PREPARES …

What is the training and expertise required to become a playful therapist? There are many paths. They can include taking courses in expressive or play therapy, sharing jokes and stories, taking an improvisational class, take an acting or stand-up comedy class, or seeking and recognizing humor wherever and whenever it occurs in life beyond the therapy room; it is bringing this practice and learned expertise into counseling. It is these learned skills, along with a bag full of humor and play tools, that prepare the therapist to deploy humor at the most opportune moments. The key, of course, is for the therapist to align personal humor with his or her personality. Without this alignment, attempts at humor will be exactly that, attempts.

The ideal here is for the therapist to integrate humor into his or her own life so that it becomes a completely natural component when it is used within the therapeutic context. The lightness that develops when a therapist becomes comfortable with humor greatly enhances both the personal and professional life of the therapist.

Once humor is introduced into therapy, the therapist needs to be alert to client responses. Did they laugh? Did they lighten up? If they did not, was the resistance the result of a poorly executed intervention, or is the couple so deeply embedded in negative patterns that they simply cannot respond to humor?

The therapist also needs to know why he or she used humor in the first place. If the goal was to prevent the affective intensity from overheating, did the intervention work? Even if the couple did not laugh, was the affective intensity reduced to a more tolerable level? If the goal was instead to help reframe a couple's point of view, did it succeed? Did one or both people begin to talk differently about the subject at hand? If the goal, on the other hand, was to create a hook, did the couple use the hook outside the therapy room?

Occasionally, a particular client will have a negative reaction to a humorous or playful intervention. Every therapist who uses humor and playfulness will eventually provoke a negative response. This is one of the risks of creative intervention. The client's reactions should always be explored. What about the intervention that triggered the negative reaction? Was the therapist insensitive, flip, or glib? What did it evoke in the client? Who or what did it remind them of? Did it touch on a pattern resident in the couple's own relationship? All these are questions that can bring further light and understanding to the situation at hand. In the event of an intervention that turns into a therapeutic "blunder," an apology for bad timing or insensitivity may be useful and even necessary. A nondefensive apology can serve as a highly valuable example for clients to model. With such a demonstration, they come to witness a person who can be present, sensitive, compassionate, authentic, and playful, exactly what they themselves need to become in their relationship.

When a negative reaction happens, an important question to ask from the perspective of clinician development is, To what degree did the client response shut down the therapist? One of the great blocks to creativity is our own fear of making mistakes (von Oech, 1998). But, "mistakes" are highly useful. The playful therapist can use them as training and development. While the use of humor can be effective, therapists need to be aware of their motivation for using humor at a given moment as well. It is important for therapists to be aware of their own tendencies. As we all know, the therapist's ego is also present in the room. If client responses are too often ambivalent or negative, if the therapist's humor is being received as glib, these are invitations to engage in accurate and careful assessment of technique and timing. Adjustments can be made in response.

The therapist's intervention motivations are the key element here. Schaefer (2003) distinguished between the therapeutic humor that emanates from a clinician's empathy and desire to be helpful and toxic humor, which instead stems from a therapist's own personal needs. There are any number of such personal needs that may motivate a therapist to use humor in a manner that is not helpful. Perhaps chief among them is the therapist's unconscious anxiety, tension, and a personal desire to avoid conflict.

When this happens, the therapist is lowering the therapeutic heat in the room but doing so from personal needs. The playful therapist needs to reflect frequently on this dynamic. Self-monitoring can bring an accurate assessment of whether such humor interventions are rooted in personal feelings of anxiety, frustration, or anger or whether they are simply and honestly in the service of client needs.

In addition to monitoring their own levels of humor or playfulness, therapists need to assess client levels of receptivity to humor. Such an assessment is critical to the therapist's decisions about which humor tools and interventions best fit the style of the clients. One way to do this is to have clients describe some specific examples of things they find funny. Such examples will show the therapist the style of humor each is comfortable with and which types of humor resonate with them both as a couple.

There is the joke about 84-year-old Ivan, who enters a retirement home for comedians; the joke well illustrates the issues at hand.

> Ivan is sitting with his friend when he hears someone yell out, "27." Everyone laughs. Then a few moments later, somebody else says, "52." Even more people laugh this time. He turns to his friend and says, "Morty, what is with the all the numbers and the laughing?" Morty explains that instead of telling the same joke over and over, the retired comedians have chosen to use numbers as a shortcut. Ivan considers, then stands up and yells, "13." Nobody laughs. Now thoroughly confused, he turns back to Morty and asks, "What gives?" Morty responds, "C'mon, Ivan. You know timing is everything."

For the playful therapist, timing truly is everything. Early in the therapeutic relationship, the use of humor is tricky because the therapist and the couple do not know each other particularly well, and a level of trust and rapport has not yet been established. This does not mean humor should not be used. In fact, this is one of the best times to use it because the risk it involves can build and model trust. If you are nervous, here are a few guidelines:

1. Do not use humor and playfulness if someone is telling his or her story for the first time, someone is describing pain or trauma, or you are uncomfortable.
2. Do use humor and playfulness if you are providing a normalizing frame for a problem (e.g., gender differences), the joke or humorous issue is the elephant in the room and not to use it would indicate fear and withdrawal, or the couple has shown a propensity to use humor as one of their coping strategies.

If using these guidelines does not produce a clear view, take the conservative approach and, temporarily at least, forgo the use of humor until greater clarity emerges.

As we have been maintaining, the use of humor and playfulness is so effective in couples therapy because, among many other benefits, it helps them arrive at the 5:1 ratio of positive to negative experiences.

In this chapter, we turned our gaze away from our clients by turning it back on ourselves, as therapists. We have underlined the fact that if we are to success-fully engender and support an attitude of play in the relationships of our clients, we must ourselves first embrace the message by bringing an attitude and sense of play along with us when we step into our offices. Marshall McCluhan's (1964) dictum is surely relevant and appropriate advice for us here: "The medium is the message." It is by fully embracing the power of play in our lives, both personal and professional, that we best qualify ourselves as suitable model candidates for conveying our message. As Gandhi demonstrated for the child, we must be the first to embrace our own prescriptions for play.

Afterword

The work that is captured in a book is really never finished. As we have said all along, cultivating a marriage is never finished. So, we have created two Web sites:

www.wearenofunanymore.com
www.play4couples.com

The first site, www.wearenofunanymore.com is more for marriage educators and therapists. You can

- Purchase user-friendly copies of the various assessments in this book.
- Order additional copies of the book.
- Watch videos of how to do some of the exercises that we described.
- Discover additional approaches to helping people reconnect with their ability to be joyous.
- Read and contribute to a blog dedicated to this type of work.

The second site, www.play4couples.com, is a site for referring your couples. The goal is to provide support for the ideas that we are espousing.
We have plans for

- videos that they can watch about some of the exercises
- deck of fun activity cards
- fun and humorous activities for the month
- information and discounts to local fun activities so that they can more easily go out
- humor of the day e-mails

Since you have purchased this book, you can use the code Hahaha to save $5.00 off your first purchase.
If you want to refer a couple to the www.play4couples.com site, they can get 10% off by using the code: fun4us.

References

Abrams, R. (1997). *The playful self: Why women need play in their lives*. London: Fourth Estate.

Ackerman, D. (1999). *Deep play*. New York: Random House.

Ainsworth, M., Blehar, M., Waters, E., & Wall, S. (1978). *Patterns of attachment*. Hillsdale, NJ: Erlbaum.

Ainsworth, T. Nobile, A. (2009). *I'd trade my husband for a housekeeper: Loving your marriage after the baby carriage*. San Francisco: Chronicle Books.

Alexander, F. (1961). *The scope of psychoanalysis*. New York: Basic Books.

Aron, A., & Aron, E. N. (1986). *Love as the expansion of self: Understanding attraction and satisfaction*. New York: Hemisphere.

Aron, A., Norman, C. C., Aron, E. N., McKenna, C., & Heyman, R. (2000). Couples shared participation in novel and arousing activities and experienced relationship quality. *Journal of Personality and Social Psychology, 78*, 273–283.

Aslanian, S. Rewiring the brain: Romania's orphan story 1996–2006. *American Public Media*; retreived 4/13/11 from http://americanradioworks.publicradio.org/features/romania/b1.html

Aune, R. K., Aune, K. S., Dawson, E. 1., & Pena, E. F. (1993). Relational messages associated with persona-sharing. *Communication Research Reports, 10*, 129–139.

Aune, K.S and Wong, N.C. (2002). Antecedents and consequences of adult play in romantic relationships. *Personal Relationships, 9*, 279–286.

Bateson, G. (1972). A theory of play and fantasy. In *Steps to an ecology of mind* (pp. 177–193). Lincoln, NE: Chandler.

Baxter, L. A. (1992). Forms and functions of intimate play in personal relationships. *Human Communication Research, 18*, 336–363.

Berk, L. S., Tan, S. A., Nehlsen-Cannarella, S., Napier, B. J. Lewis, J. E., J. W. Lee and Eby, W. C. (1988). Humor associated laughter decreases cortisol and increases spontaneous lymphocte blastogenesis. *Clinical Research, 36*, 435A.

Berk, L. S., Tan, S. A., Fry, B. J. Napier, B. J., Lee, J. W., Hubbard, R. W., Lewis, J. E., and Eby, W. C. (1989). Eustress of mirthful laughter modifies natural killer cell activity. *Clinical Research, 37*, 115A.

Berk, L. S., Tan, S. A., Berk, D. B., and Eby, W. C. (1991). Immune system changes during humor associated laughter. *Clinical Research, 39*, 124A.

Berne, E. (1973). *What do you say after you say hello?* New York: Grove.

Blanchard, K., & Johnson, S. (1982). *The one minute manager*. New York: Morrow.

Blatner, A., & Blatner, A. (1997). *The art of play: Helping adults reclaim imagination and spontaneity*. New York: Brunner/Mazel. (Original work published 1988 by Human Sciences Press).

Boszormenyi, I. & Spark, G. (1984). *Invisible loyalties*. New York: Brunner/Mazel.

Bowlby, J. (1969). *Attachment*. New York: Basic Books.

Brannan, B. (2002). *The gift of play: Why adult women stop playing and how to start again* Bloomington, IN: iUniverse.

Briere, J. (1992). *Child abuse trauma: Theory and treatment of the lasting effects*. London: Sage.

Briere, J. (1996). *Therapy for adults molested as children*, Second Edition. New York: Springer Publishing Co.

Brown, S. (2009). *Play: How it shapes the brain, opens the imagination, and invigorates the soul*. New York: Penguin Books.

Burns, A. B., Brown, J. S., Sachs-Ericsson, N., Plant, E. A., Curtis, J. T., Fredrickson, B. L., et al. (2008). Upward spirals of positive emotion and coping: Replication, extension, and initial exploration of neurochemical substrates. *Personality and Individual Differences, 44*, 360–370.

Campbell, L., Martin, R. A., & Ward, J. R. (2008). An observational study of humor use while resolving conflict in dating couples. *Personal Relationships, 15*, 41–55.

Cann, A., Calhoun, L. G., & Banks, J. S. (1997). On the role of humor appreciation in interpersonal attraction: It's no joking matter. *Humor: International Journal of Humor Research, 10*, 77–89.

Carlson, R. (1997). *Don't sweat the small stuff … and it's all small stuff*. New York: Hyperion.

Caro, T. M. (1988). Adaptive significance of play: Are we getting closer? *Tree, 3*, 50–54.

Casado-Kehoe, M., Vanderbleek, L., & Thanasiu, P. (2007). Play in couples counseling. *The Family Journal, 15*, 133–136.

Chapman, G. (1992). *The five languages of love: How to express heartfelt commitment to your mate*. Chicago: Northfield.

Cohn, M. A., Brown, S. L., Fredrickson, B. L., Mikels, J. A., Conway, A. M. (2009). Happiness unpacked: Positive emotions increase life satisfaction by building resilience, *Emotion, 9 (3)*, 361–368.

Collins, N. L. (1996). Working models of attachment: Implications for explanation, emotion, and behavior. *Journal of Personality and Social Psychology, 71*, 810–832.

Collins, N. L., & Feeney, B. C. (2000). A safe haven: An attachment theory perspective on support seeking and caregiving in intimate relationships. *Journal of Personality and Social Psychology, 78*, 1053–1073.

Collins, N. L., Ford, M. B., Guichard, A. C., & Allard, L. M. (2006). Working models of attachment and attribution processes in intimate relationships. *Personality and Social Psychology Bulletin, 32*, 201–219.

Corey, G. (2009). *Theory and practice of counselling* and *psychotherapy*. Belmount, CA: Thomson Brooks/Cole.

Courtois, C. A. (1988). *Healing the incest wound: Adult survivors in therapy*. New York: Norton.

Cousins, N. (1979). *Anatomy of an illness as perceived by the patient: Reflections on healing and regeneration*. New York: Norton.

Csikszentmihalyi, M. (1990). *Flow: The psychology of optimal experience*. New York: HarperCollins.

Davidson, R. J., Kabat-Zinn, J., Schumacher, J., Rosenkranz, M., Muller, D., Santorelli, S.F., et al. (2003). Alterations in brain and immune function produced by mindfulness meditation. *Psychosomatic Medicine, 65*, 564–570.

De Shazer, S. (1985). *Keys to solution in brief therapy*. New York: Norton.

De Shazer, S. (1988). *Clues: Investigating solutions in brief therapy*. New York: Norton.

Diepold, J., Britt, V., & Bender, S. (2004). *Evolving thought field therapy: The clinician's handbook of diagnosis, treatment and theory*. New York: Norton.

Dillon, K.M., Minchoff, B., Baker, K. H. (1985). Positive emotional states and enhancement of the immune system. *International Journal of Psychiatry in Medicine, 15*, 13–17.

Dillon, K. M. and Trotten, M. C. (1989). Psychological factors, immunocompetence, and health breast-feeding mothers and their infants. *Journal of Genetic Psychology, 150*, 155–162.

Doherty, W. (2001). *Take back your marriage: Sticking together in a world that pulls us apart.* New York: Guilford Press.

Doidge, N. (2007). *The brain that changes itself: stories of personal triumph from the frontier of brain science.* New York: Penguin.

Dolan, Y. (1991). *Resolving sexual abuse: Solution-focused therapy and Ericksonian hypnosis for adult survivors.* New York: Norton.

Dolhinow, P. J. (1987). At play in the fields. In H. Topoff (Ed.), *The natural history reader in animal behavior* (pp. 229–237). New York: Columbia University Press.

Donaldson, O. F. (1993). *Playing by heart: The vision and practice of belonging.* Nevada City, California: In-Joy.

Erickson, M. H. (1980). *The collected papers of Milton H. Erickson on hypnosis* (E. L. Rossi, Ed.). New York: Irvington.

Feinstein, D. (2004). *Energy psychology interactive.* Ashland, OR: Innersource.

Fisher, H. (2001). *Why we love.* New York: Holt.

Fisher, H. E. (1992). *Anatomy of love: A natural history of mating, marriage, and why we stray.* New York: Random House.

Fraley, B., & Aron, A. (2004). The effect of a shared humorous experience on closeness in initial encounters. *Personal Relationships, 11*, 61–78.

Frederickson, B. L. (1998). What good are positive emotions? *Review of General Psychology,* 300–319.

Fredrickson, B. (2009). *Positivity: Groundbreaking research reveals how to embrace the hidden strength of positive emotions, overcome negativity, and thrive.* New York: Crown.

Fredrickson, B. L. (2001). The role of positive emotions in positive psychology: The broaden-and-build theory of positive emotions. *American Psychologist, 56*, 218–226.

Fredrickson, B. L., & Branigan, C. A. (2005). Positive emotions broaden the scope of attention and thought-action repertoires. *Cognition and Emotion, 19*, 313–332.

Fredrickson, B. L., & Joiner, T. (2002). Positive emotions trigger upward spirals toward emotional well-being. *Psychological Science, 13*, 172–175.

Fredrickson, B. L., & Levenson, R. W. (1998). Positive emotions speed recovery from the cardiovascular sequelae of negative emotions. *Cognition and Emotion, 12*, 191–220.

Gallo, F. P. (1999). *Energy psychology: Explorations at the interface of energy cognition, behavior and health.* NewYork: CRC Press.

Gentzler, A. L., & Kerns, K. A. (2006). Adult attachment and memory of emotional reactions to negative and positive events. *Cognition and Emotion, 20*, 20–42.

Goleman, D. (2006). *Social intelligence: New science of human relationships.* New York: Bantam Books.

Gordon, G. (2006). What is play? In search of a universal definition (self-published). http://www.gwengordonplay.com/pdf/what is_play.pdf. Retrieved April 24, 2010.

Gordon, G., & Esbjorn-Hargens, S. (2007). Are we having fun yet? An exploration of the transformative power of play. *Journal of Humanistic Psychology, 47*, 198–222.

Gordon, L. (1993). *Passage to intimacy: Uniquely effective concepts and skills from the dynamic internationally acclaimed PAIRS program.*

Gottman, J. M. (1994). *Why marriages succeed or fail .... and how you can make yours last.* New York: Simon and Schuster.

Gottman, J. M. (1999). *The seven principles for making marriage work.* New York: Crown.

Gottman, J. M., & Gottman, J. (2010). *Level 1 training: Bridging the couple chasm.* Seattle, WA: Gottman Institute.

Goulding, M., & Goulding, R. (1979). *Changing lives through redecision therapy*. New York: Bruner/Mazel.

Gray, J. (1992). *Men are from Mars, women are from Venus: A practical guide for improving communication and getting what you want in your relationship*. New York: Harper Collins.

Gray, J. (1995). *Mars and Venus in the bedroom: A guide to lasting romance and passion*. New York: Harper Collins.

Gray, J. (2003). *Mars and Venus diet and exercise solution*. New York: St. Martins Press.

Haley, J. (1993). *Uncommon therapy: The psychiatric techniques of Milton H. Erickson*. New York: Norton. (Original work published 1973).

Hanson, R (2009). *Buddha's Brain: The practical neuroscience of happiness, love and wisdom*. Oakland, CA: New Harbinger.

Harley, W. F. (Sherllred) (2007). *His needs, her needs: Building an affair proof marriage*. Michigan: Revell.

Hayes, S. C., & Strosahl, K. D. (2004). *A practical guide to acceptance and commitment therapy*. New York: Springer Science and Business Media.

Hendrix, H. (1998). *Getting the love you want*. New York: Holt.

Herman, J. L (1992). *Trauma and recover: The aftermath of violence from domestic abuse to political terror*. New York: Basic.

Hicks, A. M., & Diamond, L. M. (2008). How was your day? Couples' affect when telling and hearing daily events. *Personal Relationships, 15*, 205–228.

Huizinga, J. (1949). *Homo Ludens: A study of the play element in culture*. New York: Routledge.

Isen, A. M. (1990). The influence of positive and negative affect on cognitive organization: Some implications for development. In N. Stein, B. Leventhal, & T. Trabasso (Eds.), *Psychological and biological approaches to emotion* (pp. 75–94). Hillsdale, NJ: Erlbaum.

Johnson, S. (2004). *The practice of emotionally focused couple therapy: Creating connection*. New York: Brunner/Mazel.

Johnson, S. (2008). *Hold me tight: Seven conversations for a lifetime of love*. New York: Little, Brown.

Kopecky, G. (1996). Make time for play. *American Health, 15*(4), 65–67.

Lankton, S. R., & Lankton, C. (1983). *The answer within: A clinical framework of Ericksonian hypnotherapy*. New York: Bruner/Mazel.

Lankton, S. R., & Lankton, C. (1987). *Enchantment and intervention*. New York: Bruner/Mazel.

Lauer, J. C., & Lauer, R. H. (2002). *The play solution: How to put the fun and excitement back into your marriage*. New York: McGraw Hill.

Levine, P. (1997). *Waking the tiger*. Berkeley, CA: North Atlantic Books.

Lewandowski, G. W., & Aron, A. (2004). Distinguishing arousal from novelty and challenge in initial romantic attraction between strangers. *Social Behavior and Personality, 32*, 361–372.

Lipton, B. (2005). *The biology of belief: Unleashing the power of consciousness, matter, and miracles*. Mountain of Love. Santa Rosa. CA.

Love, P., & Robinson, J. (1994). *Hot monogamy*. New York: Penguin.

Luskin, F. (2007). *Forgive for love: The missing ingredient for a healthy and lasting relationship*. New York: Harper Collins.

Lyubomirsky, S. (2007). *The how of happiness: A scientific approach to getting the life you want*. New York: Penguin.

Maltz, W. (1992). *The sexual healing journey: A guide for survivors of sexual abuse*. New York: Harper.

Marano, H. (2004). Marriages fall into the danger zone of divorce when ratio of positive to negative interactions dips below five to one. *Psychology Today,* March 16. Retrieved October 15, 2010 from http://www.psychologytoday.com/articles/200403/marriage-math.

Markman, H. Stanley, S., Jenkins, C., Blumberg, S., Whitely, C. (2004). *12 Hours to a great marriage: A step by step guide to making love last.* San Fransisco: JohnWiley.

Markman, H. J., Stanley, S. M., & Blumberg, S. L. (2010). *Fighting for your marriage: Bestseller for enhancing marriage and preventing divorce* (3rd ed.). San Francisco: Jossey Bass.

Martin, R A. and Dobbins, J. P. (1988). Sense of humor, hassles and immunoglobulin A — Evidence for a stress moderating effect of humor. *International Journal of Psychiatry in Medicine, 18,* 93–105.

McCarthy, B., & McCarthy, E. (2003). *Rekindling desire: A step-by-set program to help low-sex and no-sex marriages.* New York: Brunner-Routledge.

McCluhan, M. (1964). *Understanding media.* London: Routledge.

McGoldrick, M., & Gerson, R. (1985). *Genograms in family assessment.* New York: Norton.

Mikulincer, M. & Sheffi, E. (2002). Adult attachment style and cognitive reactions to positive affect: A test of solving. *Motivation and Emotion, 24* (3), 149–174,

Millar, S. (1968). *The psychology of play.* New York: Penguin.

Minuchin, S., & Fishman, H. C. (1981). *Family therapy techniques.* Cambridge, MA: Harvard University Press.

Morreall, J. (1997). *Humor works.* Amherst, MA: HRD Press.

Nochmanovitch, S. (1990). *Free play: Improvisation in life and art.* New York: Penguin Putnam.

O'Hanlon, W. (1987). *Taproots: Underlying principles of Milton Erickson's therapy and hypnosis.* New York: Norton.

Panksepp, J. (1998). *Affective neuroscience: The foundations of human and animal emotions.* New York: Oxford University Press.

Perel, E. (2006). *Mating in captivity: Unlocking erotic intelligence.* New York: Harper Collins.

Perls, F. (1973). *The Gestalt approach & eye witness to therapy.* Palo Alto, CA: Science and Behavior Books.

Pert, C. B. (1997). *Molecules of emotion.* New York: Scribner.

Pietromonaco, P. R., & Feldman Barrett, L. (1997). Working models of attachment and daily social interactions. *Journal of Personality and Social Psychology, 73,* 1409–1423.

Provine, R. R. (2000). *Laughter: A scientific investigation.* New York: Penguin.

Reissman, C., Aron, A., & Bergen, M. (1993). Shared activities and marital satisfaction: Causal direction and self-expansion versus boredom. *Journal of Social and Personal Relationships, 10,* 243–254.

Rubin, K. H. (1982). Early play theories revisited: Contributions to contemporary research and theory. *Contributions to Human Development, 6,* 4–14.

Satir, V. (1983). *Conjoint family therapy.* New York: Science and Behavior Books.

Schachter, S., & Singer, J. (1962). Cognitive, social, and physiological determinants of emotional state. *Psychological Review, 69,* 379–399.

Schaefer, C. (2003). *Play therapy with adults.* Hoboken, NJ: Wiley.

Schnarch, D. (2002). *Resurrecting sex. Keeping love and intimacy alive in committed relationships.* New York: Harper Collins.

Schwarz, R. A. (2002). *Tools for transforming trauma.* New York: Brunner-Routledge.

Seligman, M. E. P. and Maier, S. F. (1967). Failure to escape traumatic shock. *Journal of Experimental Psychology, 74,* 1–9.

Seligman, M. E. (2002). *Authentic happiness: Using the new positive psychology to realize your potential for lasting fulfillment.* New York: Free Press.

Seligman, M. E., & Csikszentmihalyi, M. (2000). Positive psychology: An introduction. *American Psychologist, 55*, 5–14.

Shapiro, F. (1995). *Eye movement desensitization and reprocessing: Basic principles, protocols and procedures.* New York: Guilford.

Shaver, C., & Hazen, P. (1987). Romantic love conceptualized as an attachment process. *Journal of Personality and Social Psychology, 52*, 511–524.

Sherrod, L. R., & Singer, J. L (1989). The development of make believe play. In J. Goldstein (Ed.), *Sports, games and play* (pp. 1–38). Hillsdale, NJ: Erlbaum.

Siegel, D. J. (1999). *The developing mind: How relationships and the brain interact to shape who we are.* New York: Guilford Press.

Siegel, D. J. (2010). *Mindsight: The new science of transformation of personal transformation.* New York: Bantam.

Siegel, D. J. (2010). *Mindsight: The new science of transformation of personal transformation.* NewYork: Bantam.

Steiner, C. (1974). *Scripts people live: Transactional analysis of life scripts.* New York: Grove.

Stern, D. (1994). *The present moment in psychotherapy and everyday life.* NewYork: Norton.

Sutton-Smith, B. (1997). *The ambiguity of play.* Cambridge, MA: Harvard University Press.

Tannen, D. (1990). *You just don't understand.* New York. Ballantine Books.

Terr, L. (1999). . *Beyond love and work: Why adults need to play.* New York: Scribner.

Tolle, E. (2005). *A new earth: Awakening to your life's purpose.* New York: Penguin Group.

Tsapelas, I., Aron, A., & Orbuch, T. (2009). Marital boredom now predicts less satisfaction 9 years later. *Psychological Science, 20*, 532–545.

Van der Kolk, B. A. (1987). *Psychological trauma.* Washington, DC: American Psychiatric Press.

Voltaire. (n.d.). BrainyQuote.com. Retrieved October 20, 2010, from http://www.brainy-quote.com/quotes/quotes/v/voltaire106709.html.

Von Oech, R. (1983). *A whack on the side of the head: How you can be more creative.* New York: Warner Books.

Von Oech, R. (1998). *A whack on the side of the head: How you can be more creative.* New York: Warner Books.

Webster's new world college dictionary (3rd ed.). (1988). New York: Simon & Schuster.

Weiner, D. J. (1994). *Rehearsals for growth: Theater improvisation for psychotherapists.* New York: Norton.

Weiner-Davis, M. (2003). *The sex starved marriage: Boosting your marriage libido.* New York: Simon & Schuster.

White, M., & Epston, D. (1990). *Narrative means to therapeutic ends.* New York: Norton.

Winnicott, D. W. (1971*). Playing and reality.* New York: Basic Books.

Witaker, C. (1982). *From psycheto system: The evolving therapy of Carl Whitaker* (J. Neil & Kniskern Eds). New York: Guilford Press.

Zeig, J. K. (1985). *Experiencing Erickson: An introduction to the man and his work.* New York: Bruner/Mazel.

Index